HARBINGER

OMEGA
RISING

JOSHUA DYSART | KHARI EVANS | LEWIS LAROSA | IAN HANNIN

CONTENTS

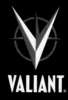

VALIANT

Peter Cuneo
Chairman

Dinesh Shamdasani
CEO and Chief Creative Officer

Gavin Cuneo
CFO and Head of Strategic Development

Fred Pierce
Publisher

Warren Simons
VP Executive Editor

Walter Black
VP Operations

Hunter Gorinson
Marketing and Communications Manager

Atom! Freeman
Sales Manager

Travis Escarfullery
Production and Design Manager

Rian Hughes/Device
Trade Dress and Book Design

Jody LeHeup
Associate Editor

Josh Johns
Assistant Editor

Peter Stern
Operations Coordinator

Ivan Cohen
Collection Editor

Russell Brown
President, Consumer Products,
Promotions & Ad Sales

Harbinger®: Omega Rising.
Published by Valiant Entertainment, LLC. Office of Publication: 424 West 33rd Street, New York, NY 10001.

Printed in the U.S.A. Second Printing.
ISBN: 9780979640957.

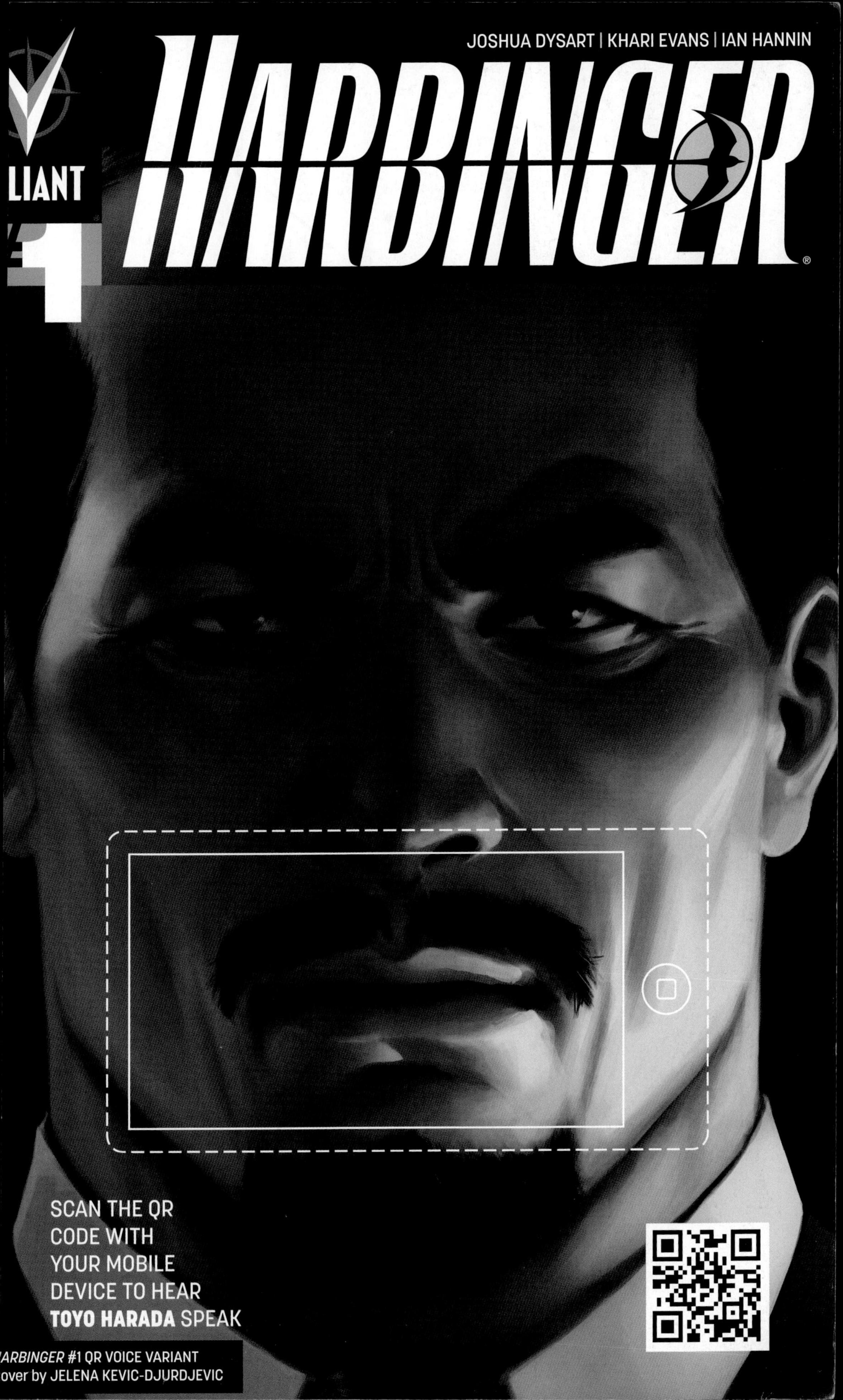
VALIANT
#1
JOSHUA DYSART | KHARI EVANS | IAN HANNIN
HARBINGER®
SCAN THE QR CODE WITH YOUR MOBILE DEVICE TO HEAR **TOYO HARADA** SPEAK
HARBINGER #1 QR VOICE VARIANT
Cover by JELENA KEVIC-DJURDJEVIC

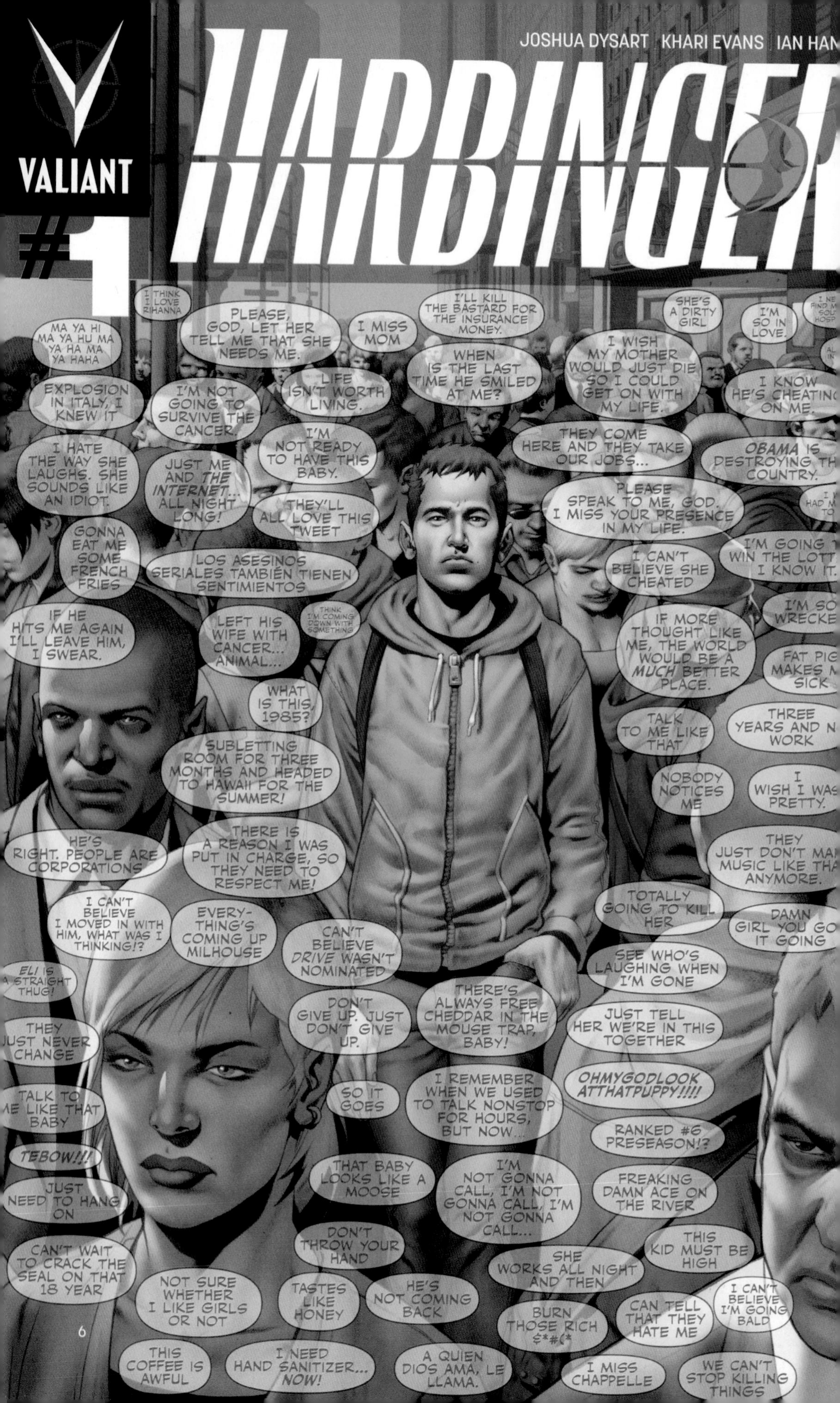
VALIANT
#1
JOSHUA DYSART | KHARI EVANS | IAN HAN
HARBINGER
I THINK I LOVE RIHANNA
MA YA HI MA YA HU MA YA HA MA YA HAHA
PLEASE, GOD, LET HER TELL ME THAT SHE NEEDS ME.
I MISS MOM
I'LL KILL THE BASTARD FOR THE INSURANCE MONEY.
SHE'S A DIRTY GIRL
I'M SO IN LOVE.
I WISH MY MOTHER WOULD JUST DIE SO I COULD GET ON WITH MY LIFE.
WHEN IS THE LAST TIME HE SMILED AT ME?
LIFE ISN'T WORTH LIVING.
EXPLOSION IN ITALY, I KNEW IT
I'M NOT GOING TO SURVIVE THE CANCER.
I KNOW HE'S CHEATING ON ME.
I'M NOT READY TO HAVE THIS BABY.
THEY COME HERE AND THEY TAKE OUR JOBS...
I HATE THE WAY SHE LAUGHS. SHE SOUNDS LIKE AN IDIOT.
JUST ME AND THE INTERNET... ALL NIGHT LONG!
OBAMA IS DESTROYING TH COUNTRY.
THEY'LL ALL LOVE THIS TWEET
PLEASE SPEAK TO ME, GOD. I MISS YOUR PRESENCE IN MY LIFE.
GONNA EAT ME SOME FRENCH FRIES
LOS ASESINOS SERIALES TAMBIÉN TIENEN SENTIMIENTOS
I CAN'T BELIEVE SHE CHEATED
I'M GOING T WIN THE LOTT I KNOW IT.
IF HE HITS ME AGAIN I'LL LEAVE HIM, I SWEAR.
LEFT HIS WIFE WITH CANCER... ANIMAL...
THINK I'M COMING DOWN WITH SOMETHING
IF MORE THOUGHT LIKE ME, THE WORLD WOULD BE A MUCH BETTER PLACE.
I'M SO WRECKE
FAT PIG MAKES M SICK
WHAT IS THIS, 1985?
TALK TO ME LIKE THAT
THREE YEARS AND N WORK
SUBLETTING ROOM FOR THREE MONTHS AND HEADED TO HAWAII FOR THE SUMMER!
NOBODY NOTICES ME
I WISH I WAS PRETTY.
HE'S RIGHT. PEOPLE ARE CORPORATIONS
THERE IS A REASON I WAS PUT IN CHARGE, SO THEY NEED TO RESPECT ME!
THEY JUST DON'T MA MUSIC LIKE THA ANYMORE.
TOTALLY GOING TO KILL HER
I CAN'T BELIEVE I MOVED IN WITH HIM, WHAT WAS I THINKING!?
EVERY-THING'S COMING UP MILHOUSE
CAN'T BELIEVE DRIVE WASN'T NOMINATED
DAMN GIRL YOU GO IT GOING
ELI IS A STRAIGHT THUG!
SEE WHO'S LAUGHING WHEN I'M GONE
DON'T GIVE UP. JUST DON'T GIVE UP.
THERE'S ALWAYS FREE CHEDDAR IN THE MOUSE TRAP, BABY!
JUST TELL HER WE'RE IN THIS TOGETHER
THEY JUST NEVER CHANGE
TALK TO ME LIKE THAT BABY
SO IT GOES
I REMEMBER WHEN WE USED TO TALK NONSTOP FOR HOURS, BUT NOW...
OHMYGODLOOK ATTHATPUPPY!!!!
RANKED #6 PRESEASON!?
TEBOW!!!
THAT BABY LOOKS LIKE A MOOSE
I'M NOT GONNA CALL, I'M NOT GONNA CALL, I'M NOT GONNA CALL...
FREAKING DAMN ACE ON THE RIVER
JUST NEED TO HANG ON
DON'T THROW YOUR HAND
THIS KID MUST BE HIGH
CAN'T WAIT TO CRACK THE SEAL ON THAT 18 YEAR
SHE WORKS ALL NIGHT AND THEN
NOT SURE WHETHER I LIKE GIRLS OR NOT
TASTES LIKE HONEY
HE'S NOT COMING BACK
BURN THOSE RICH $*#(*
CAN TELL THAT THEY HATE ME
I CAN'T BELIEVE I'M GOING BALD
THIS COFFEE IS AWFUL
I NEED HAND SANITIZER... NOW!
A QUIEN DIOS AMA, LE LLAMA.
I MISS CHAPPELLE
WE CAN'T STOP KILLING THINGS

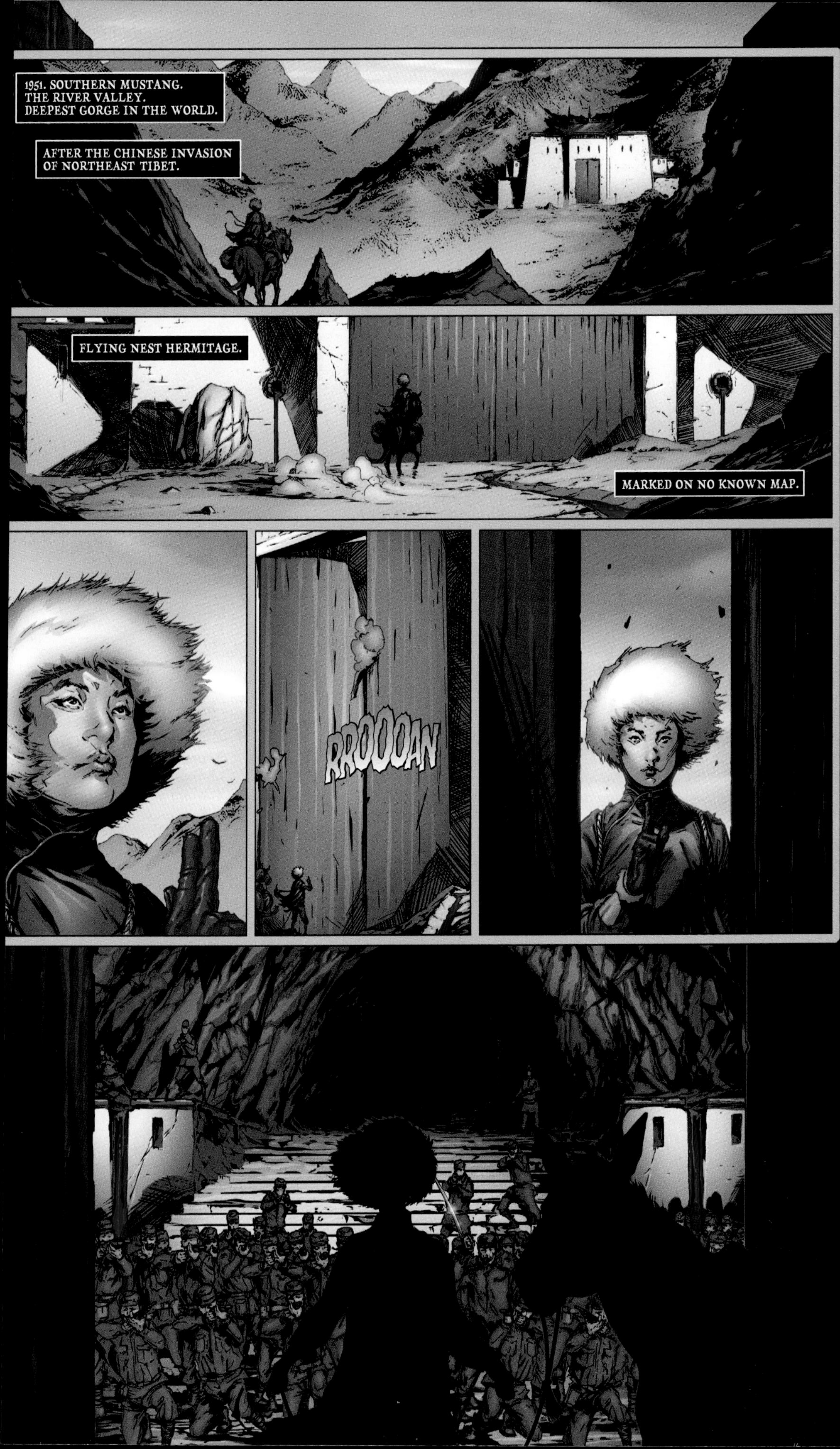
1951. SOUTHERN MUSTANG.
THE RIVER VALLEY.
DEEPEST GORGE IN THE WORLD.
AFTER THE CHINESE INVASION
OF NORTHEAST TIBET.
FLYING NEST HERMITAGE.
MARKED ON NO KNOWN MAP.
RROOOAN

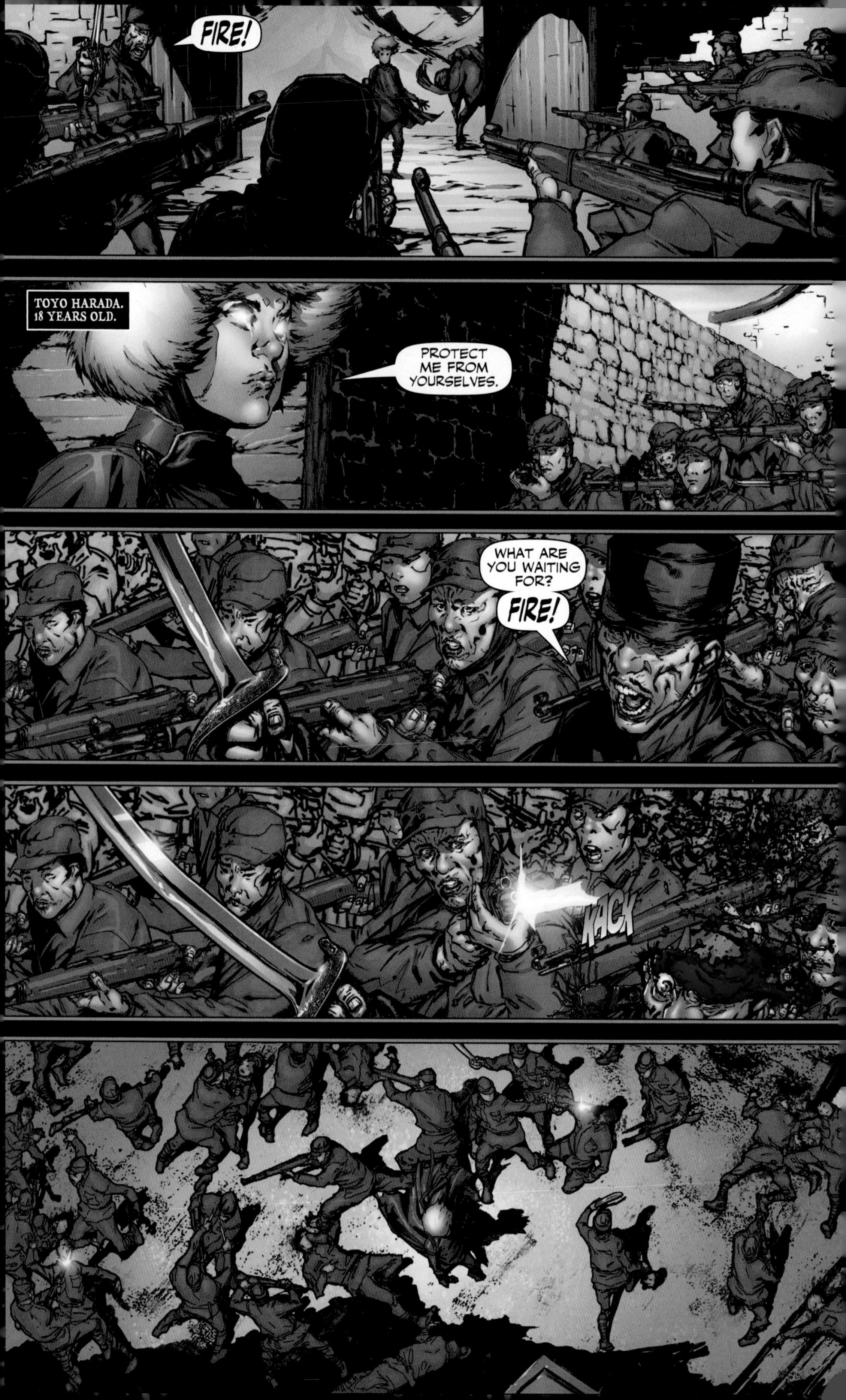
FIRE!
TOYO HARADA.
18 YEARS OLD.
PROTECT ME FROM YOURSELVES.
WHAT ARE YOU WAITING FOR?
FIRE!
KACK

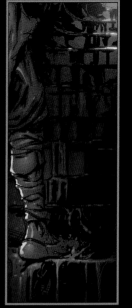

WELCOME, HARADA TOYO.

YOU'RE REAL... I DREAMED OF YOU... THE BLEEDING MONK WHO DOES NOT DIE. I CAME ALL THIS WAY, THOUGH I DIDN'T KNOW IF...I DIDN'T KNOW...

IT IS NOT FOR ME TO SPEAK ON WHAT IS REAL.

BUT YOU SAW MY COMING? YOU CAN SEE MY FUTURE?

YES, HARBINGER, I SEE YOUR FUTURE...

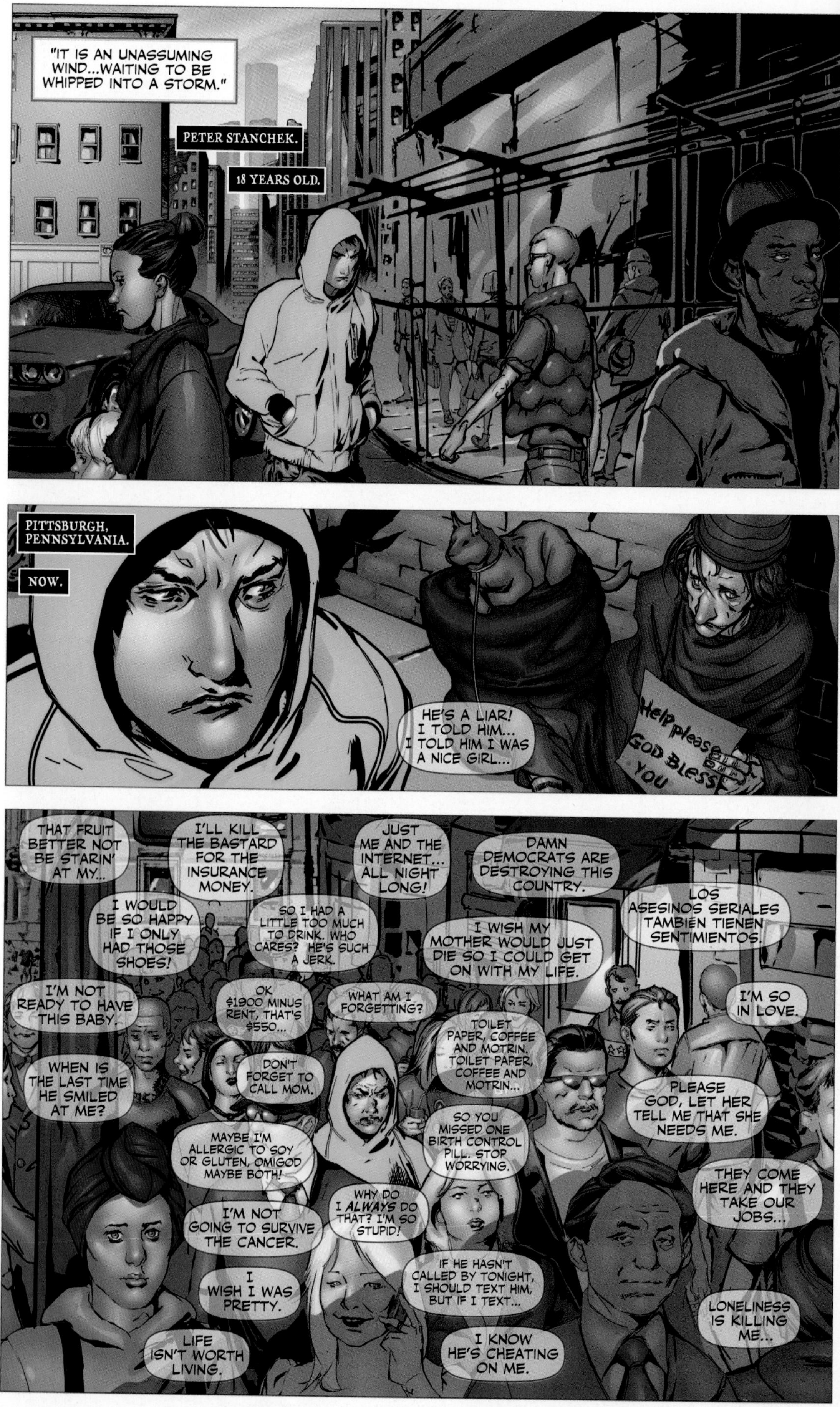

"IT IS AN UNASSUMING WIND...WAITING TO BE WHIPPED INTO A STORM."
PETER STANCHEK.
18 YEARS OLD.
PITTSBURGH, PENNSYLVANIA.
NOW.
HE'S A LIAR! I TOLD HIM... I TOLD HIM I WAS A NICE GIRL...
Help please GOD BLESS YOU
THAT FRUIT BETTER NOT BE STARIN' AT MY...
I'LL KILL THE BASTARD FOR THE INSURANCE MONEY.
JUST ME AND THE INTERNET... ALL NIGHT LONG!
DAMN DEMOCRATS ARE DESTROYING THIS COUNTRY.
I WOULD BE SO HAPPY IF I ONLY HAD THOSE SHOES!
SO I HAD A LITTLE TOO MUCH TO DRINK. WHO CARES? HE'S SUCH A JERK.
I WISH MY MOTHER WOULD JUST DIE SO I COULD GET ON WITH MY LIFE.
LOS ASESINOS SERIALES TAMBIÉN TIENEN SENTIMIENTOS.
I'M NOT READY TO HAVE THIS BABY.
OK $1900 MINUS RENT, THAT'S $550...
WHAT AM I FORGETTING?
I'M SO IN LOVE.
TOILET PAPER, COFFEE AND MOTRIN. TOILET PAPER, COFFEE AND MOTRIN...
WHEN IS THE LAST TIME HE SMILED AT ME?
DON'T FORGET TO CALL MOM.
PLEASE GOD, LET HER TELL ME THAT SHE NEEDS ME.
MAYBE I'M ALLERGIC TO SOY OR GLUTEN, OMIGOD MAYBE BOTH!
SO YOU MISSED ONE BIRTH CONTROL PILL. STOP WORRYING.
THEY COME HERE AND THEY TAKE OUR JOBS...
I'M NOT GOING TO SURVIVE THE CANCER.
WHY DO I ALWAYS DO THAT? I'M SO STUPID!
I WISH I WAS PRETTY.
IF HE HASN'T CALLED BY TONIGHT, I SHOULD TEXT HIM, BUT IF I TEXT...
LONELINESS IS KILLING ME...
LIFE ISN'T WORTH LIVING.
I KNOW HE'S CHEATING ON ME.

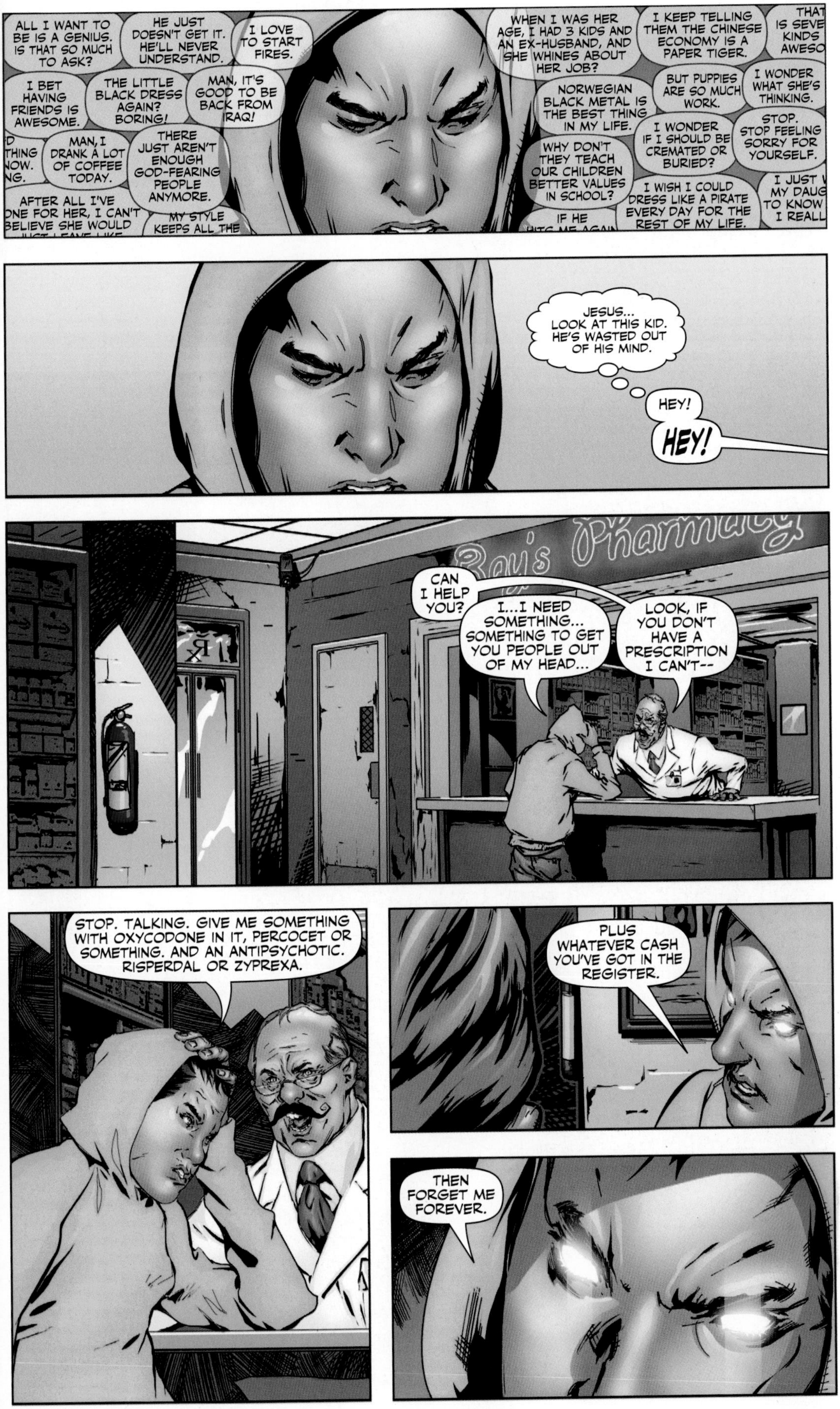

ALL I WANT TO BE IS A GENIUS. IS THAT SO MUCH TO ASK?
HE JUST DOESN'T GET IT. HE'LL NEVER UNDERSTAND.
I LOVE TO START FIRES.
I BET HAVING FRIENDS IS AWESOME.
THE LITTLE BLACK DRESS AGAIN? BORING!
MAN, IT'S GOOD TO BE BACK FROM IRAQ!
MAN, I DRANK A LOT OF COFFEE TODAY.
THERE JUST AREN'T ENOUGH GOD-FEARING PEOPLE ANYMORE.
WHEN I WAS HER AGE, I HAD 3 KIDS AND AN EX-HUSBAND, AND SHE WHINES ABOUT HER JOB?
I KEEP TELLING THEM THE CHINESE ECONOMY IS A PAPER TIGER.
NORWEGIAN BLACK METAL IS THE BEST THING IN MY LIFE.
BUT PUPPIES ARE SO MUCH WORK.
I WONDER WHAT SHE'S THINKING.
WHY DON'T THEY TEACH OUR CHILDREN BETTER VALUES IN SCHOOL?
I WONDER IF I SHOULD BE CREMATED OR BURIED?
STOP. STOP FEELING SORRY FOR YOURSELF.
I WISH I COULD DRESS LIKE A PIRATE EVERY DAY FOR THE REST OF MY LIFE.
JESUS... LOOK AT THIS KID. HE'S WASTED OUT OF HIS MIND.
HEY!
HEY!
Ray's Pharmacy
CAN I HELP YOU?
I...I NEED SOMETHING... SOMETHING TO GET YOU PEOPLE OUT OF MY HEAD...
LOOK, IF YOU DON'T HAVE A PRESCRIPTION I CAN'T--
STOP. TALKING. GIVE ME SOMETHING WITH OXYCODONE IN IT, PERCOCET OR SOMETHING. AND AN ANTIPSYCHOTIC. RISPERDAL OR ZYPREXA.
PLUS WHATEVER CASH YOU'VE GOT IN THE REGISTER.
THEN FORGET ME FOREVER.

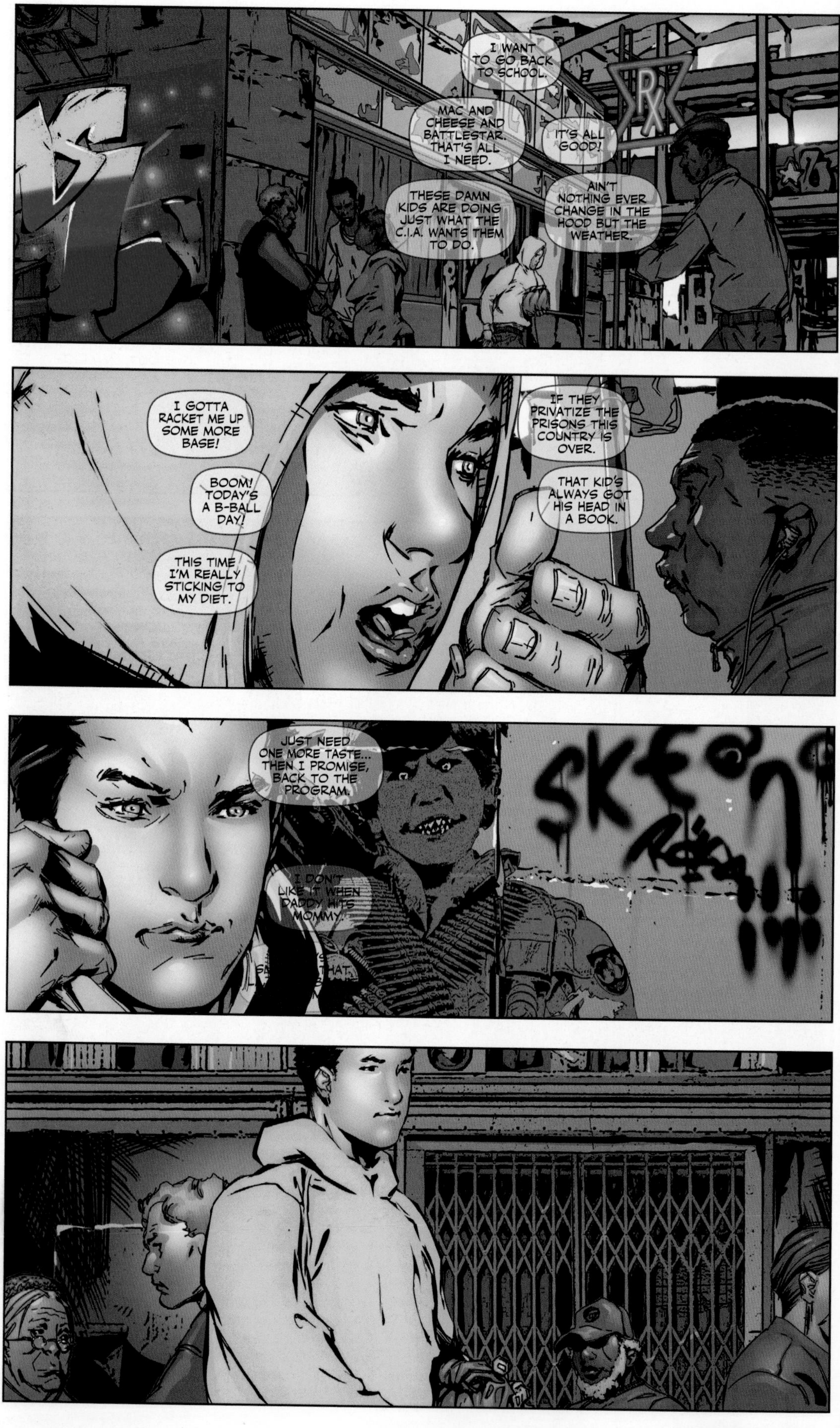
I WANT TO GO BACK TO SCHOOL.
MAC AND CHEESE AND BATTLESTAR. THAT'S ALL I NEED.
IT'S ALL GOOD!
THESE DAMN KIDS ARE DOING JUST WHAT THE C.I.A. WANTS THEM TO DO.
AIN'T NOTHING EVER CHANGE IN THE HOOD BUT THE WEATHER.
I GOTTA RACKET ME UP SOME MORE BASE!
BOOM! TODAY'S A B-BALL DAY!
THIS TIME I'M REALLY STICKING TO MY DIET.
IF THEY PRIVATIZE THE PRISONS THIS COUNTRY IS OVER.
THAT KID'S ALWAYS GOT HIS HEAD IN A BOOK.
JUST NEED ONE MORE TASTE... THEN I PROMISE, BACK TO THE PROGRAM.
I DON'T LIKE IT WHEN DADDY HITS MOMMY.

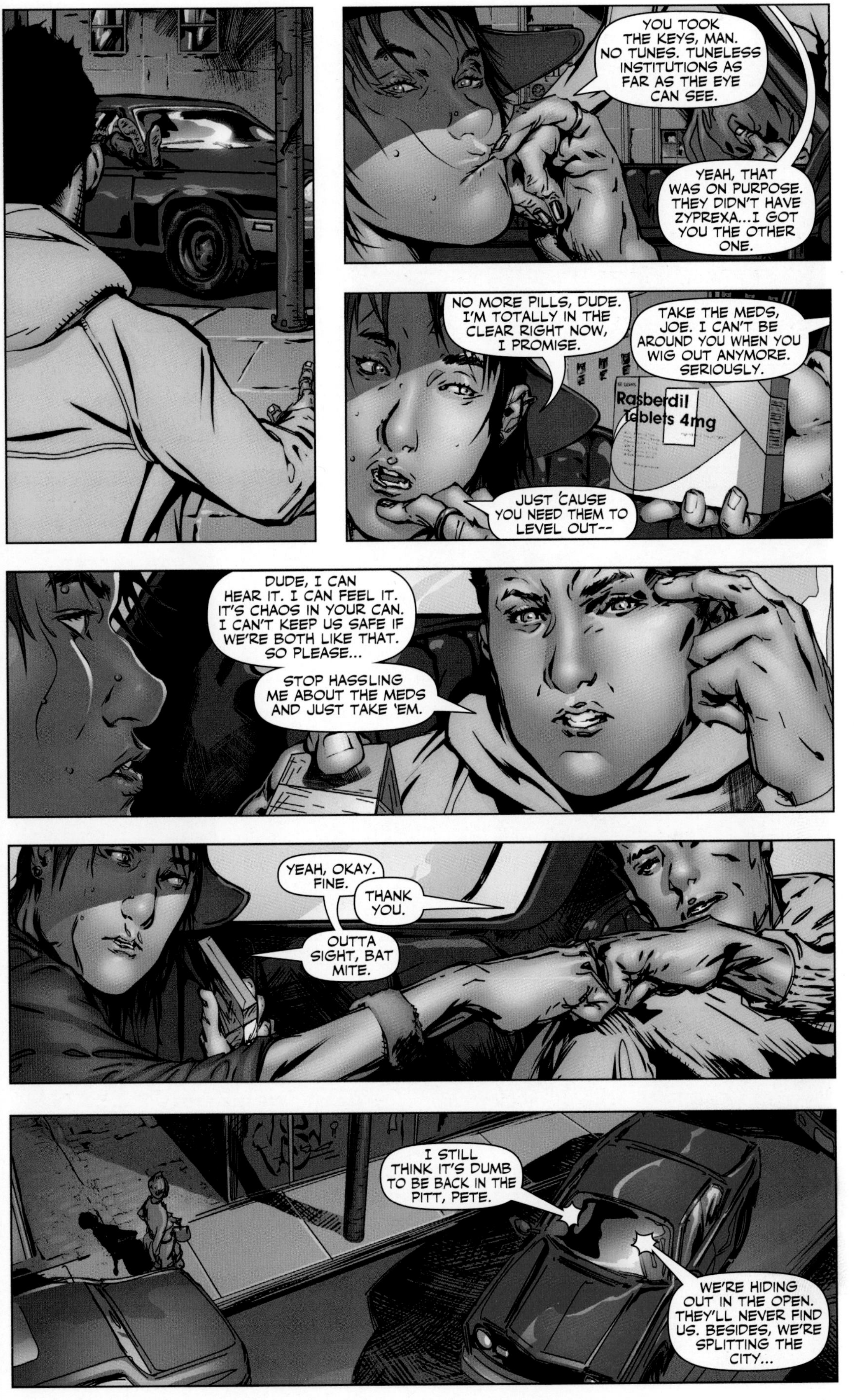
YOU TOOK THE KEYS, MAN. NO TUNES. TUNELESS INSTITUTIONS AS FAR AS THE EYE CAN SEE.
YEAH, THAT WAS ON PURPOSE. THEY DIDN'T HAVE ZYPREXA...I GOT YOU THE OTHER ONE.
NO MORE PILLS, DUDE. I'M TOTALLY IN THE CLEAR RIGHT NOW, I PROMISE.
TAKE THE MEDS, JOE. I CAN'T BE AROUND YOU WHEN YOU WIG OUT ANYMORE. SERIOUSLY.
Rasberdil Tablets 4mg
JUST 'CAUSE YOU NEED THEM TO LEVEL OUT--
DUDE, I CAN HEAR IT. I CAN FEEL IT. IT'S CHAOS IN YOUR CAN. I CAN'T KEEP US SAFE IF WE'RE BOTH LIKE THAT. SO PLEASE...
STOP HASSLING ME ABOUT THE MEDS AND JUST TAKE 'EM.
YEAH, OKAY. FINE.
THANK YOU.
OUTTA SIGHT, BAT MITE.
I STILL THINK IT'S DUMB TO BE BACK IN THE PITT, PETE.
WE'RE HIDING OUT IN THE OPEN. THEY'LL NEVER FIND US. BESIDES, WE'RE SPLITTING THE CITY...

"WE'RE GOING TO THE BURBS."

FORECLOSURE
FOR SALE
BANK OWNED

THIS IS WAY NOT COOL, PETE!

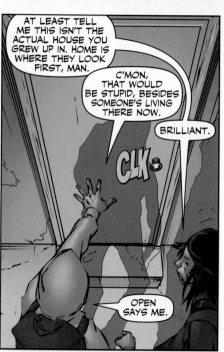

AT LEAST TELL ME THIS ISN'T THE ACTUAL HOUSE YOU GREW UP IN. HOME IS WHERE THEY LOOK FIRST, MAN.

C'MON, THAT WOULD BE STUPID, BESIDES SOMEONE'S LIVING THERE NOW.

BRILLIANT.

CLK

OPEN SAYS ME.

PETE, FOR REAL, WHAT ARE WE DOING HERE? IT'S LIKE YOU'RE MAKING IT EASY FOR HIM.

I DON'T KNOW. I MEAN, SIX CITIES IN SEVEN MONTHS. HOW MUCH LONGER CAN WE STAY ON THE RUN...

I'M JUST TIRED, I GUESS. I WANTED TO SEE HOME, BEFORE WE'RE TOO FAR GONE OR...WHATEVER.

WELL, I'M ON YOUR SIDE, MAN. ALWAYS. BUT THERE'S NO WAY I'M GOING BACK TO THE HOSPITAL.

NO MORE HOSPITALS. I PROMISE.

AT LEAST IT'S NICE TO BE INDOORS.

LIVING LARGE, BABY. THIS IS HOW WE DO IT...

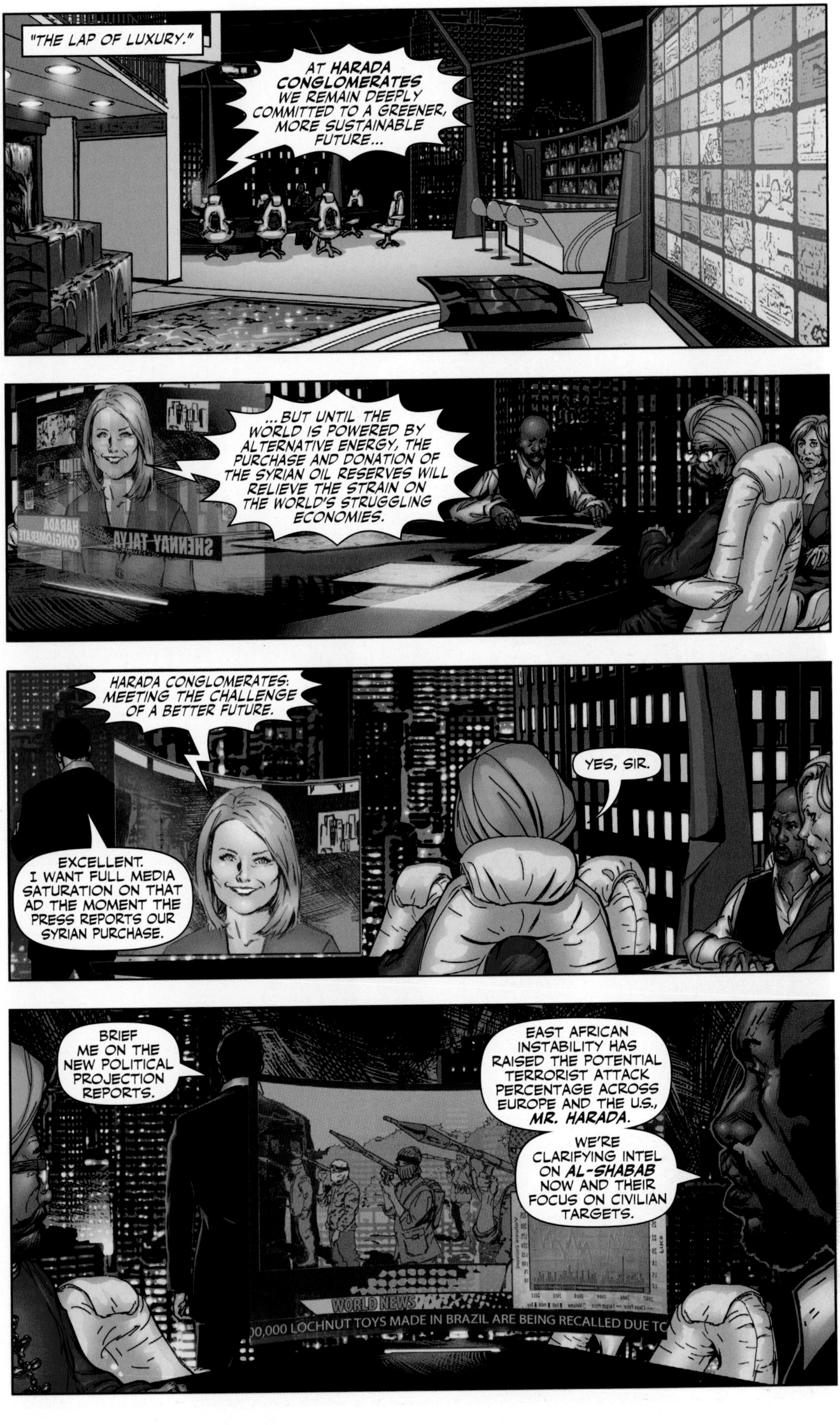

"THE LAP OF LUXURY."
AT HARADA CONGLOMERATES WE REMAIN DEEPLY COMMITTED TO A GREENER, MORE SUSTAINABLE FUTURE...
HARADA CONGLOMERATE
SHENNAY TALYA
...BUT UNTIL THE WORLD IS POWERED BY ALTERNATIVE ENERGY, THE PURCHASE AND DONATION OF THE SYRIAN OIL RESERVES WILL RELIEVE THE STRAIN ON THE WORLD'S STRUGGLING ECONOMIES.
HARADA CONGLOMERATES: MEETING THE CHALLENGE OF A BETTER FUTURE.
EXCELLENT. I WANT FULL MEDIA SATURATION ON THAT AD THE MOMENT THE PRESS REPORTS OUR SYRIAN PURCHASE.
YES, SIR.
BRIEF ME ON THE NEW POLITICAL PROJECTION REPORTS.
EAST AFRICAN INSTABILITY HAS RAISED THE POTENTIAL TERRORIST ATTACK PERCENTAGE ACROSS EUROPE AND THE U.S., MR. HARADA.
WE'RE CLARIFYING INTEL ON AL-SHABAB NOW AND THEIR FOCUS ON CIVILIAN TARGETS.
WORLD NEWS
00,000 LOCHNUT TOYS MADE IN BRAZIL ARE BEING RECALLED DUE TO

EXCELLENT. AND WHERE DO WE STAND ON GETTING THE *MEDICAL BOTS* ONLINE AND DEPLOYED IN THE REGION?

THE BBC REPORT FROM SUDAN IS SCHEDULED FOR MONDAY. WE'RE VERY EXCITED.

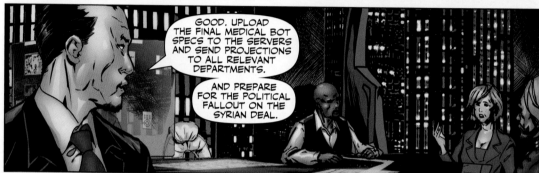

GOOD. UPLOAD THE FINAL MEDICAL BOT SPECS TO THE SERVERS AND SEND PROJECTIONS TO ALL RELEVANT DEPARTMENTS.

AND PREPARE FOR THE POLITICAL FALLOUT ON THE SYRIAN DEAL.

YOU'RE ALL EXCUSED.

SHOW ME...

...PETER STANCHEK.

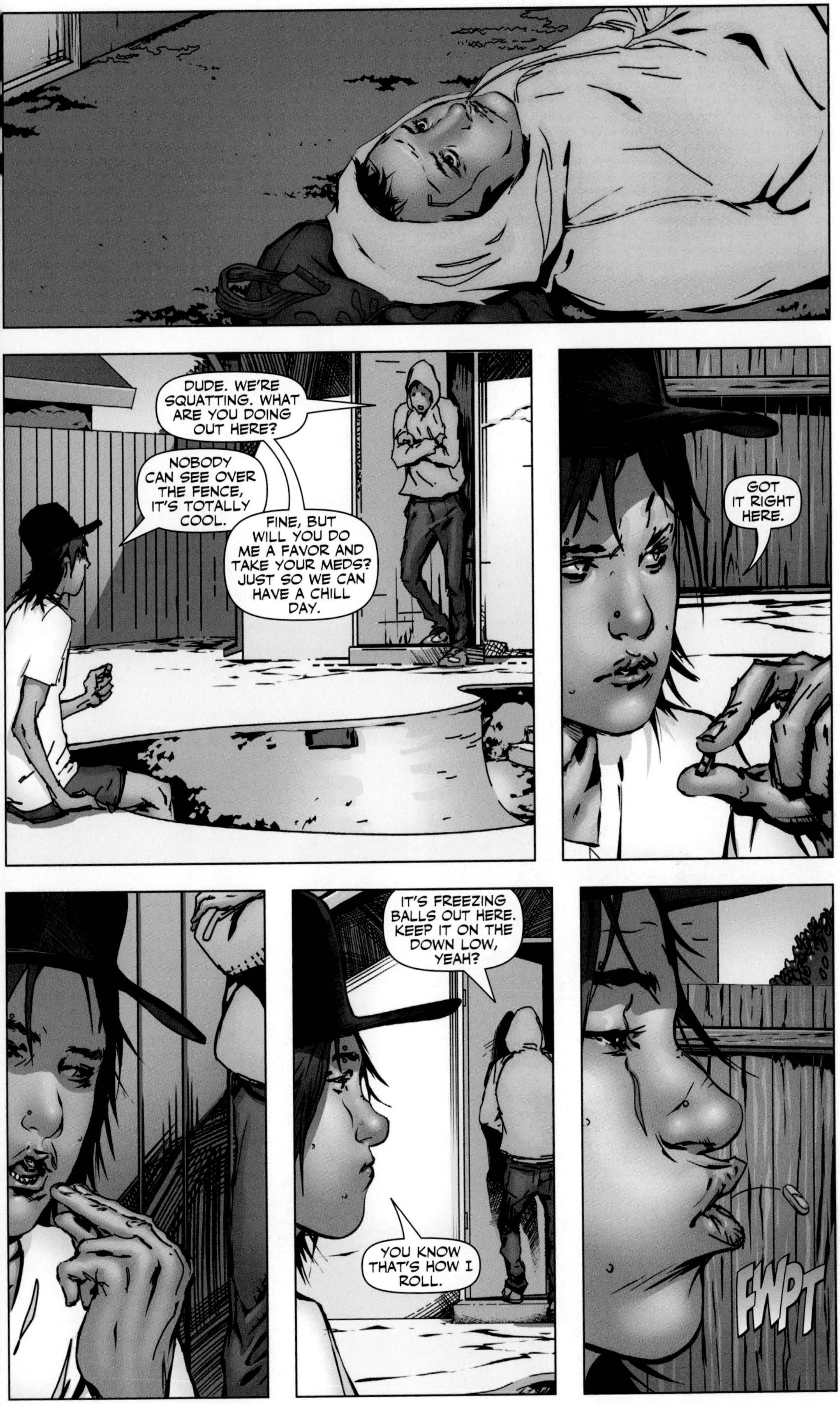
DUDE. WE'RE SQUATTING. WHAT ARE YOU DOING OUT HERE?
NOBODY CAN SEE OVER THE FENCE, IT'S TOTALLY COOL.
FINE, BUT WILL YOU DO ME A FAVOR AND TAKE YOUR MEDS? JUST SO WE CAN HAVE A CHILL DAY.
GOT IT RIGHT HERE.
IT'S FREEZING BALLS OUT HERE. KEEP IT ON THE DOWN LOW, YEAH?
YOU KNOW THAT'S HOW I ROLL.
FWPT

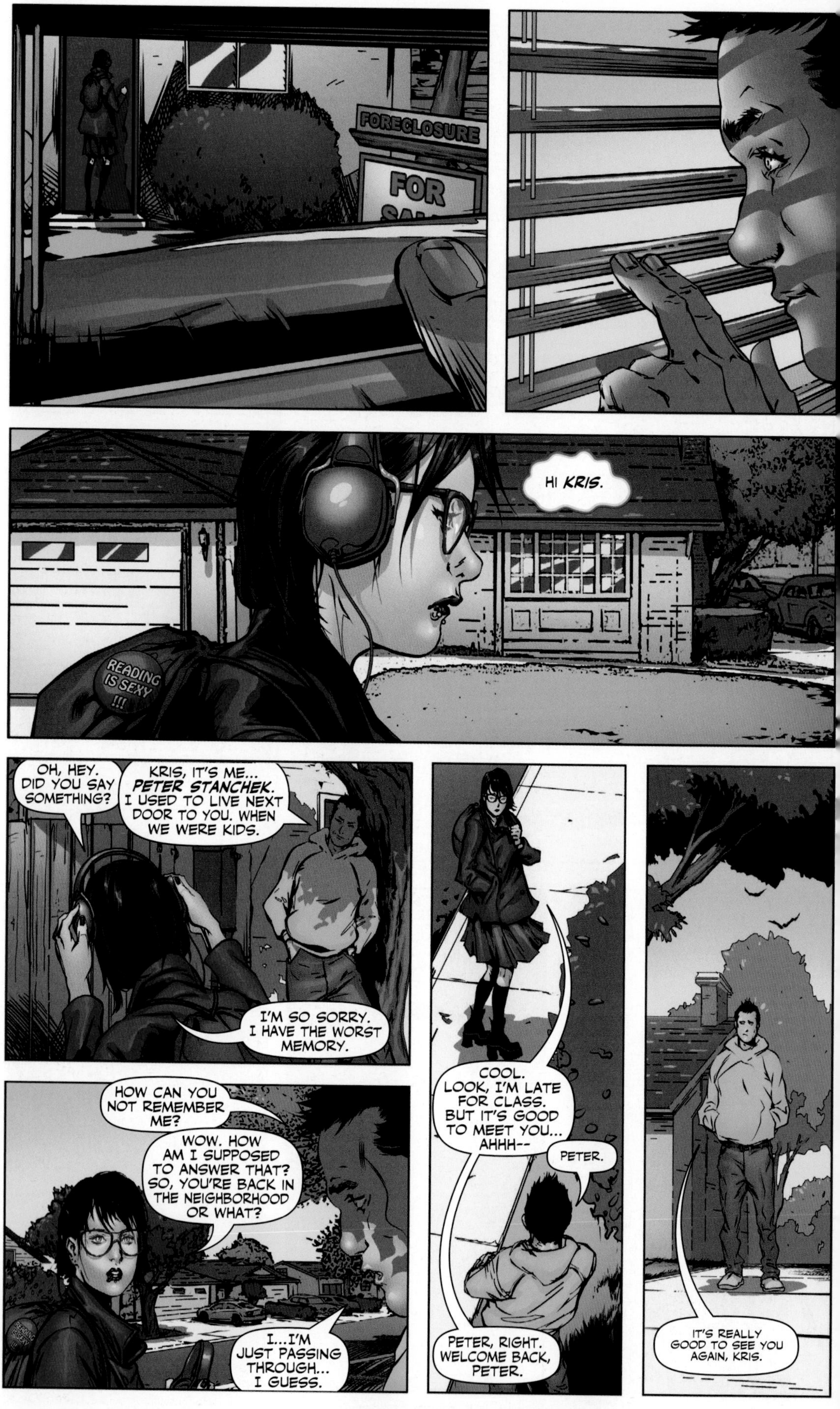
FORECLOSURE
FOR
HI KRIS.
READING IS SEXY !!!
OH, HEY. DID YOU SAY SOMETHING?
KRIS, IT'S ME... PETER STANCHEK. I USED TO LIVE NEXT DOOR TO YOU. WHEN WE WERE KIDS.
I'M SO SORRY. I HAVE THE WORST MEMORY.
HOW CAN YOU NOT REMEMBER ME?
WOW. HOW AM I SUPPOSED TO ANSWER THAT? SO, YOU'RE BACK IN THE NEIGHBORHOOD OR WHAT?
I...I'M JUST PASSING THROUGH... I GUESS.
COOL. LOOK, I'M LATE FOR CLASS. BUT IT'S GOOD TO MEET YOU... AHHH--
PETER.
PETER, RIGHT. WELCOME BACK, PETER.
IT'S REALLY GOOD TO SEE YOU AGAIN, KRIS.

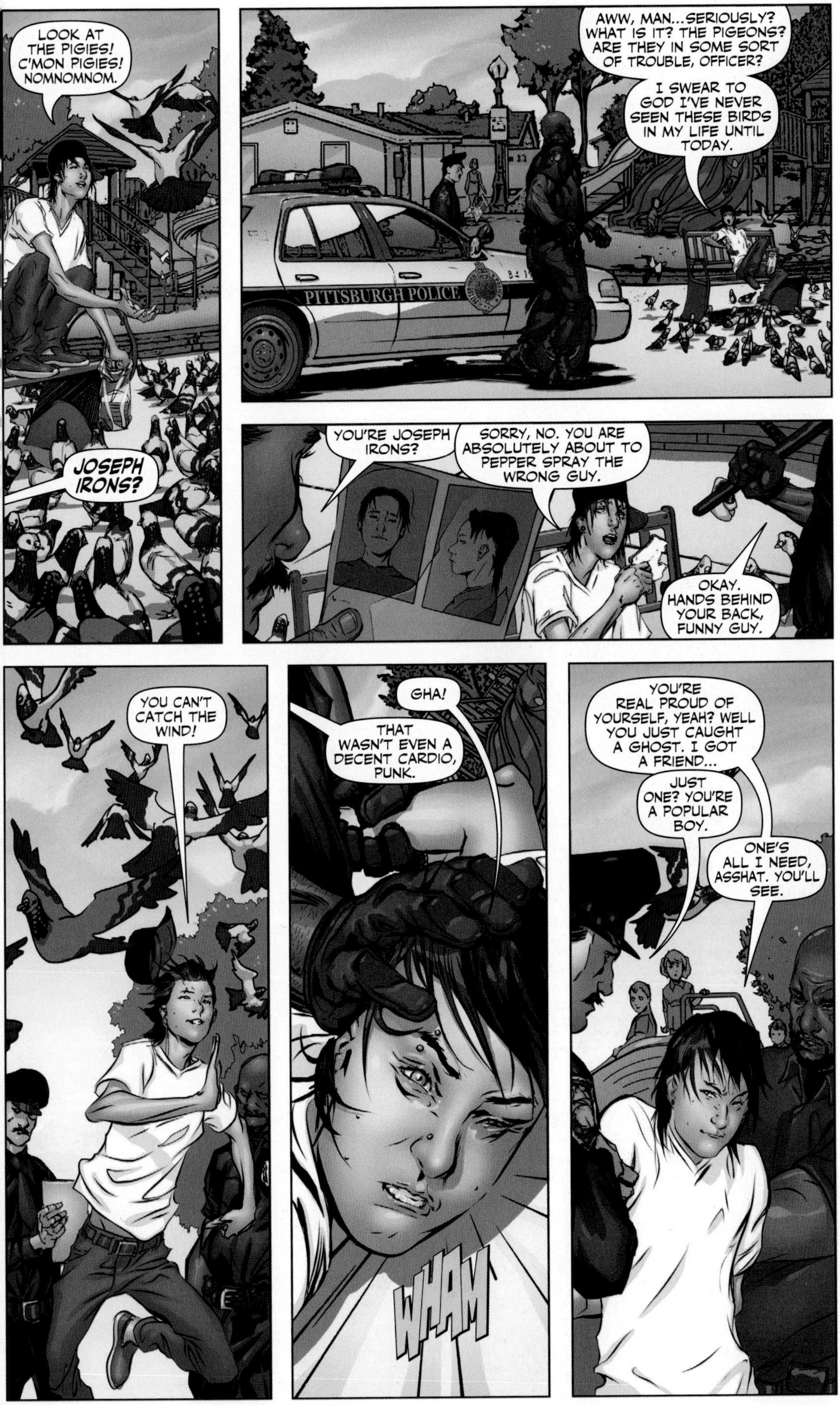
LOOK AT THE PIGIES! C'MON PIGIES! NOMNOMNOM.
JOSEPH IRONS?
AWW, MAN...SERIOUSLY? WHAT IS IT? THE PIGEONS? ARE THEY IN SOME SORT OF TROUBLE, OFFICER?
I SWEAR TO GOD I'VE NEVER SEEN THESE BIRDS IN MY LIFE UNTIL TODAY.
PITTSBURGH POLICE
YOU'RE JOSEPH IRONS?
SORRY, NO. YOU ARE ABSOLUTELY ABOUT TO PEPPER SPRAY THE WRONG GUY.
OKAY. HANDS BEHIND YOUR BACK, FUNNY GUY.
YOU CAN'T CATCH THE WIND!
GHA!
THAT WASN'T EVEN A DECENT CARDIO, PUNK.
WHAM
YOU'RE REAL PROUD OF YOURSELF, YEAH? WELL YOU JUST CAUGHT A GHOST. I GOT A FRIEND...
JUST ONE? YOU'RE A POPULAR BOY.
ONE'S ALL I NEED, ASSHAT. YOU'LL SEE.

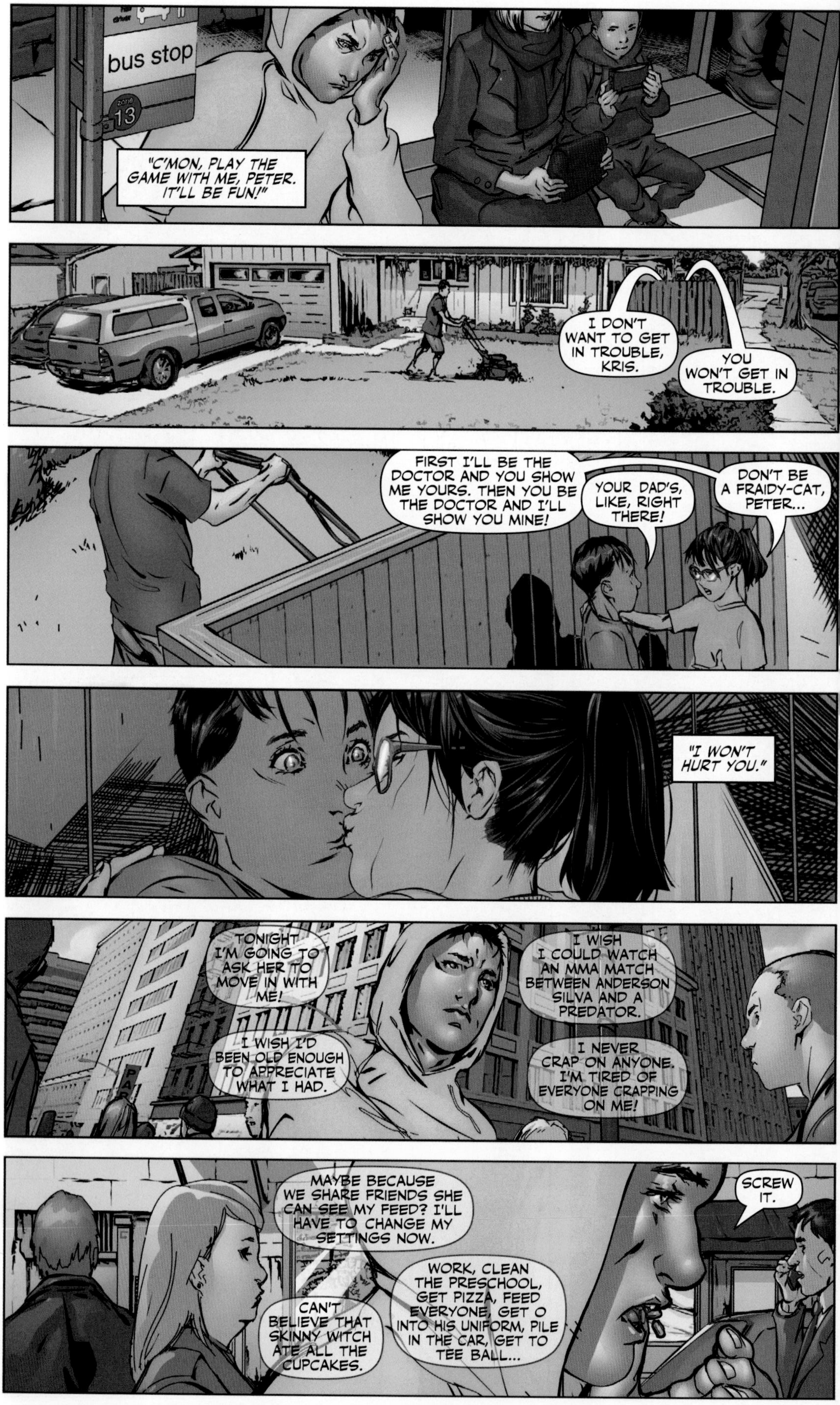
bus stop
13
"C'MON, PLAY THE GAME WITH ME, PETER. IT'LL BE FUN!"
I DON'T WANT TO GET IN TROUBLE, KRIS.
YOU WON'T GET IN TROUBLE.
FIRST I'LL BE THE DOCTOR AND YOU SHOW ME YOURS. THEN YOU BE THE DOCTOR AND I'LL SHOW YOU MINE!
YOUR DAD'S, LIKE, RIGHT THERE!
DON'T BE A FRAIDY-CAT, PETER...
"I WON'T HURT YOU."
TONIGHT I'M GOING TO ASK HER TO MOVE IN WITH ME!
I WISH I'D BEEN OLD ENOUGH TO APPRECIATE WHAT I HAD.
I WISH I COULD WATCH AN MMA MATCH BETWEEN ANDERSON SILVA AND A PREDATOR.
I NEVER CRAP ON ANYONE. I'M TIRED OF EVERYONE CRAPPING ON ME!
MAYBE BECAUSE WE SHARE FRIENDS SHE CAN SEE MY FEED? I'LL HAVE TO CHANGE MY SETTINGS NOW.
CAN'T BELIEVE THAT SKINNY WITCH ATE ALL THE CUPCAKES.
WORK, CLEAN THE PRESCHOOL, GET PIZZA, FEED EVERYONE, GET O INTO HIS UNIFORM, PILE IN THE CAR, GET TO TEE BALL...
SCREW IT.

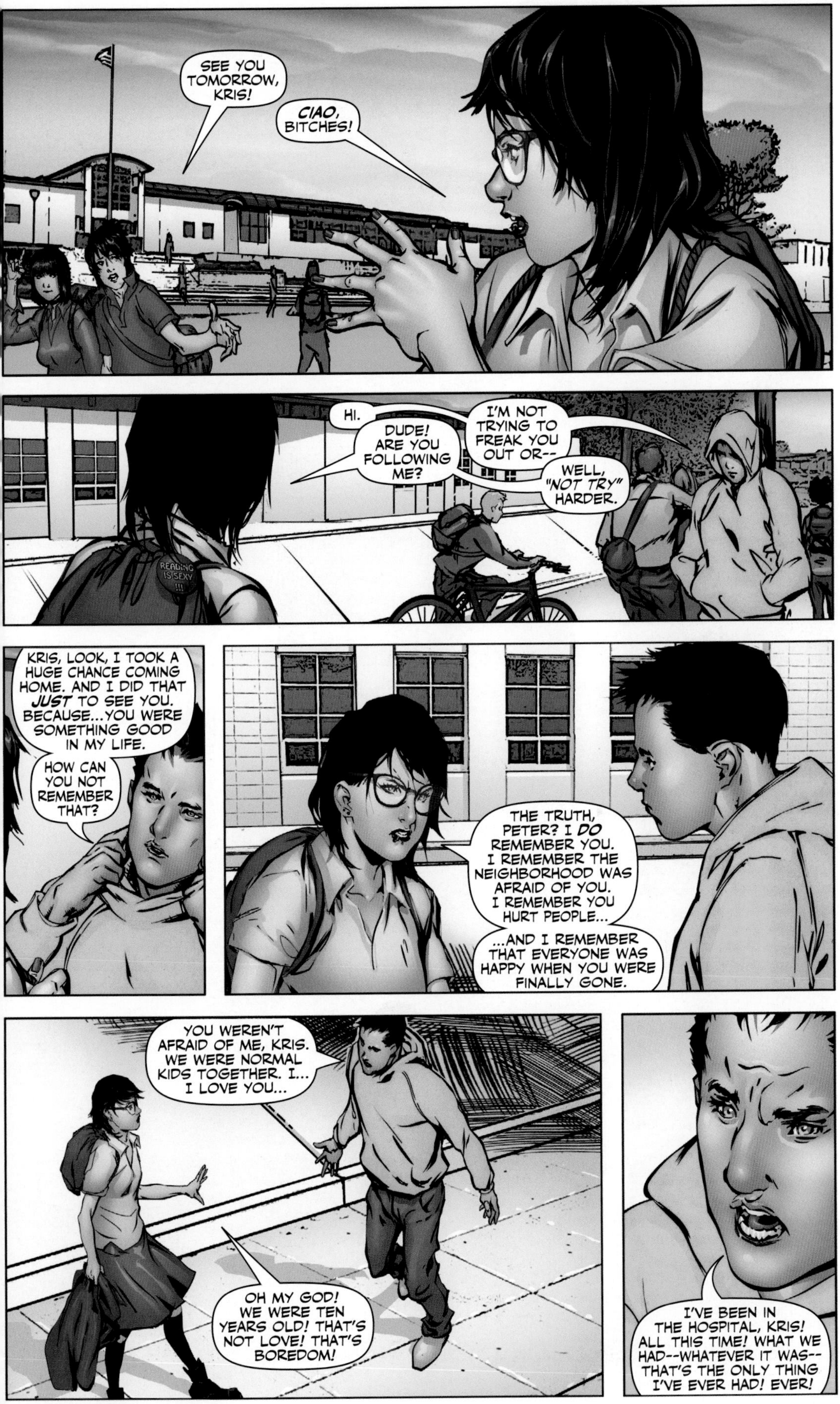

SEE YOU TOMORROW, KRIS!
CIAO, BITCHES!
HI.
DUDE! ARE YOU FOLLOWING ME?
I'M NOT TRYING TO FREAK YOU OUT OR--
WELL, "NOT TRY" HARDER.
READING IS SEXY !!!
KRIS, LOOK, I TOOK A HUGE CHANCE COMING HOME. AND I DID THAT JUST TO SEE YOU. BECAUSE...YOU WERE SOMETHING GOOD IN MY LIFE.
HOW CAN YOU NOT REMEMBER THAT?
THE TRUTH, PETER? I DO REMEMBER YOU. I REMEMBER THE NEIGHBORHOOD WAS AFRAID OF YOU. I REMEMBER YOU HURT PEOPLE...
...AND I REMEMBER THAT EVERYONE WAS HAPPY WHEN YOU WERE FINALLY GONE.
YOU WEREN'T AFRAID OF ME, KRIS. WE WERE NORMAL KIDS TOGETHER. I... I LOVE YOU...
OH MY GOD! WE WERE TEN YEARS OLD! THAT'S NOT LOVE! THAT'S BOREDOM!
I'VE BEEN IN THE HOSPITAL, KRIS! ALL THIS TIME! WHAT WE HAD--WHATEVER IT WAS--THAT'S THE ONLY THING I'VE EVER HAD! EVER!

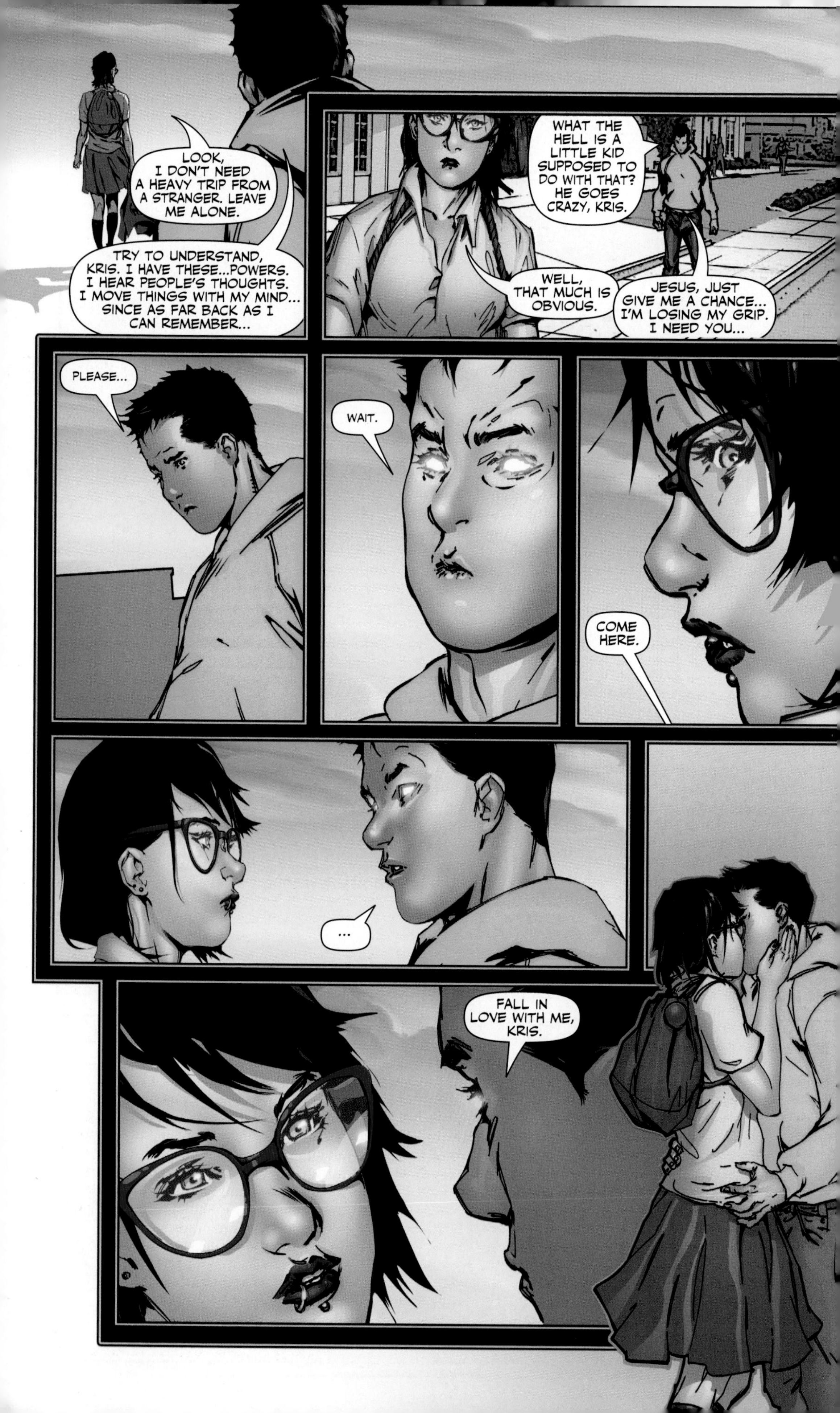
LOOK, I DON'T NEED A HEAVY TRIP FROM A STRANGER. LEAVE ME ALONE.
TRY TO UNDERSTAND, KRIS. I HAVE THESE...POWERS. I HEAR PEOPLE'S THOUGHTS. I MOVE THINGS WITH MY MIND... SINCE AS FAR BACK AS I CAN REMEMBER...
WHAT THE HELL IS A LITTLE KID SUPPOSED TO DO WITH THAT? HE GOES CRAZY, KRIS.
WELL, THAT MUCH IS OBVIOUS.
JESUS, JUST GIVE ME A CHANCE... I'M LOSING MY GRIP. I NEED YOU...
PLEASE...
WAIT.
COME HERE.
...
FALL IN LOVE WITH ME, KRIS.

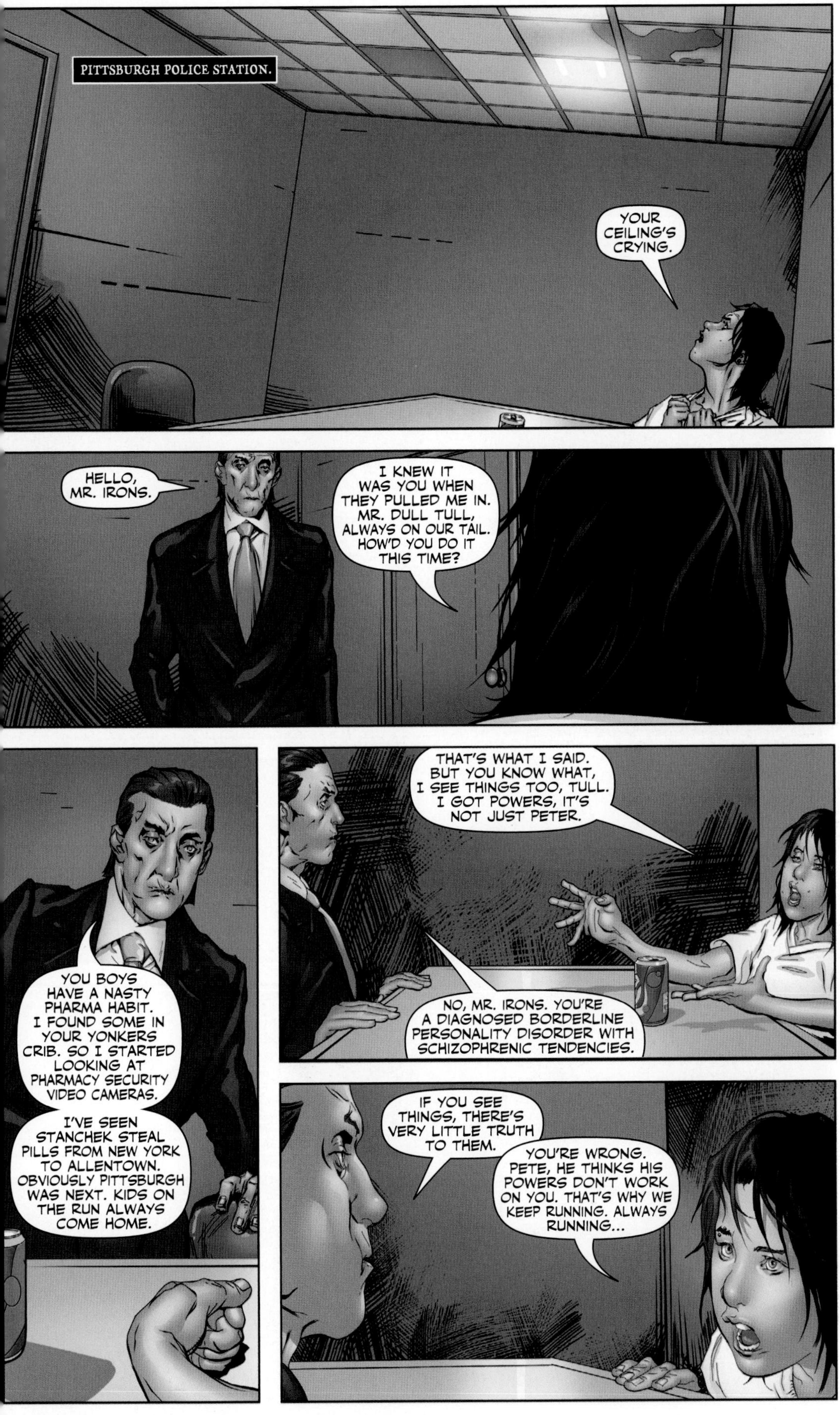

PITTSBURGH POLICE STATION.
YOUR CEILING'S CRYING.
HELLO, MR. IRONS.
I KNEW IT WAS YOU WHEN THEY PULLED ME IN. MR. DULL TULL, ALWAYS ON OUR TAIL. HOW'D YOU DO IT THIS TIME?
YOU BOYS HAVE A NASTY PHARMA HABIT. I FOUND SOME IN YOUR YONKERS CRIB. SO I STARTED LOOKING AT PHARMACY SECURITY VIDEO CAMERAS.
I'VE SEEN STANCHEK STEAL PILLS FROM NEW YORK TO ALLENTOWN. OBVIOUSLY PITTSBURGH WAS NEXT. KIDS ON THE RUN ALWAYS COME HOME.
THAT'S WHAT I SAID. BUT YOU KNOW WHAT, I SEE THINGS TOO, TULL. I GOT POWERS, IT'S NOT JUST PETER.
NO, MR. IRONS. YOU'RE A DIAGNOSED BORDERLINE PERSONALITY DISORDER WITH SCHIZOPHRENIC TENDENCIES.
IF YOU SEE THINGS, THERE'S VERY LITTLE TRUTH TO THEM.
YOU'RE WRONG. PETE, HE THINKS HIS POWERS DON'T WORK ON YOU. THAT'S WHY WE KEEP RUNNING. ALWAYS RUNNING...

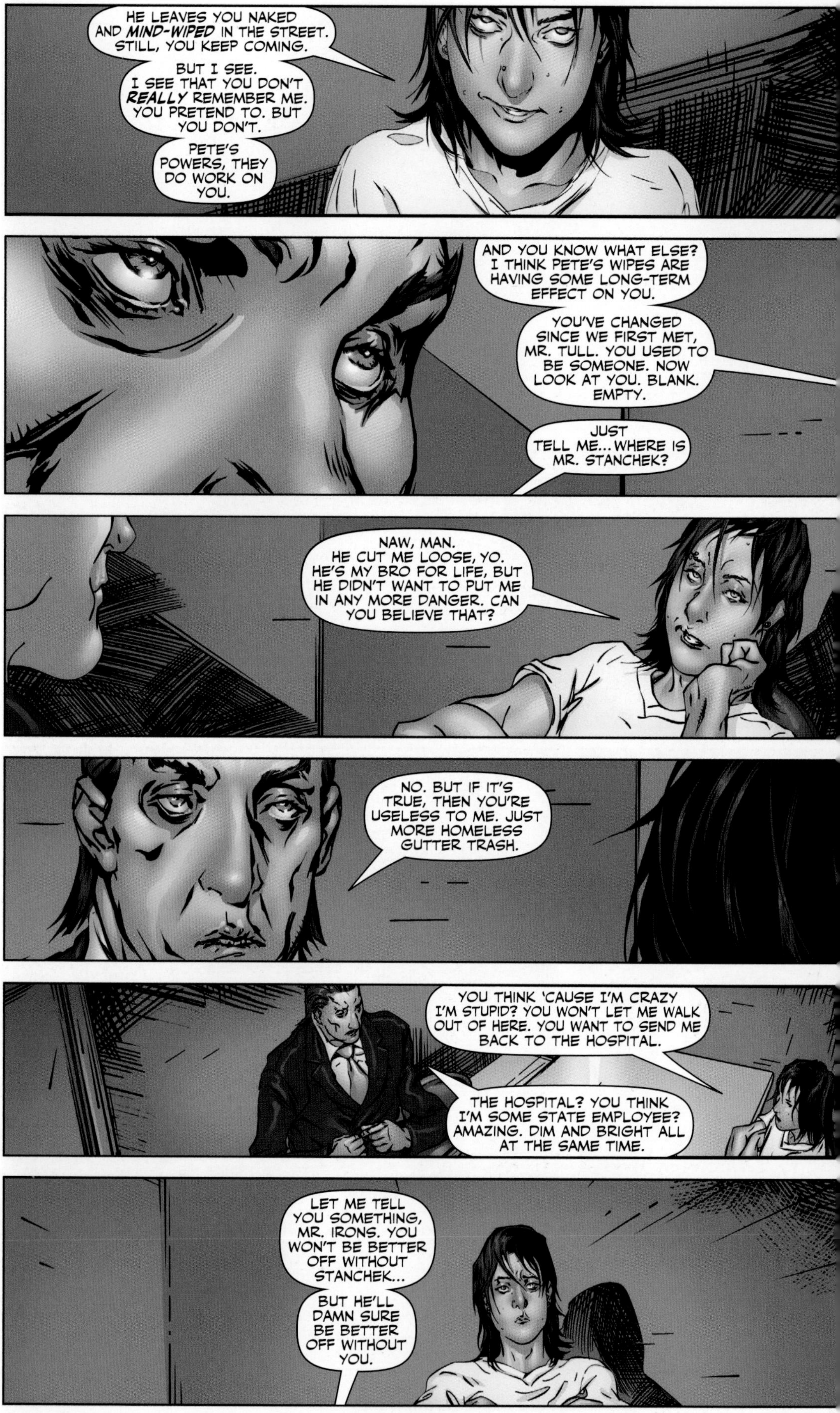
HE LEAVES YOU NAKED AND *MIND-WIPED* IN THE STREET. STILL, YOU KEEP COMING.
BUT I SEE. I SEE THAT YOU DON'T *REALLY* REMEMBER ME. YOU PRETEND TO. BUT YOU DON'T.
PETE'S POWERS, THEY DO WORK ON YOU.
AND YOU KNOW WHAT ELSE? I THINK PETE'S WIPES ARE HAVING SOME LONG-TERM EFFECT ON YOU.
YOU'VE CHANGED SINCE WE FIRST MET, MR. TULL. YOU USED TO BE SOMEONE. NOW LOOK AT YOU. BLANK. EMPTY.
JUST TELL ME...WHERE IS MR. STANCHEK?
NAW, MAN. HE CUT ME LOOSE, YO. HE'S MY BRO FOR LIFE, BUT HE DIDN'T WANT TO PUT ME IN ANY MORE DANGER. CAN YOU BELIEVE THAT?
NO. BUT IF IT'S TRUE, THEN YOU'RE USELESS TO ME. JUST MORE HOMELESS GUTTER TRASH.
YOU THINK 'CAUSE I'M CRAZY I'M STUPID? YOU WON'T LET ME WALK OUT OF HERE. YOU WANT TO SEND ME BACK TO THE HOSPITAL.
THE HOSPITAL? YOU THINK I'M SOME STATE EMPLOYEE? AMAZING. DIM AND BRIGHT ALL AT THE SAME TIME.
LET ME TELL YOU SOMETHING, MR. IRONS. YOU WON'T BE BETTER OFF WITHOUT STANCHEK...
BUT HE'LL DAMN SURE BE BETTER OFF WITHOUT YOU.

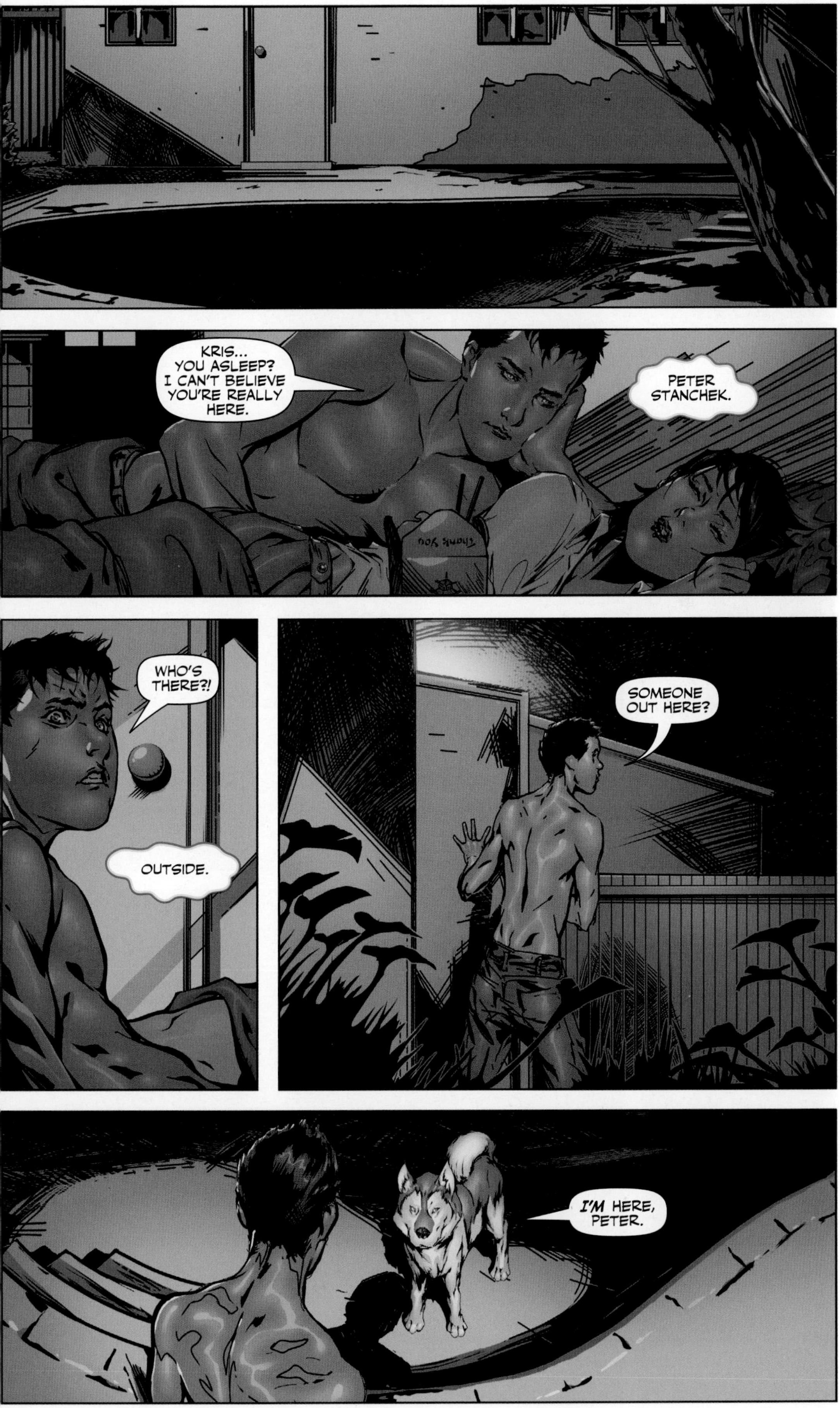
KRIS... YOU ASLEEP? I CAN'T BELIEVE YOU'RE REALLY HERE.
PETER STANCHEK.
WHO'S THERE?!
OUTSIDE.
SOMEONE OUT HERE?
I'M HERE, PETER.

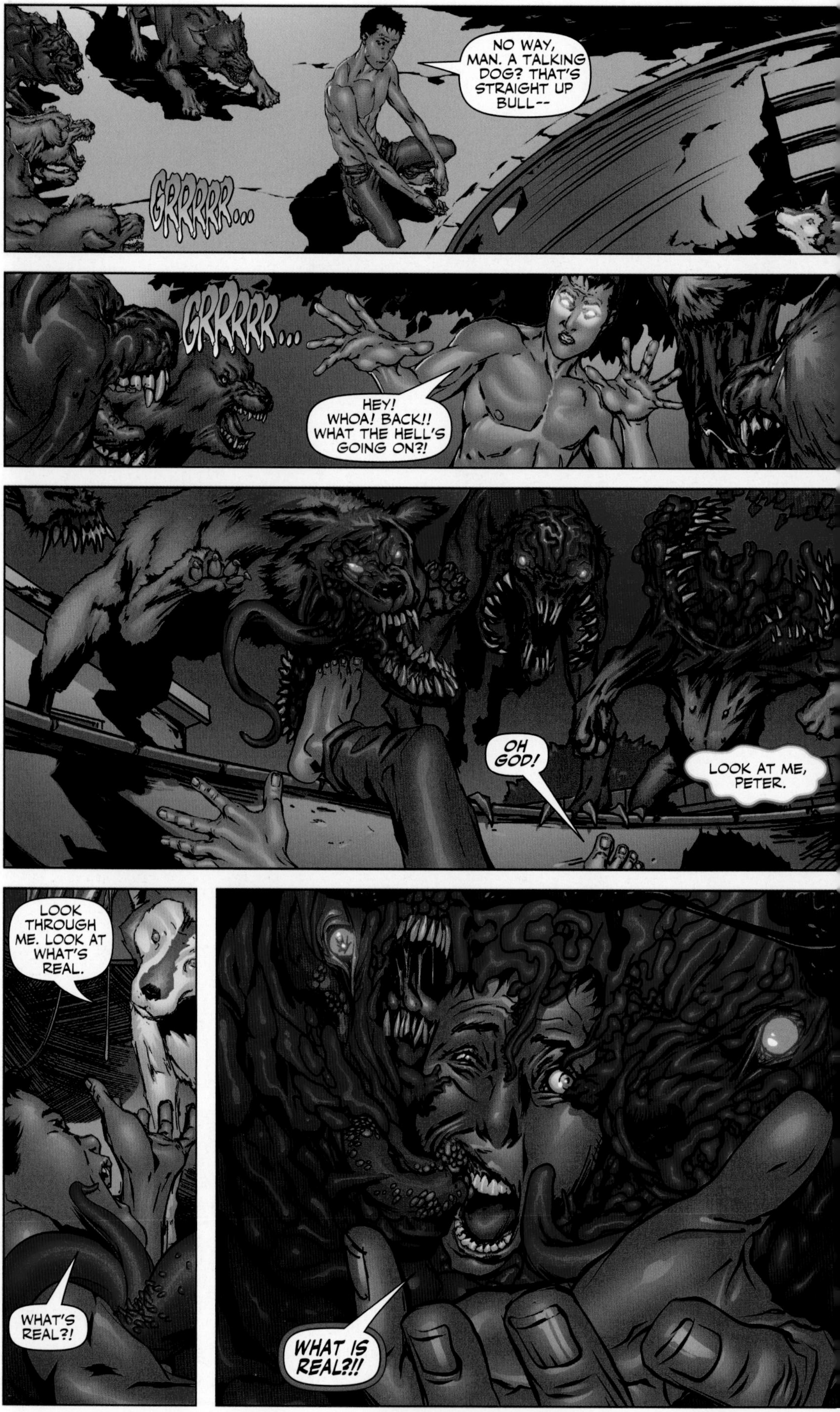
NO WAY, MAN. A TALKING DOG? THAT'S STRAIGHT UP BULL--
GRRRRR...
GRRRRR...
HEY! WHOA! BACK!! WHAT THE HELL'S GOING ON?!
OH GOD!
LOOK AT ME, PETER.
LOOK THROUGH ME. LOOK AT WHAT'S REAL.
WHAT'S REAL?!
WHAT IS REAL?!!

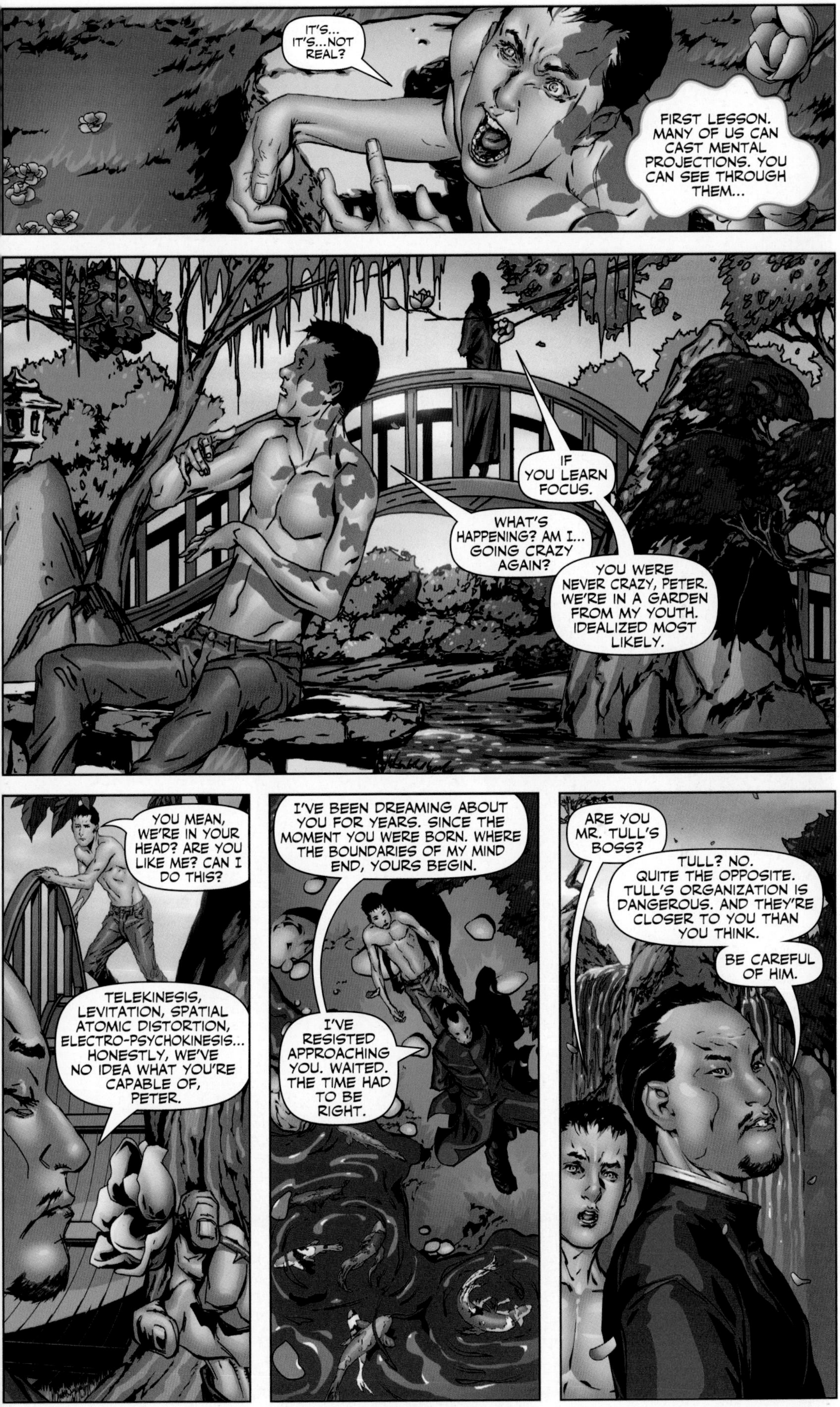
IT'S... IT'S...NOT REAL?
FIRST LESSON. MANY OF US CAN CAST MENTAL PROJECTIONS. YOU CAN SEE THROUGH THEM...
IF YOU LEARN FOCUS.
WHAT'S HAPPENING? AM I... GOING CRAZY AGAIN?
YOU WERE NEVER CRAZY, PETER. WE'RE IN A GARDEN FROM MY YOUTH. IDEALIZED MOST LIKELY.
YOU MEAN, WE'RE IN YOUR HEAD? ARE YOU LIKE ME? CAN I DO THIS?
TELEKINESIS, LEVITATION, SPATIAL ATOMIC DISTORTION, ELECTRO-PSYCHOKINESIS... HONESTLY, WE'VE NO IDEA WHAT YOU'RE CAPABLE OF, PETER.
I'VE BEEN DREAMING ABOUT YOU FOR YEARS. SINCE THE MOMENT YOU WERE BORN. WHERE THE BOUNDARIES OF MY MIND END, YOURS BEGIN.
I'VE RESISTED APPROACHING YOU. WAITED. THE TIME HAD TO BE RIGHT.
ARE YOU MR. TULL'S BOSS?
TULL? NO. QUITE THE OPPOSITE. TULL'S ORGANIZATION IS DANGEROUS. AND THEY'RE CLOSER TO YOU THAN YOU THINK.
BE CAREFUL OF HIM.

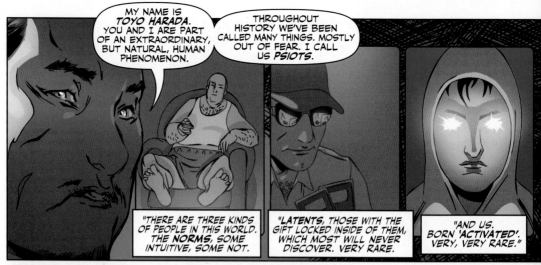

MY NAME IS *TOYO HARADA*. YOU AND I ARE PART OF AN EXTRAORDINARY, BUT NATURAL, HUMAN PHENOMENON.

THROUGHOUT HISTORY WE'VE BEEN CALLED MANY THINGS. MOSTLY OUT OF FEAR. I CALL US *PSIOTS*.

"THERE ARE THREE KINDS OF PEOPLE IN THIS WORLD. THE *NORMS*, SOME INTUITIVE, SOME NOT.

"*LATENTS*, THOSE WITH THE GIFT LOCKED INSIDE OF THEM, WHICH MOST WILL NEVER DISCOVER. VERY RARE.

"AND US. BORN '*ACTIVATED*'. VERY, VERY RARE."

YOU'RE A UNIQUE AND BEAUTIFUL THING, EVEN AMONGST UNIQUE AND BEAUTIFUL THINGS, PETER.

I DON'T GET IT. WHY DIDN'T YOU COME TO ME EARLIER? I MEAN, ALL I NEEDED WAS SOMEONE TO HELP ME UNDERSTAND.

I KNOW YOU BETTER THAN YOU KNOW YOURSELF. YOU WOULDN'T HAVE ACCEPTED MY HELP. NOT UNTIL NOW.

THIS IS AN INTERVENTION. THERE'S NOTHING LEFT ON YOUR PATH BUT ABSOLUTE SELF-DESTRUCTION.

LIVING ON THE RUN. SELF-MEDICATING. SELF-REGULATING. DAMPENING YOUR OWN POWERS.

YOU IMAGINE YOU'RE DOING THE BEST FOR JOE. BUT YOU KEEP HIM FROM GETTING GENUINE HELP...

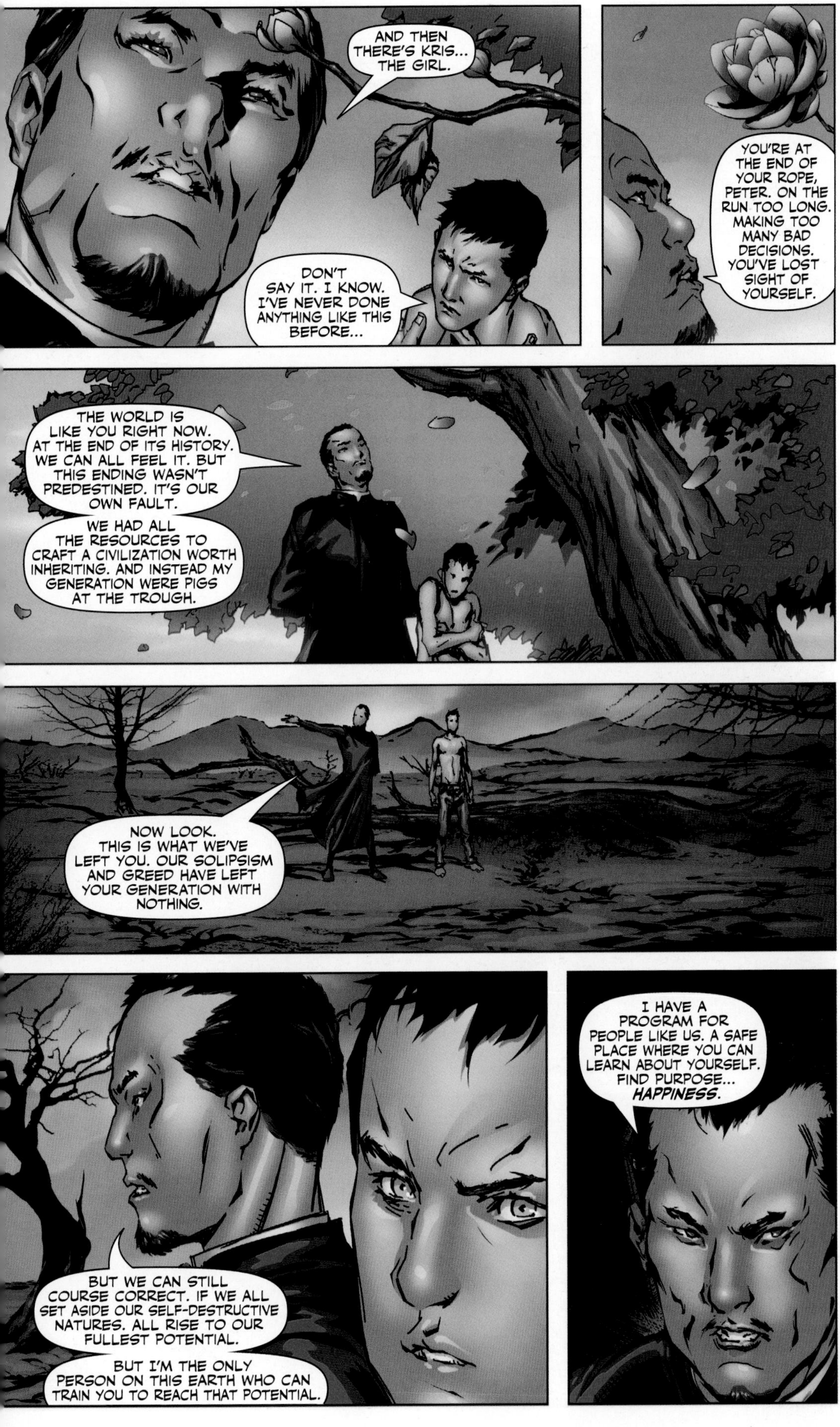
AND THEN THERE'S KRIS... THE GIRL.
DON'T SAY IT. I KNOW. I'VE NEVER DONE ANYTHING LIKE THIS BEFORE...
YOU'RE AT THE END OF YOUR ROPE, PETER. ON THE RUN TOO LONG. MAKING TOO MANY BAD DECISIONS. YOU'VE LOST SIGHT OF YOURSELF.
THE WORLD IS LIKE YOU RIGHT NOW. AT THE END OF ITS HISTORY. WE CAN ALL FEEL IT. BUT THIS ENDING WASN'T PREDESTINED. IT'S OUR OWN FAULT.
WE HAD ALL THE RESOURCES TO CRAFT A CIVILIZATION WORTH INHERITING. AND INSTEAD MY GENERATION WERE PIGS AT THE TROUGH.
NOW LOOK. THIS IS WHAT WE'VE LEFT YOU. OUR SOLIPSISM AND GREED HAVE LEFT YOUR GENERATION WITH NOTHING.
BUT WE CAN STILL COURSE CORRECT. IF WE ALL SET ASIDE OUR SELF-DESTRUCTIVE NATURES. ALL RISE TO OUR FULLEST POTENTIAL.
BUT I'M THE ONLY PERSON ON THIS EARTH WHO CAN TRAIN YOU TO REACH THAT POTENTIAL.
I HAVE A PROGRAM FOR PEOPLE LIKE US. A SAFE PLACE WHERE YOU CAN LEARN ABOUT YOURSELF. FIND PURPOSE... *HAPPINESS*.

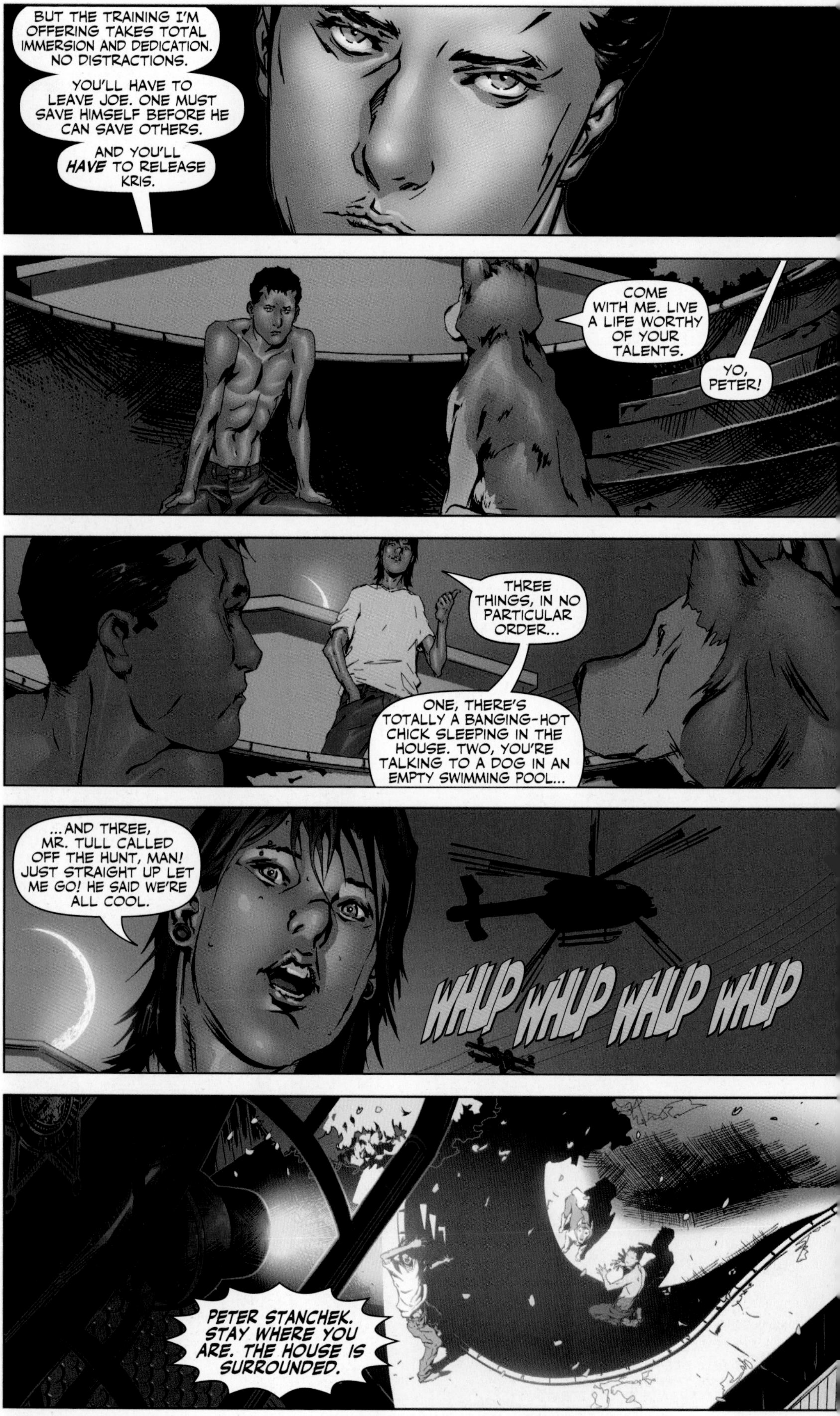
BUT THE TRAINING I'M OFFERING TAKES TOTAL IMMERSION AND DEDICATION. NO DISTRACTIONS.
YOU'LL HAVE TO LEAVE JOE. ONE MUST SAVE HIMSELF BEFORE HE CAN SAVE OTHERS.
AND YOU'LL *HAVE* TO RELEASE KRIS.
COME WITH ME. LIVE A LIFE WORTHY OF YOUR TALENTS.
YO, PETER!
THREE THINGS, IN NO PARTICULAR ORDER...
ONE, THERE'S TOTALLY A BANGING-HOT CHICK SLEEPING IN THE HOUSE. TWO, YOU'RE TALKING TO A DOG IN AN EMPTY SWIMMING POOL...
...AND THREE, MR. TULL CALLED OFF THE HUNT, MAN! JUST STRAIGHT UP LET ME GO! HE SAID WE'RE ALL COOL.
WHUP WHUP WHUP WHUP
PETER STANCHEK. STAY WHERE YOU ARE. THE HOUSE IS SURROUNDED.

GOD DAMN IT, JOE...

THEY FOLLOWED YOU.

WHUP WHUP WHUP

AWESOME! IT'S LIKE A MICHAEL BAY MOVIE!

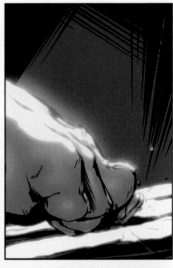

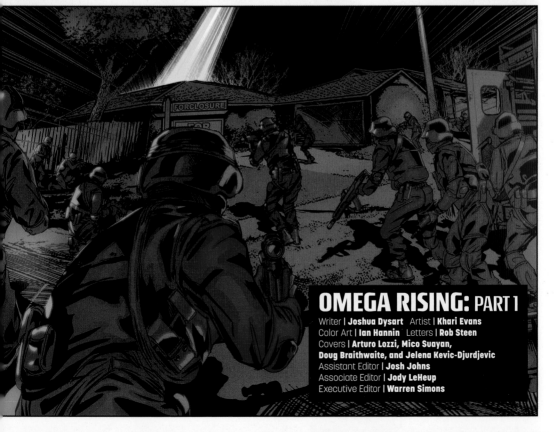

FORCLOSURE

OMEGA RISING: PART 1

Writer | **Joshua Dysart**   Artist | **Khari Evans**
Color Art | **Ian Hannin**   Letters | **Rob Steen**
Covers | **Arturo Lozzi, Mico Suayan,**
Doug Braithwaite, and Jelena Kevic-Djurdjevic
Assistant Editor | **Josh Johns**
Associate Editor | **Jody LeHeup**
Executive Editor | **Warren Simons**

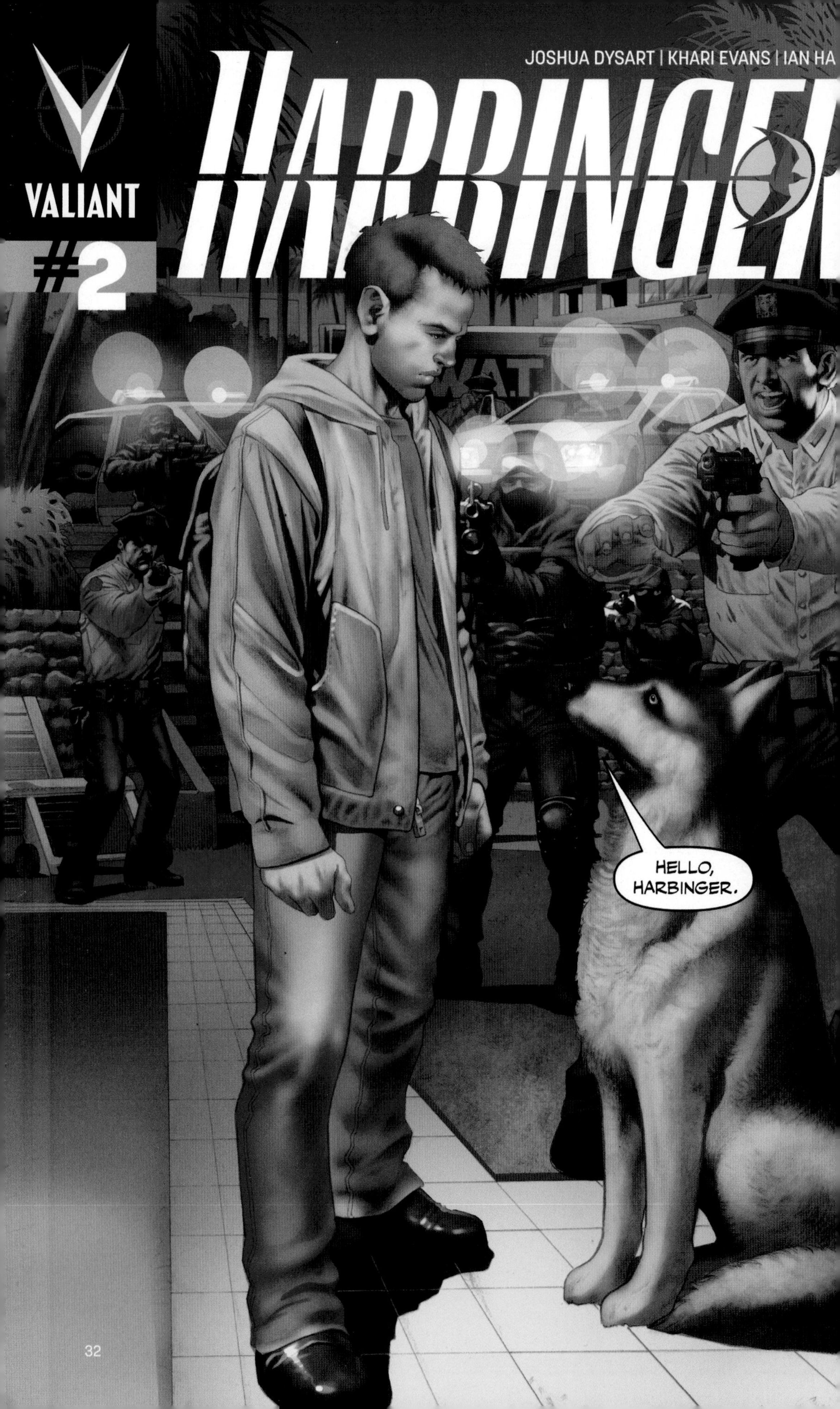
VALIANT
#2
JOSHUA DYSART | KHARI EVANS | IAN HA
HARBINGER
HELLO, HARBINGER.

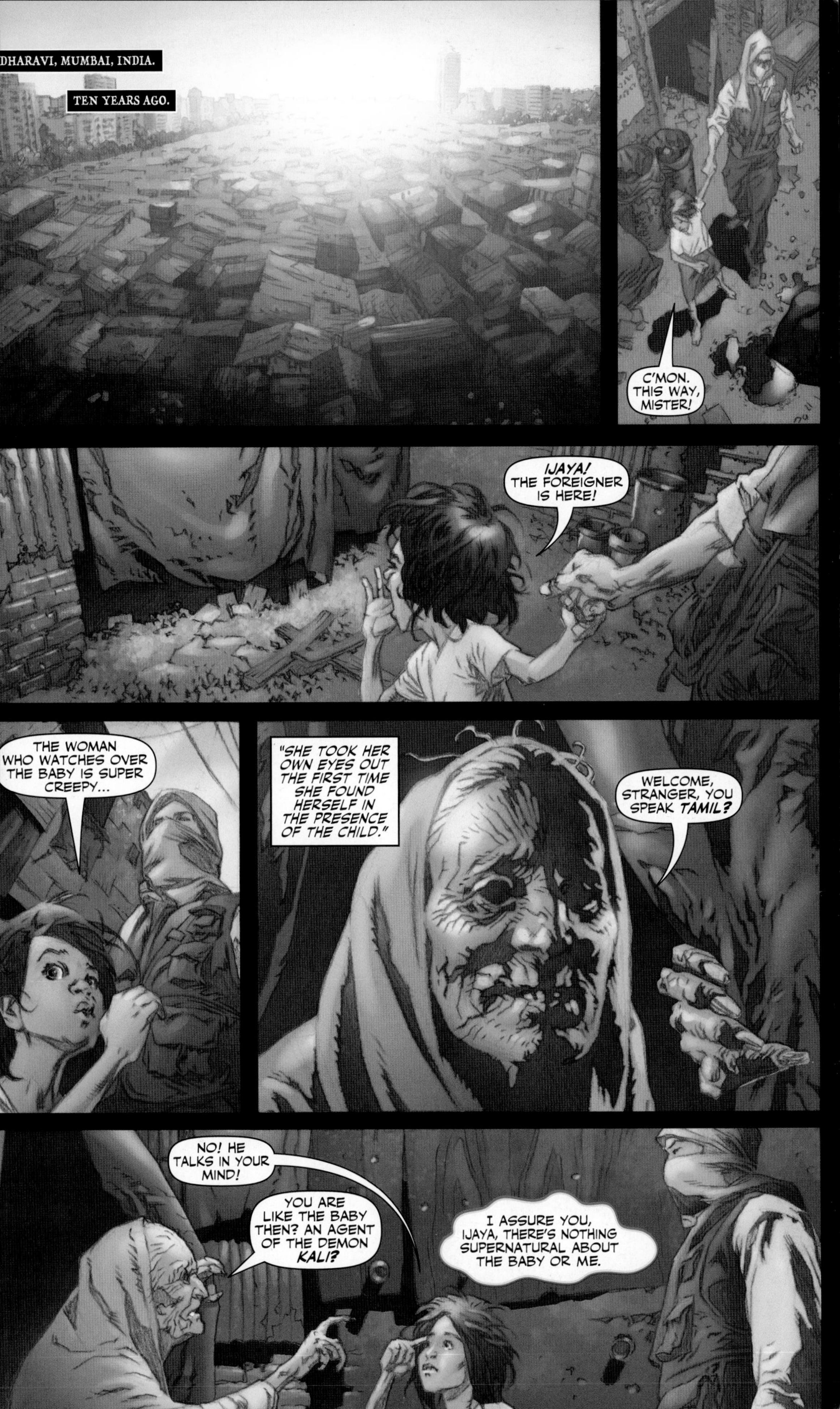

DHARAVI, MUMBAI, INDIA.
TEN YEARS AGO.
C'MON. THIS WAY, MISTER!
IJAYA! THE FOREIGNER IS HERE!
THE WOMAN WHO WATCHES OVER THE BABY IS SUPER CREEPY...
"SHE TOOK HER OWN EYES OUT THE FIRST TIME SHE FOUND HERSELF IN THE PRESENCE OF THE CHILD."
WELCOME, STRANGER, YOU SPEAK TAMIL?
NO! HE TALKS IN YOUR MIND!
YOU ARE LIKE THE BABY THEN? AN AGENT OF THE DEMON KALI?
I ASSURE YOU, IJAYA, THERE'S NOTHING SUPERNATURAL ABOUT THE BABY OR ME.

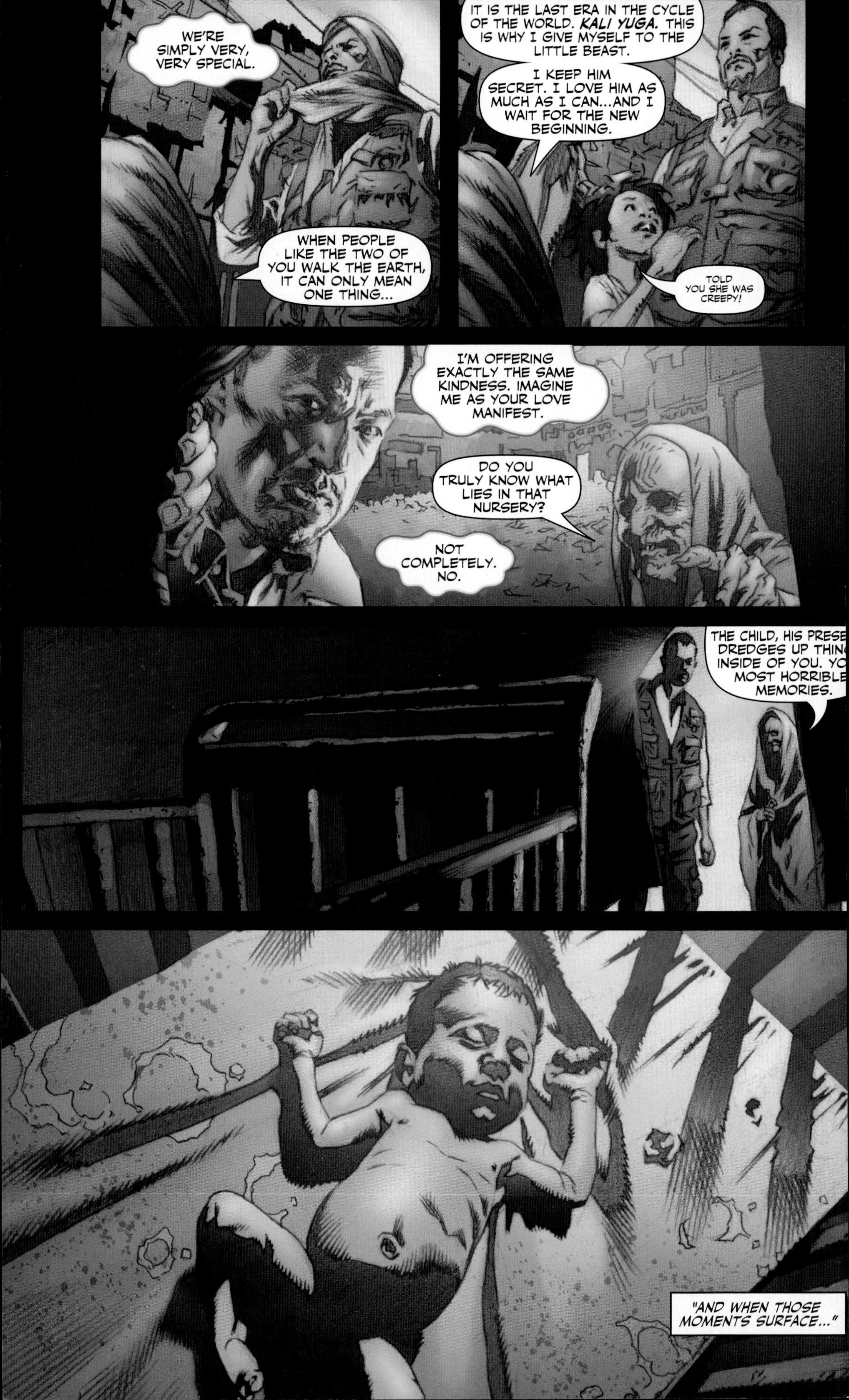
WE'RE SIMPLY VERY, VERY SPECIAL.
WHEN PEOPLE LIKE THE TWO OF YOU WALK THE EARTH, IT CAN ONLY MEAN ONE THING...
IT IS THE LAST ERA IN THE CYCLE OF THE WORLD. *KALI YUGA.* THIS IS WHY I GIVE MYSELF TO THE LITTLE BEAST.
I KEEP HIM SECRET. I LOVE HIM AS MUCH AS I CAN...AND I WAIT FOR THE NEW BEGINNING.
TOLD YOU SHE WAS *CREEPY!*
I'M OFFERING EXACTLY THE SAME KINDNESS. IMAGINE ME AS YOUR LOVE MANIFEST.
DO YOU TRULY KNOW WHAT LIES IN THAT NURSERY?
NOT COMPLETELY. NO.
THE CHILD, HIS PRESE DREDGES UP THIN INSIDE OF YOU. YO MOST HORRIBLE MEMORIES.
"AND WHEN THOSE MOMENTS SURFACE..."

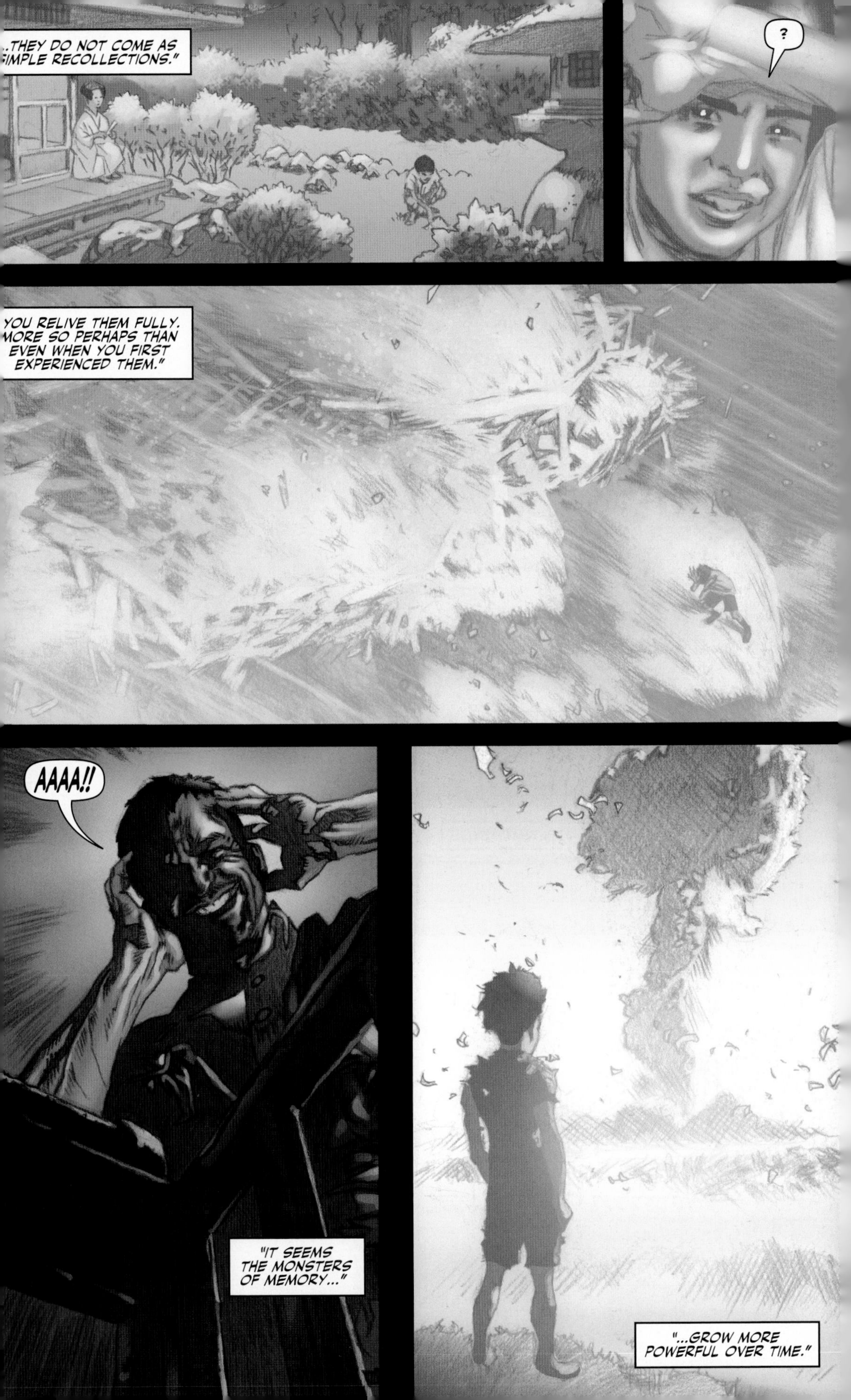
..THEY DO NOT COME AS SIMPLE RECOLLECTIONS."
?
YOU RELIVE THEM FULLY. MORE SO PERHAPS THAN EVEN WHEN YOU FIRST EXPERIENCED THEM."
AAAA!!
"IT SEEMS THE MONSTERS OF MEMORY..."
"...GROW MORE POWERFUL OVER TIME."

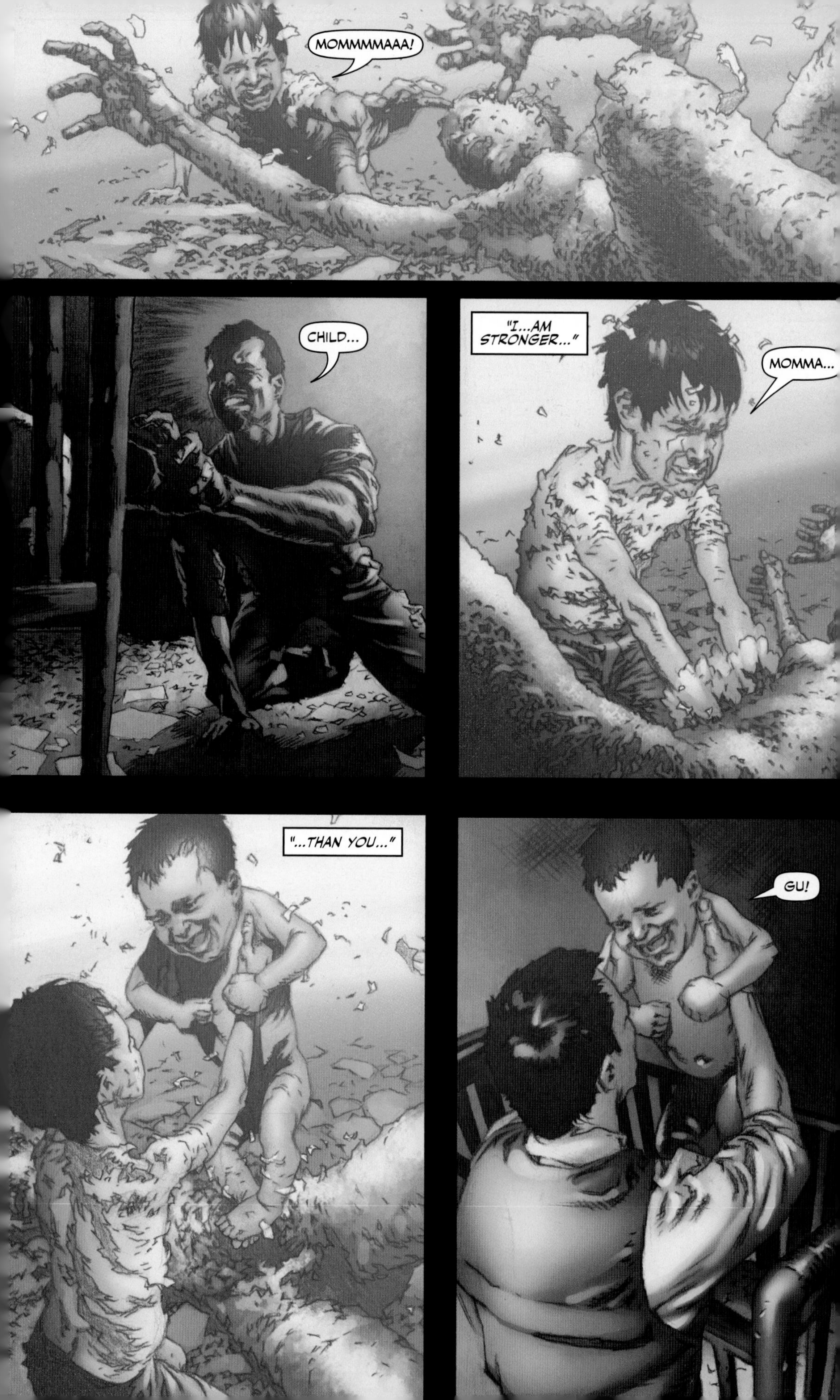
MOMMMMAAA!
CHILD...
"I...AM STRONGER..."
MOMMA...
"...THAN YOU..."
GU!

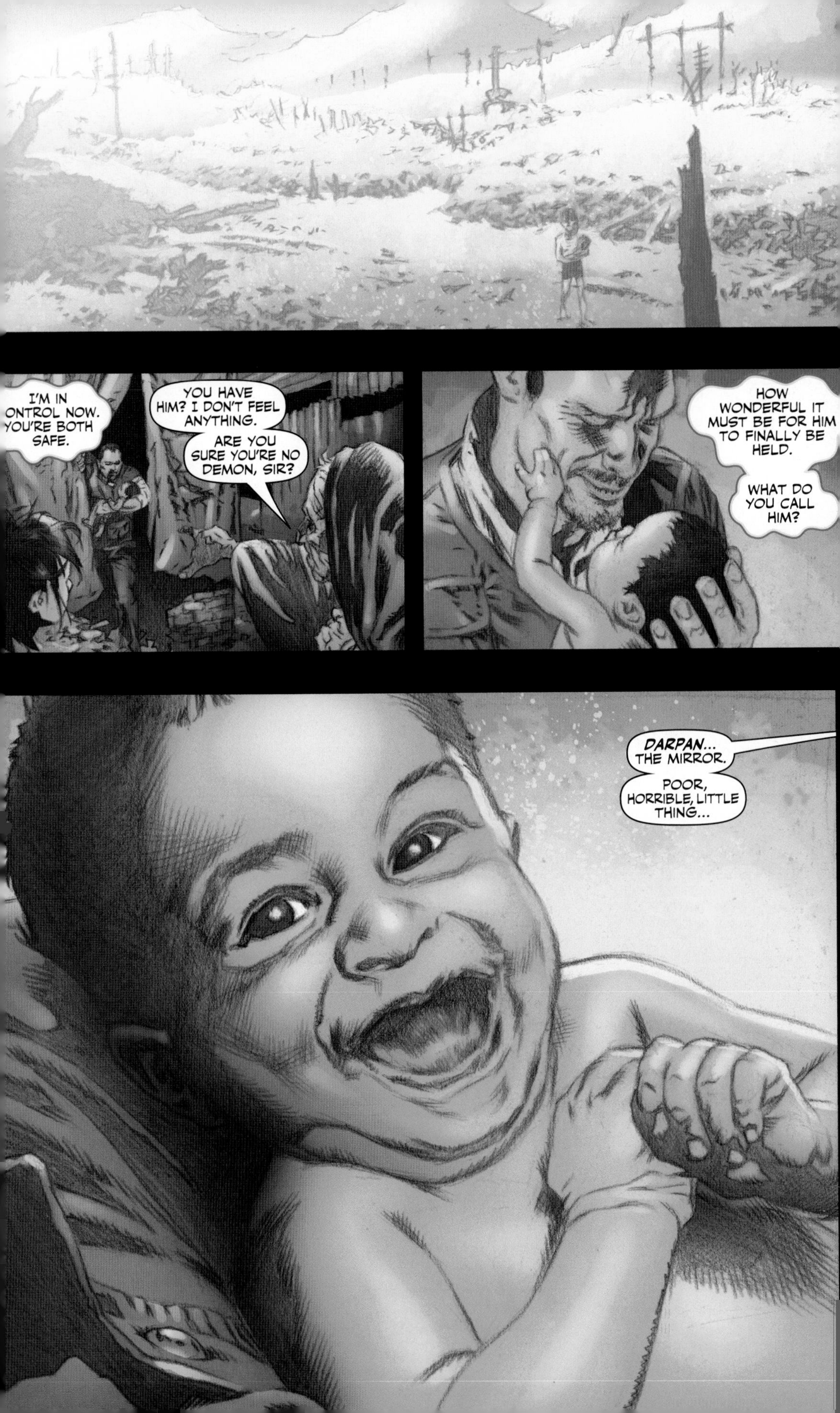
I'M IN ONTROL NOW. YOU'RE BOTH SAFE.
YOU HAVE HIM? I DON'T FEEL ANYTHING.
ARE YOU SURE YOU'RE NO DEMON, SIR?
HOW WONDERFUL IT MUST BE FOR HIM TO FINALLY BE HELD.
WHAT DO YOU CALL HIM?
DARPAN... THE MIRROR.
POOR, HORRIBLE, LITTLE THING...

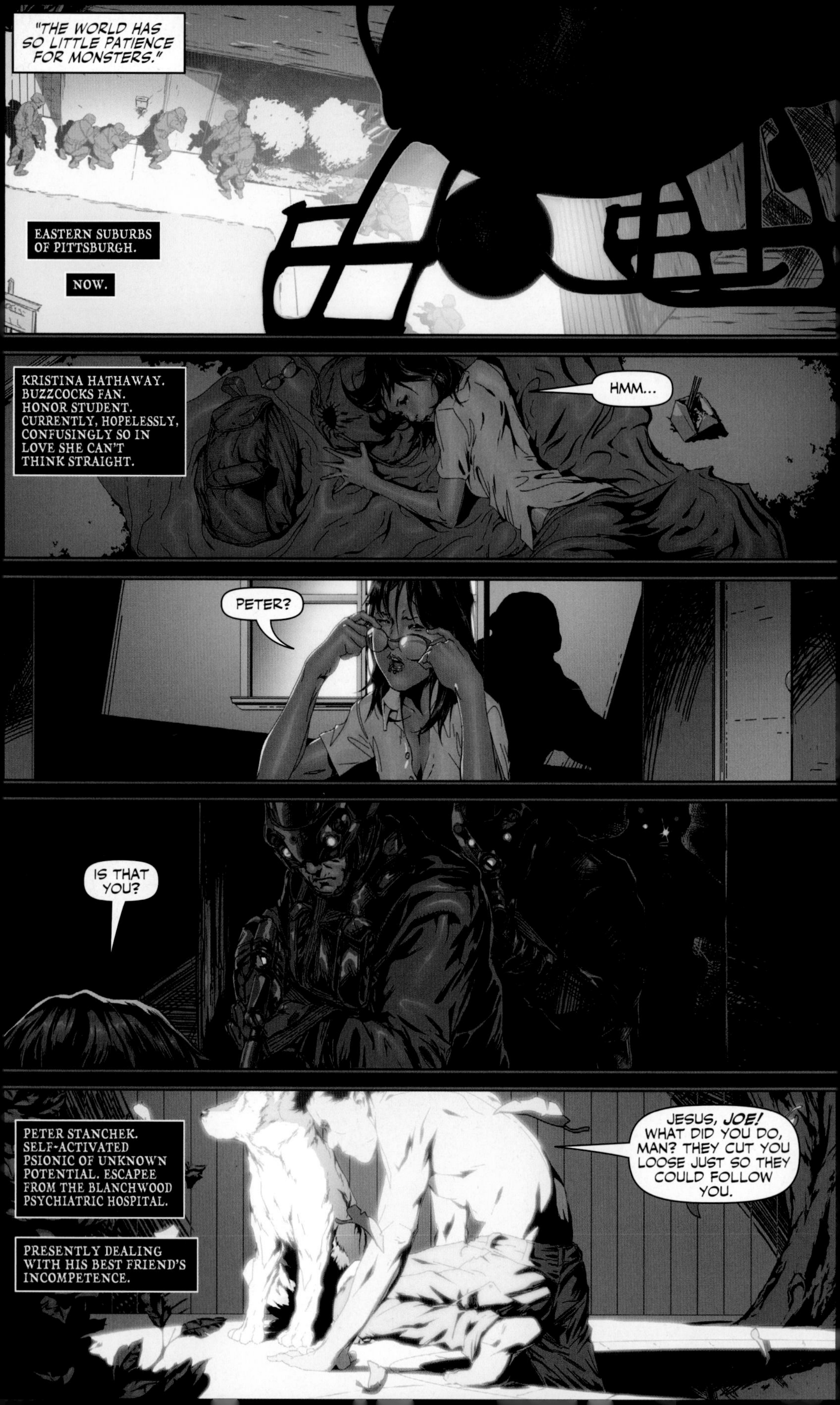

"THE WORLD HAS SO LITTLE PATIENCE FOR MONSTERS."
EASTERN SUBURBS OF PITTSBURGH.
NOW.
KRISTINA HATHAWAY. BUZZCOCKS FAN. HONOR STUDENT. CURRENTLY, HOPELESSLY, CONFUSINGLY SO IN LOVE SHE CAN'T THINK STRAIGHT.
HMM...
PETER?
IS THAT YOU?
PETER STANCHEK. SELF-ACTIVATED PSIONIC OF UNKNOWN POTENTIAL. ESCAPEE FROM THE BLANCHWOOD PSYCHIATRIC HOSPITAL.
PRESENTLY DEALING WITH HIS BEST FRIEND'S INCOMPETENCE.
JESUS, JOE! WHAT DID YOU DO, MAN? THEY CUT YOU LOOSE JUST SO THEY COULD FOLLOW YOU.

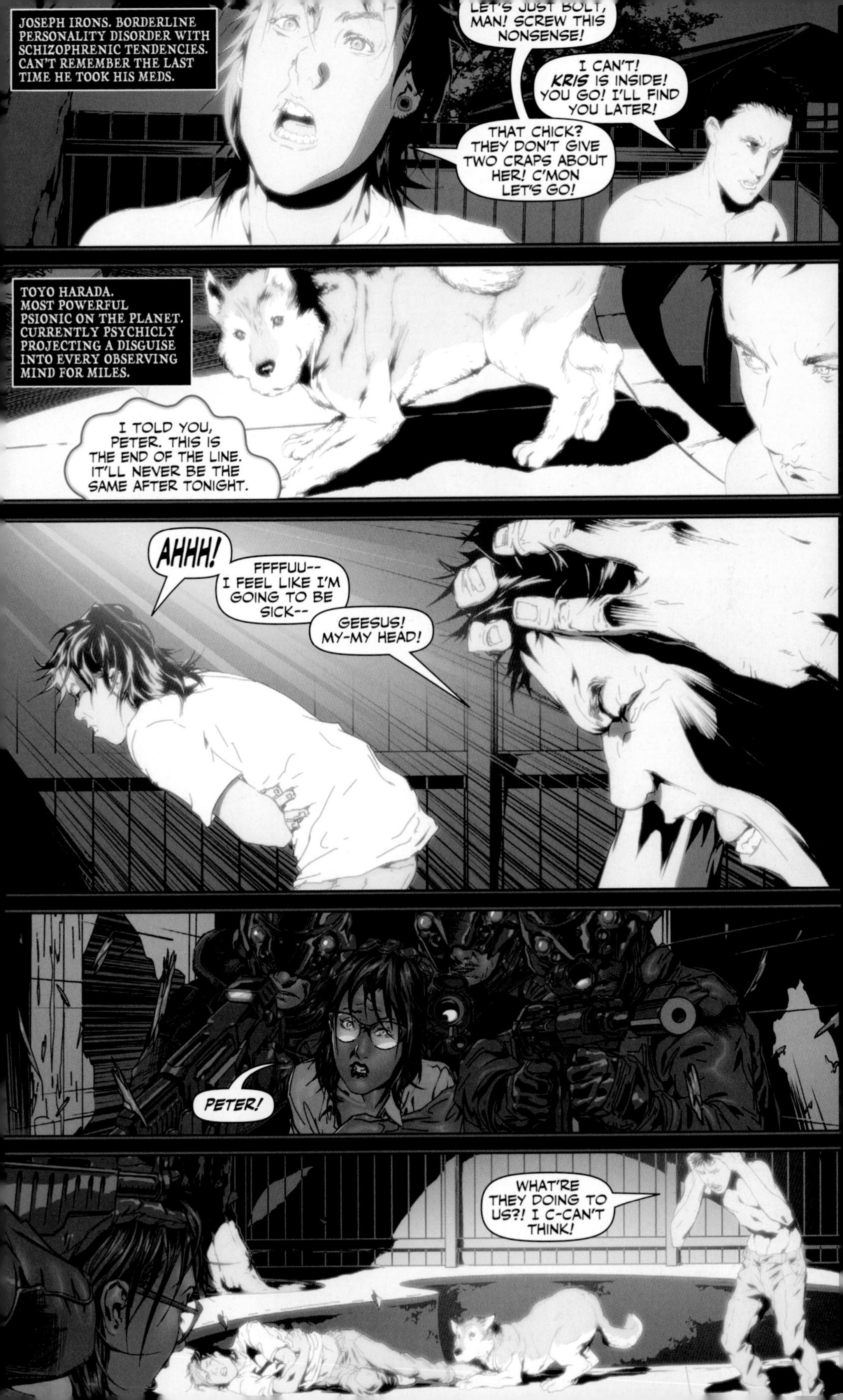
JOSEPH IRONS. BORDERLINE PERSONALITY DISORDER WITH SCHIZOPHRENIC TENDENCIES. CAN'T REMEMBER THE LAST TIME HE TOOK HIS MEDS.
LET'S JUST BOLT, MAN! SCREW THIS NONSENSE!
I CAN'T! KRIS IS INSIDE! YOU GO! I'LL FIND YOU LATER!
THAT CHICK? THEY DON'T GIVE TWO CRAPS ABOUT HER! C'MON LET'S GO!
TOYO HARADA. MOST POWERFUL PSIONIC ON THE PLANET. CURRENTLY PSYCHICLY PROJECTING A DISGUISE INTO EVERY OBSERVING MIND FOR MILES.
I TOLD YOU, PETER. THIS IS THE END OF THE LINE. IT'LL NEVER BE THE SAME AFTER TONIGHT.
AHHH!
FFFFUU-- I FEEL LIKE I'M GOING TO BE SICK--
GEESUS! MY-MY HEAD!
PETER!
WHAT'RE THEY DOING TO US?! I C-CAN'T THINK!

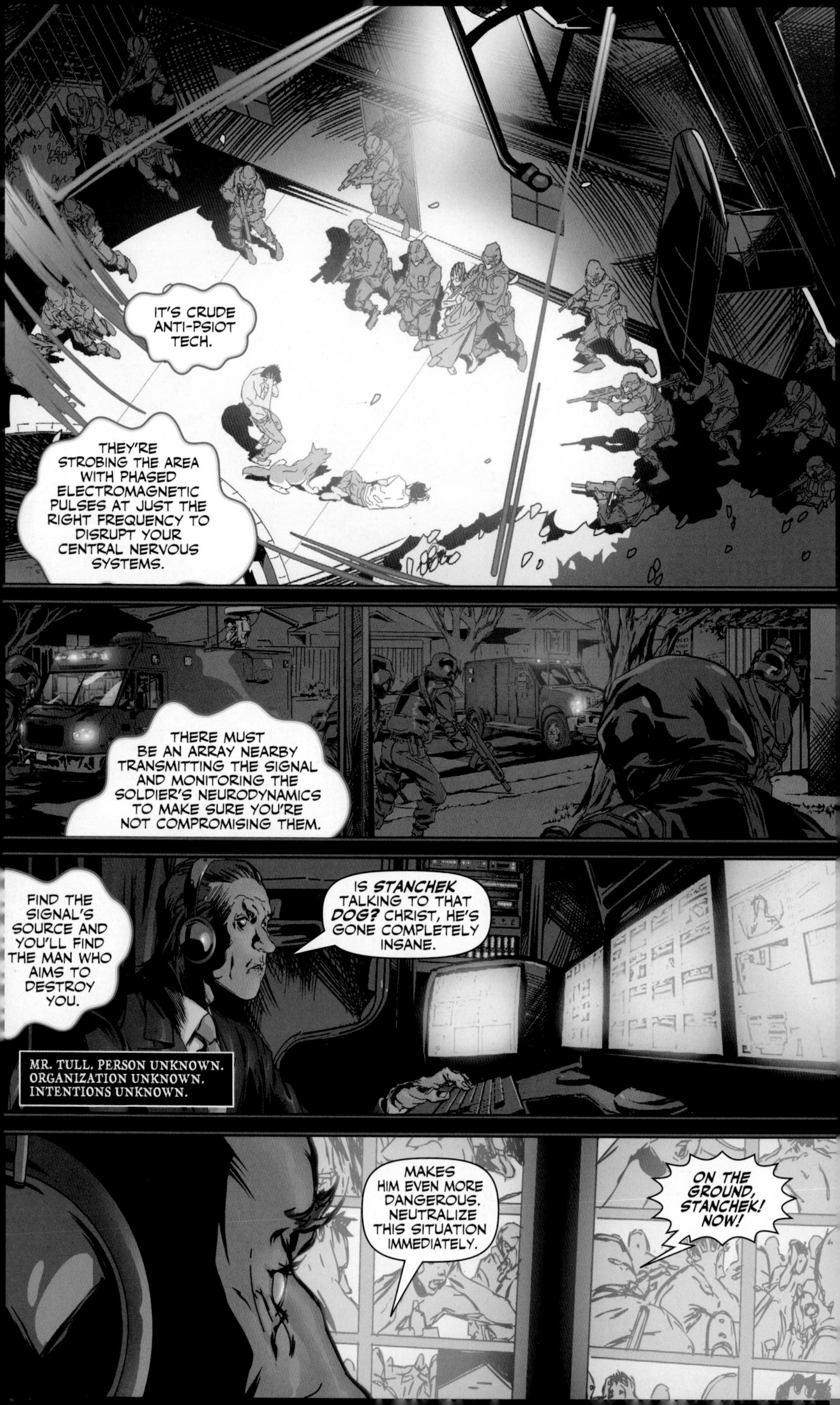

IT'S CRUDE ANTI-PSIOT TECH.
THEY'RE STROBING THE AREA WITH PHASED ELECTROMAGNETIC PULSES AT JUST THE RIGHT FREQUENCY TO DISRUPT YOUR CENTRAL NERVOUS SYSTEMS.
THERE MUST BE AN ARRAY NEARBY TRANSMITTING THE SIGNAL AND MONITORING THE SOLDIER'S NEURODYNAMICS TO MAKE SURE YOU'RE NOT COMPROMISING THEM.
FIND THE SIGNAL'S SOURCE AND YOU'LL FIND THE MAN WHO AIMS TO DESTROY YOU.
IS STANCHEK TALKING TO THAT DOG? CHRIST, HE'S GONE COMPLETELY INSANE.
MR. TULL. PERSON UNKNOWN. ORGANIZATION UNKNOWN. INTENTIONS UNKNOWN.
MAKES HIM EVEN MORE DANGEROUS. NEUTRALIZE THIS SITUATION IMMEDIATELY.
ON THE GROUND, STANCHEK! NOW!

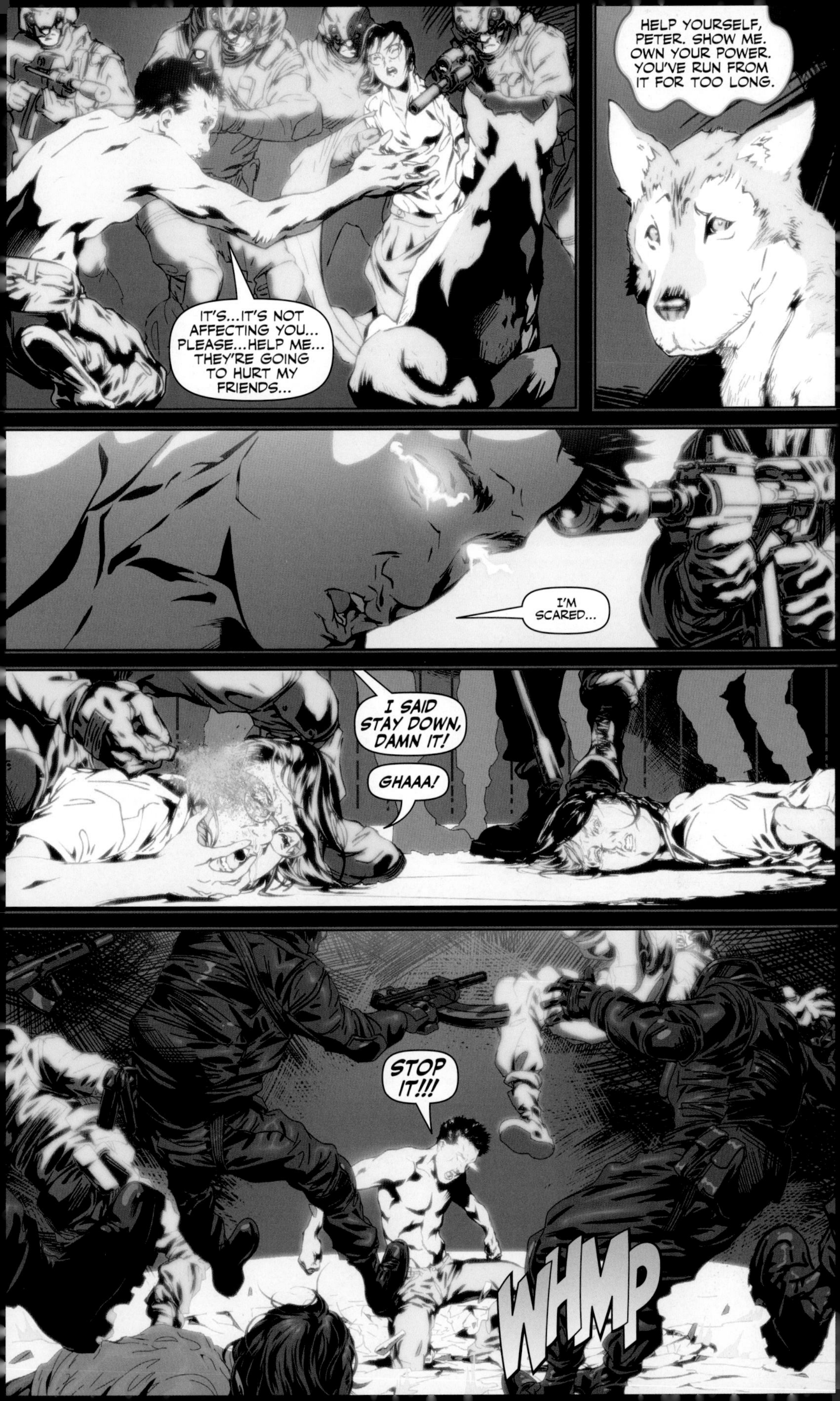
IT'S...IT'S NOT AFFECTING YOU... PLEASE...HELP ME... THEY'RE GOING TO HURT MY FRIENDS...
HELP YOURSELF, PETER. SHOW ME. OWN YOUR POWER. YOU'VE RUN FROM IT FOR TOO LONG.
I'M SCARED...
I SAID STAY DOWN, DAMN IT!
GHAAA!
STOP IT!!!
WHMP

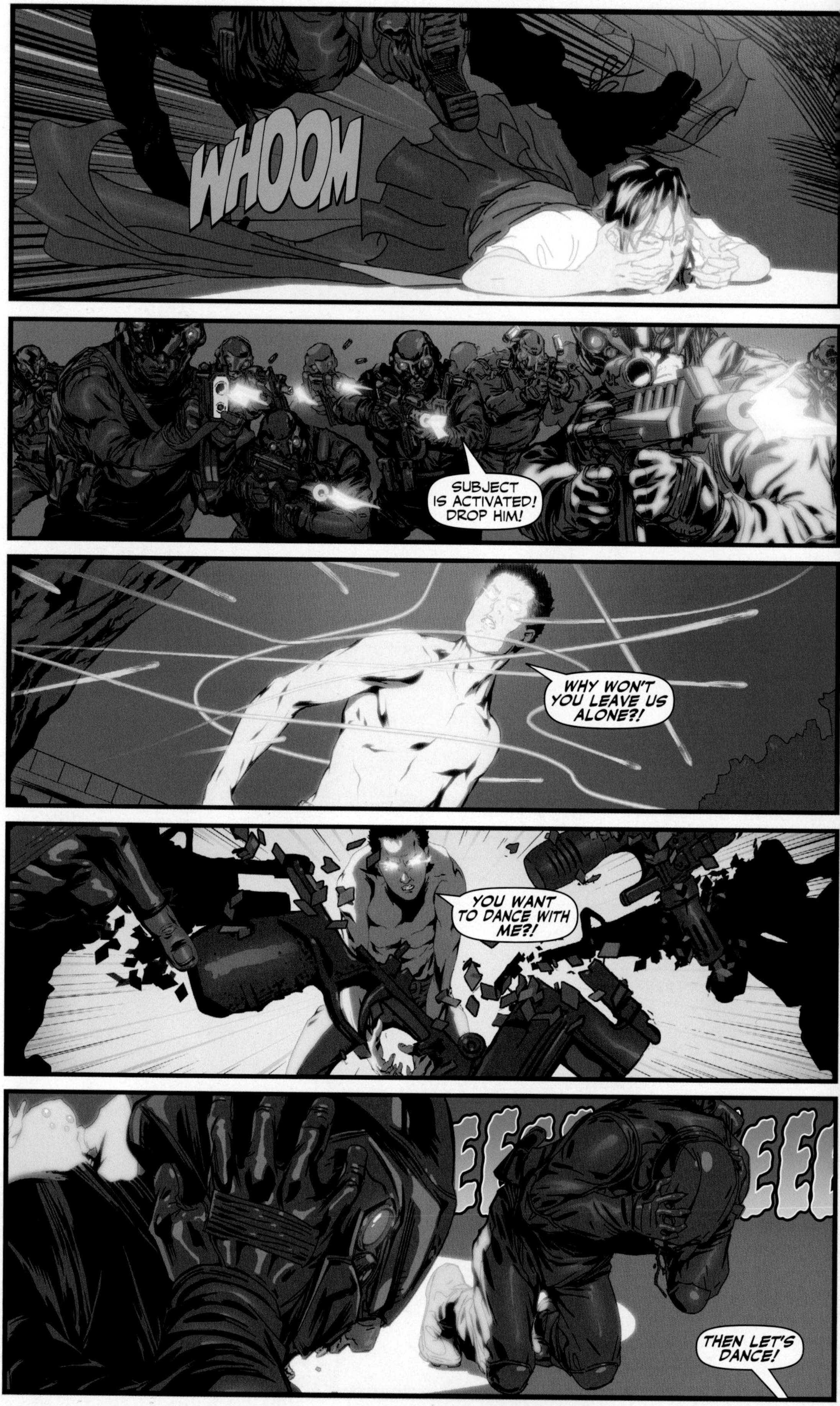
WHOOM
SUBJECT IS ACTIVATED! DROP HIM!
WHY WON'T YOU LEAVE US ALONE?!
YOU WANT TO DANCE WITH ME?!
THEN LET'S DANCE!

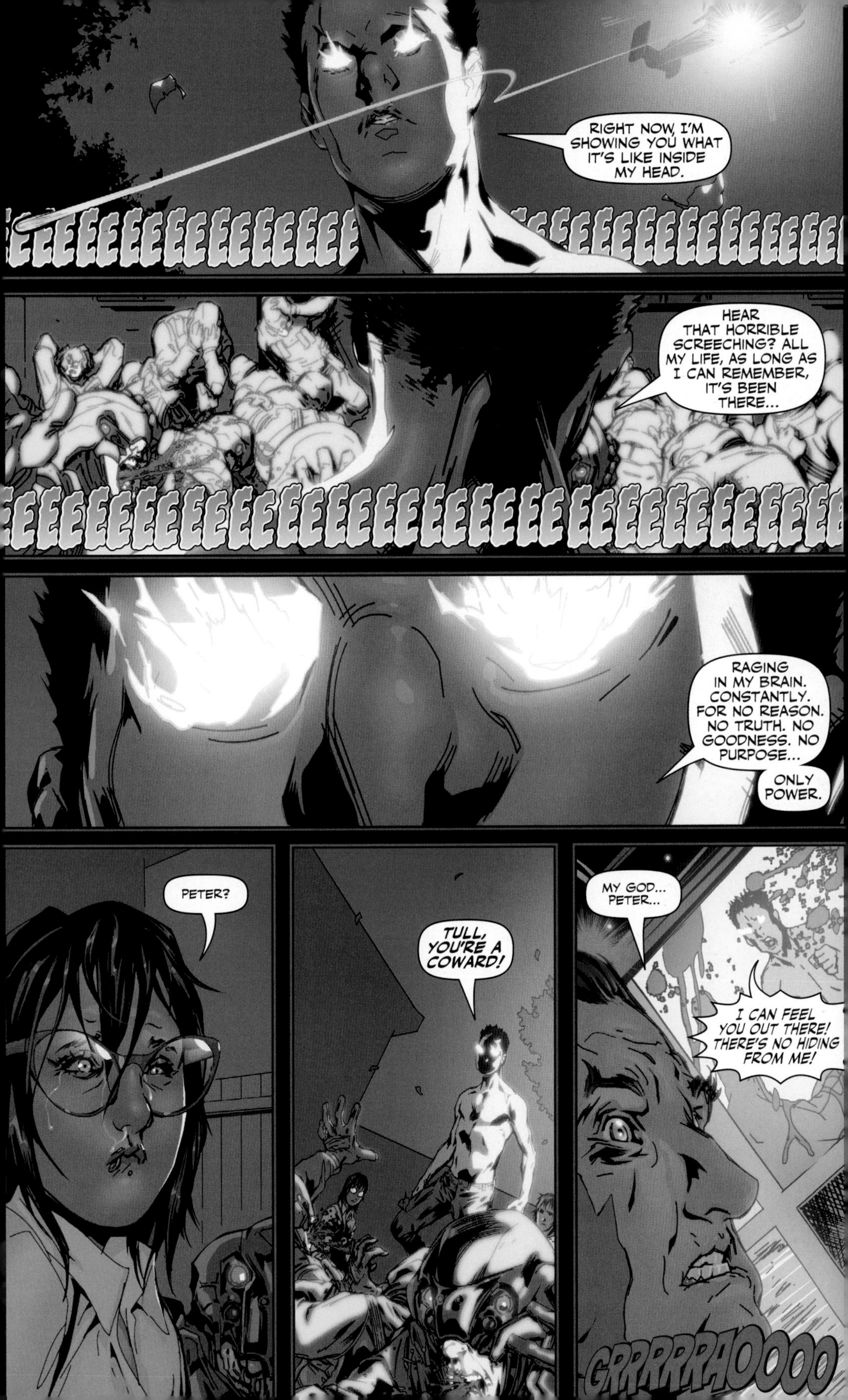
RIGHT NOW, I'M SHOWING YOU WHAT IT'S LIKE INSIDE MY HEAD.
EEEEEEEEEEEEEEE EEEEEEEEEEEEEEEEE
HEAR THAT HORRIBLE SCREECHING? ALL MY LIFE, AS LONG AS I CAN REMEMBER, IT'S BEEN THERE...
EEEEEEEEEEEEEEEEEEEEEEEEEEEEEEEEEEEEEE
RAGING IN MY BRAIN. CONSTANTLY. FOR NO REASON. NO TRUTH. NO GOODNESS. NO PURPOSE...
ONLY POWER.
PETER?
TULL, YOU'RE A COWARD!
MY GOD... PETER...
I CAN FEEL YOU OUT THERE! THERE'S NO HIDING FROM ME!
GRRRRRAOOOO

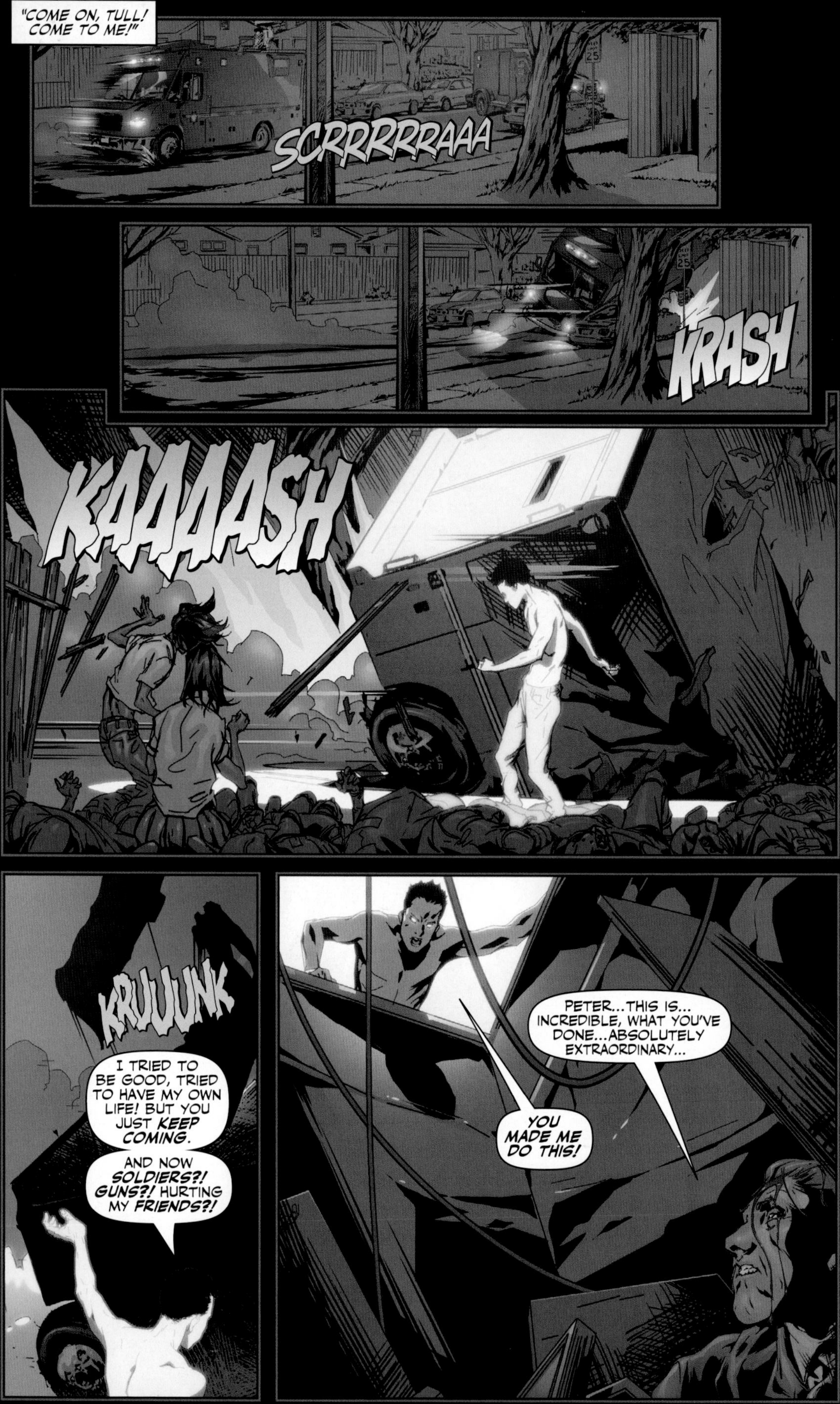
"COME ON, TULL! COME TO ME!"
SCRRRRRAAA
KRASH
KAAAAASH
KRUUUNK
I TRIED TO BE GOOD, TRIED TO HAVE MY OWN LIFE! BUT YOU JUST KEEP COMING.
AND NOW SOLDIERS?! GUNS?! HURTING MY FRIENDS?!
PETER...THIS IS... INCREDIBLE, WHAT YOU'VE DONE...ABSOLUTELY EXTRAORDINARY...
YOU MADE ME DO THIS!

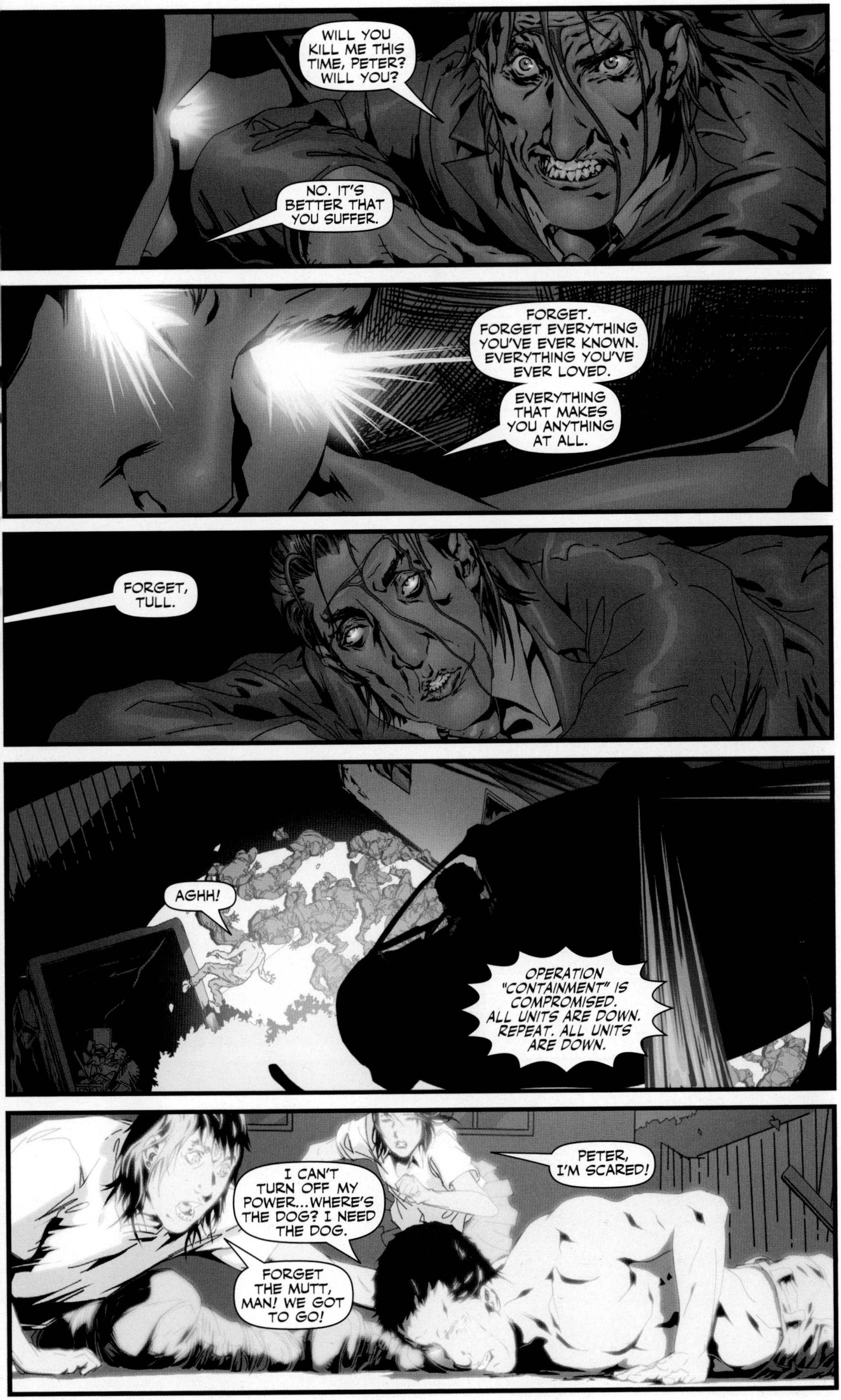

WILL YOU KILL ME THIS TIME, PETER? WILL YOU?
NO. IT'S BETTER THAT YOU SUFFER.
FORGET. FORGET EVERYTHING YOU'VE EVER KNOWN. EVERYTHING YOU'VE EVER LOVED.
EVERYTHING THAT MAKES YOU ANYTHING AT ALL.
FORGET, TULL.
AGHH!
OPERATION "CONTAINMENT" IS COMPROMISED. ALL UNITS ARE DOWN. REPEAT. ALL UNITS ARE DOWN.
I CAN'T TURN OFF MY POWER...WHERE'S THE DOG? I NEED THE DOG.
PETER, I'M SCARED!
FORGET THE MUTT, MAN! WE GOT TO GO!

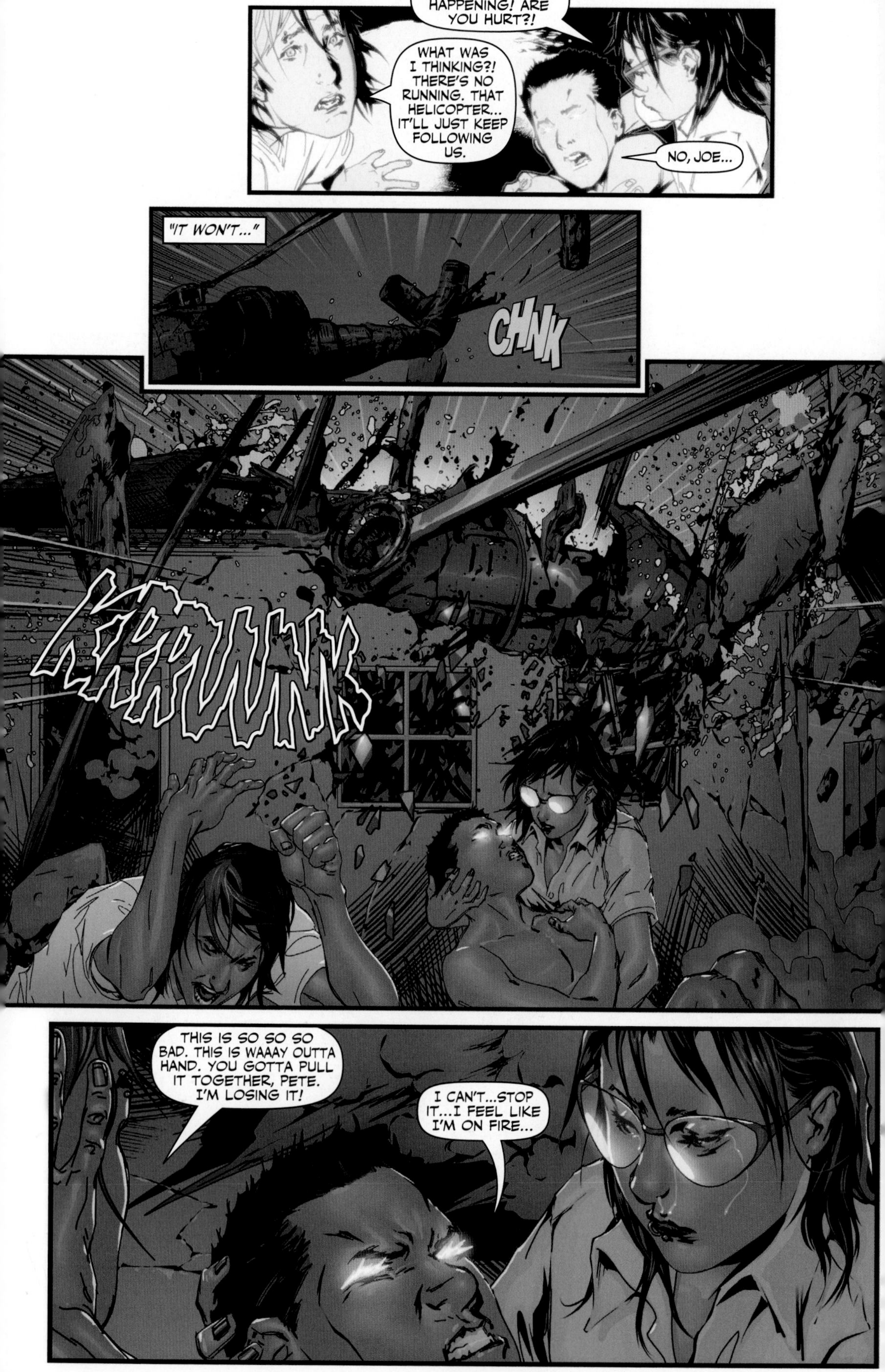
I DON'T UNDERSTAND WHAT'S HAPPENING! ARE YOU HURT?!
WHAT WAS I THINKING?! THERE'S NO RUNNING. THAT HELICOPTER... IT'LL JUST KEEP FOLLOWING US.
NO, JOE...
"IT WON'T..."
CHNK
KRRUUNK
THIS IS SO SO SO BAD. THIS IS WAAAY OUTTA HAND. YOU GOTTA PULL IT TOGETHER, PETE. I'M LOSING IT!
I CAN'T...STOP IT...I FEEL LIKE I'M ON FIRE...

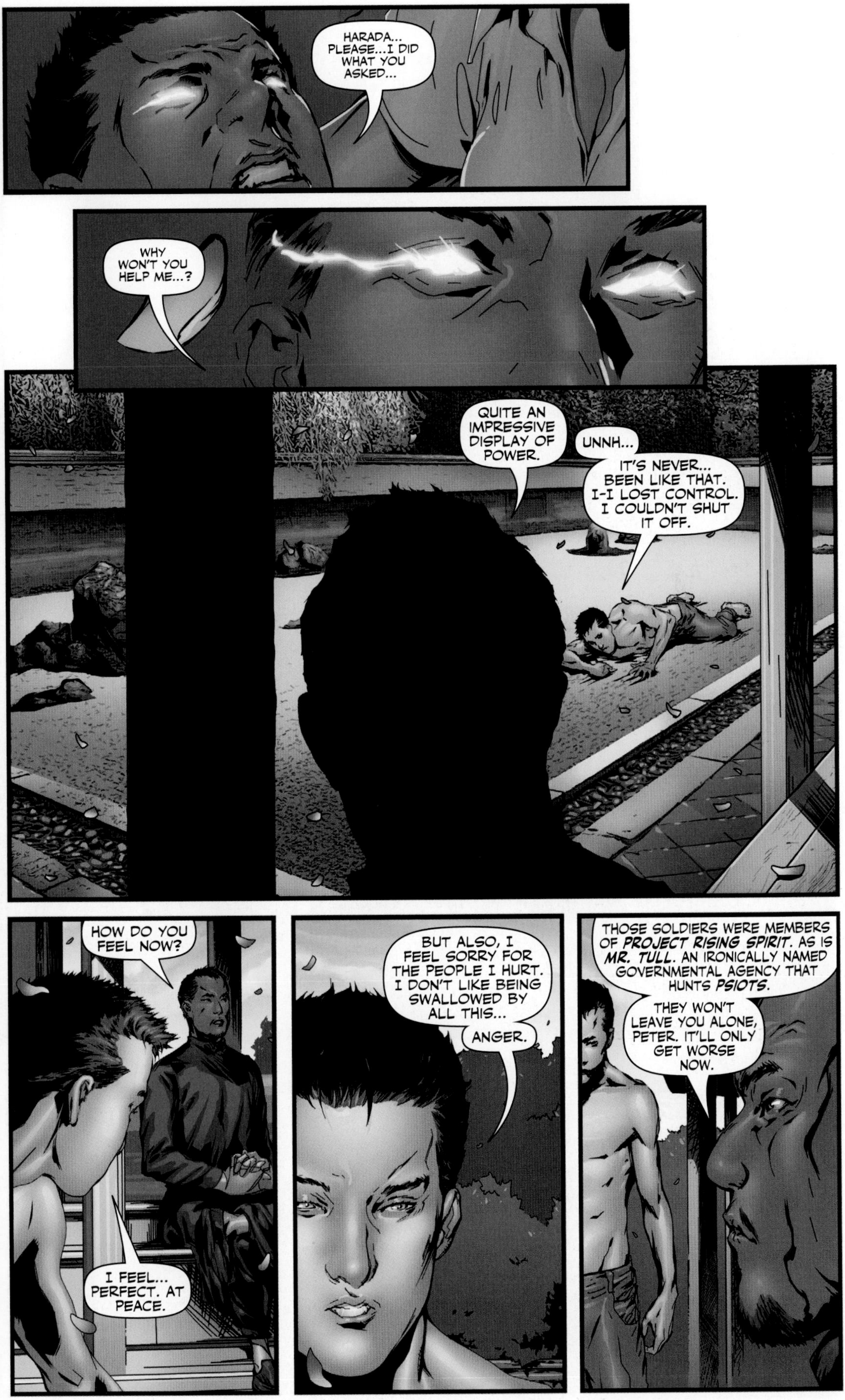
HARADA... PLEASE...I DID WHAT YOU ASKED...
WHY WON'T YOU HELP ME...?
QUITE AN IMPRESSIVE DISPLAY OF POWER.
UNNH...
IT'S NEVER... BEEN LIKE THAT. I-I LOST CONTROL. I COULDN'T SHUT IT OFF.
HOW DO YOU FEEL NOW?
I FEEL... PERFECT. AT PEACE.
BUT ALSO, I FEEL SORRY FOR THE PEOPLE I HURT. I DON'T LIKE BEING SWALLOWED BY ALL THIS...
ANGER.
THOSE SOLDIERS WERE MEMBERS OF PROJECT RISING SPIRIT. AS IS MR. TULL. AN IRONICALLY NAMED GOVERNMENTAL AGENCY THAT HUNTS PSIOTS.
THEY WON'T LEAVE YOU ALONE, PETER. IT'LL ONLY GET WORSE NOW.

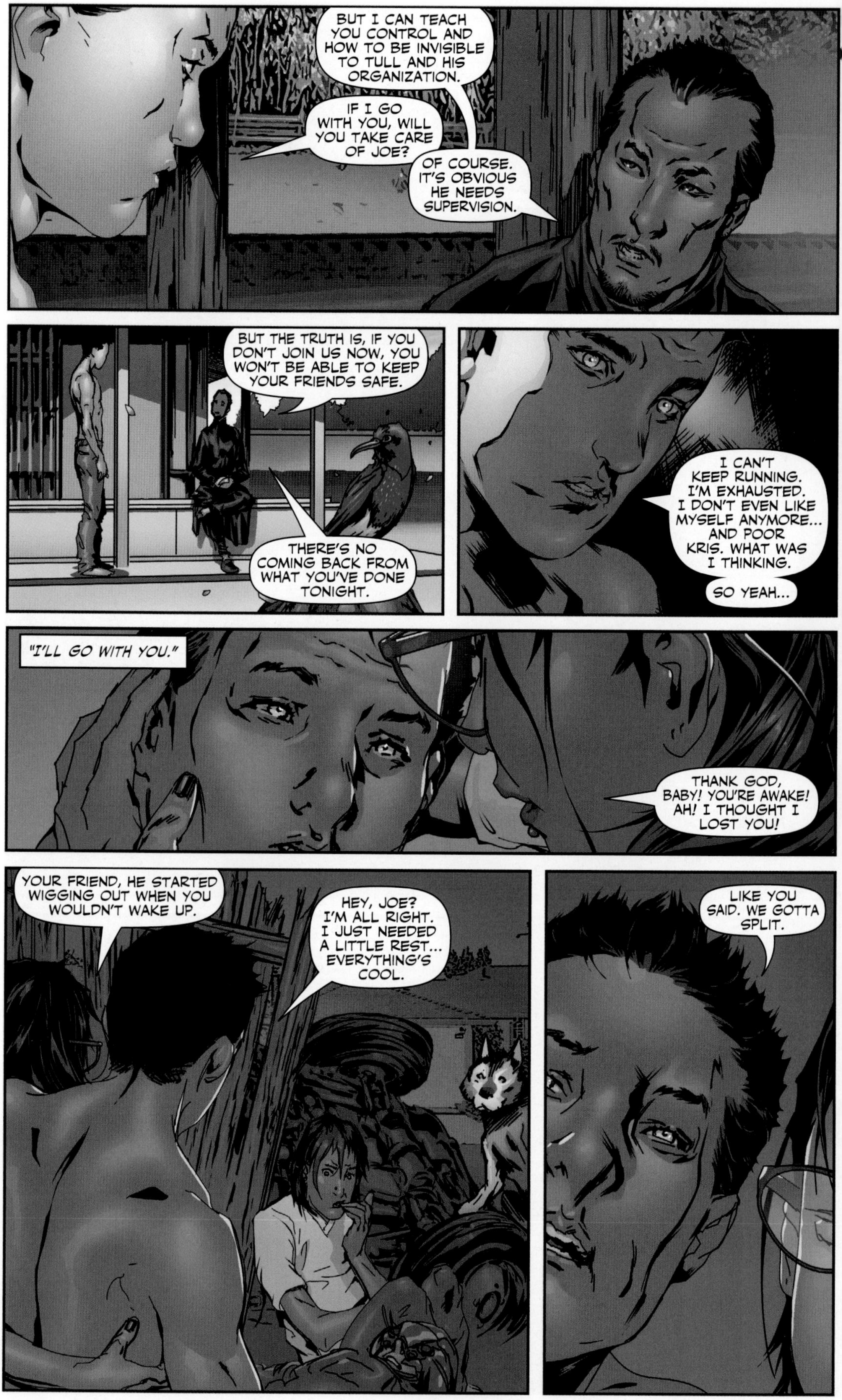

BUT I CAN TEACH YOU CONTROL AND HOW TO BE INVISIBLE TO TULL AND HIS ORGANIZATION.
IF I GO WITH YOU, WILL YOU TAKE CARE OF JOE?
OF COURSE. IT'S OBVIOUS HE NEEDS SUPERVISION.
BUT THE TRUTH IS, IF YOU DON'T JOIN US NOW, YOU WON'T BE ABLE TO KEEP YOUR FRIENDS SAFE.
THERE'S NO COMING BACK FROM WHAT YOU'VE DONE TONIGHT.
I CAN'T KEEP RUNNING. I'M EXHAUSTED. I DON'T EVEN LIKE MYSELF ANYMORE... AND POOR KRIS. WHAT WAS I THINKING.
SO YEAH...
"I'LL GO WITH YOU."
THANK GOD, BABY! YOU'RE AWAKE! AH! I THOUGHT I LOST YOU!
YOUR FRIEND, HE STARTED WIGGING OUT WHEN YOU WOULDN'T WAKE UP.
HEY, JOE? I'M ALL RIGHT. I JUST NEEDED A LITTLE REST... EVERYTHING'S COOL.
LIKE YOU SAID. WE GOTTA SPLIT.

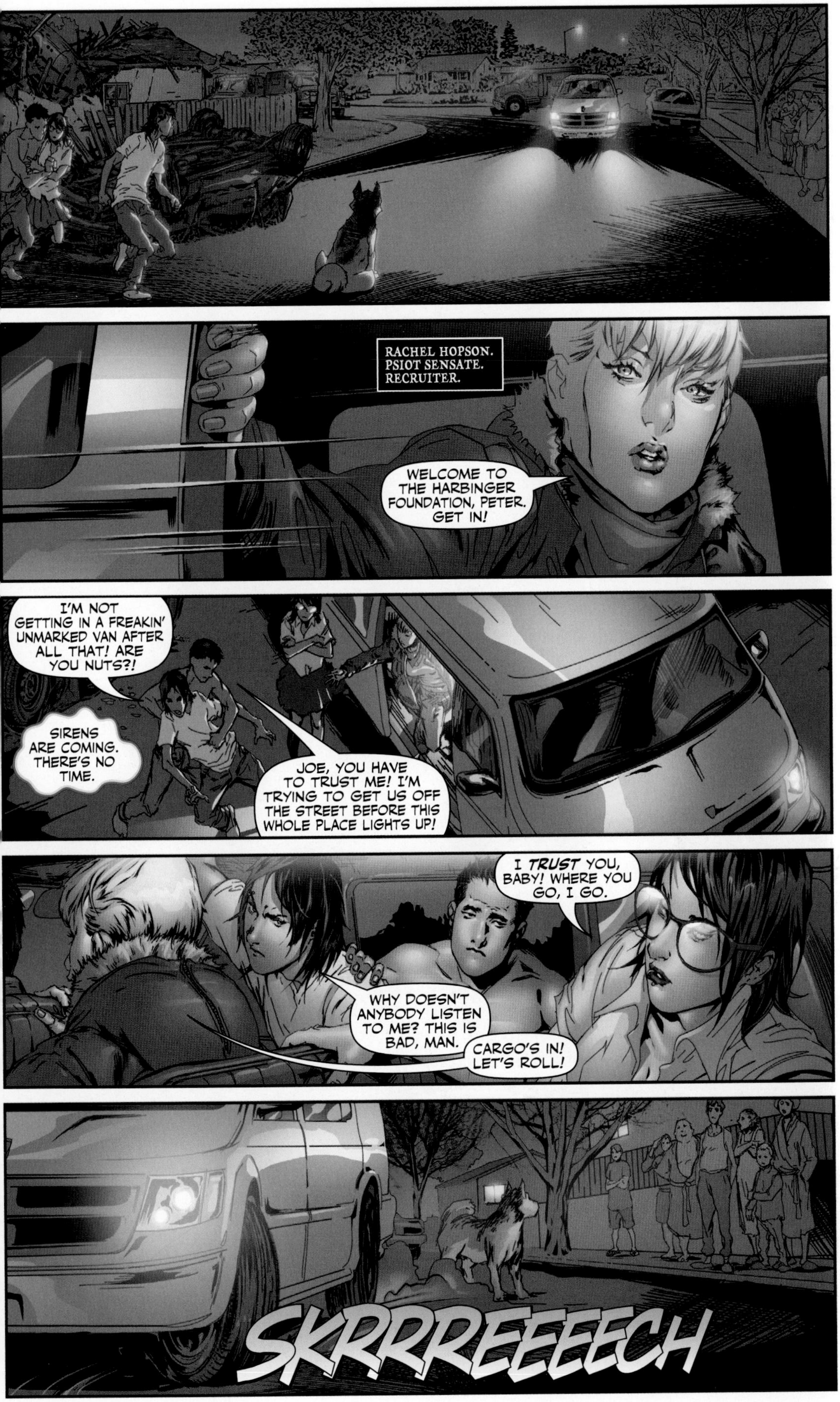
RACHEL HOPSON. PSIOT SENSATE. RECRUITER.
WELCOME TO THE HARBINGER FOUNDATION, PETER. GET IN!
I'M NOT GETTING IN A FREAKIN' UNMARKED VAN AFTER ALL THAT! ARE YOU NUTS?!
SIRENS ARE COMING. THERE'S NO TIME.
JOE, YOU HAVE TO TRUST ME! I'M TRYING TO GET US OFF THE STREET BEFORE THIS WHOLE PLACE LIGHTS UP!
I TRUST YOU, BABY! WHERE YOU GO, I GO.
WHY DOESN'T ANYBODY LISTEN TO ME? THIS IS BAD, MAN.
CARGO'S IN! LET'S ROLL!
SKRRREEEECH

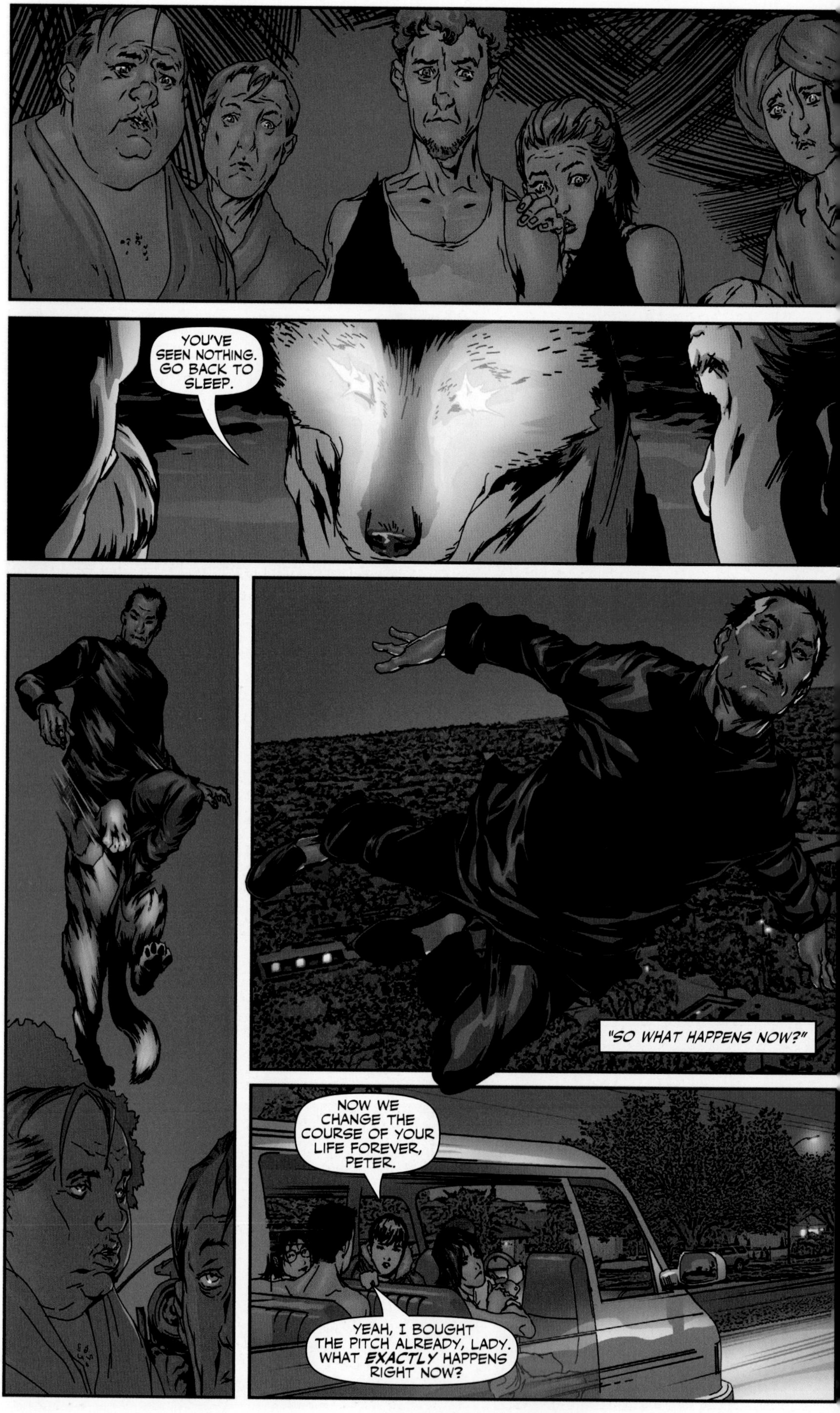
YOU'VE SEEN NOTHING. GO BACK TO SLEEP.
"SO WHAT HAPPENS NOW?"
NOW WE CHANGE THE COURSE OF YOUR LIFE FOREVER, PETER.
YEAH, I BOUGHT THE PITCH ALREADY, LADY. WHAT *EXACTLY* HAPPENS RIGHT NOW?

THIS IS NOT COOL, PETE. JUST MIND-DOUCHE THESE TOOLS AND LET'S GET OUTTA HERE.

JOE, YOU'RE HAVING A PSYCHOTIC EPISODE...

HERE, I CAN HELP YOU IF YOU LET ME TELE-LINK...

YO! PETER!!

LEAVE HIM ALONE. JUST...DON'T TOUCH HIM. OKAY? NOBODY SCREWS WITH HIS HEAD! I PROMISED HIM.

ALL RIGHT, BUT PETER, WHAT HAPPENS NEXT IS THE HARDEST PART. IT'S TIME TO LET GO OF YOUR FRIENDS NOW.

WHAT DID THAT BITCH JUST SAY?!

SEE, STRANGE-HOT-CHICK-WHO-I'M-SUDDENLY-ALLIED-WITH?! NOW YOU KNOW WHY I'M PARANOID! EVERYONE ACTUALLY IS AGAINST ME!

WAIT. DUDE, DID THE VAN JUST STOP?

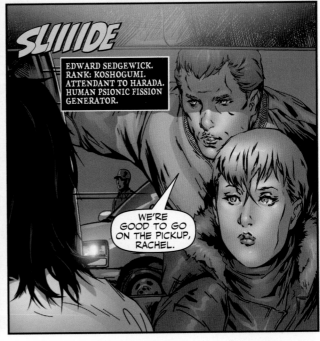

SLIIIDE

EDWARD SEDGEWICK. RANK: KOSHOGUMI. ATTENDANT TO HARADA. HUMAN PSIONIC FISSION GENERATOR.

WE'RE GOOD TO GO ON THE PICKUP, RACHEL.

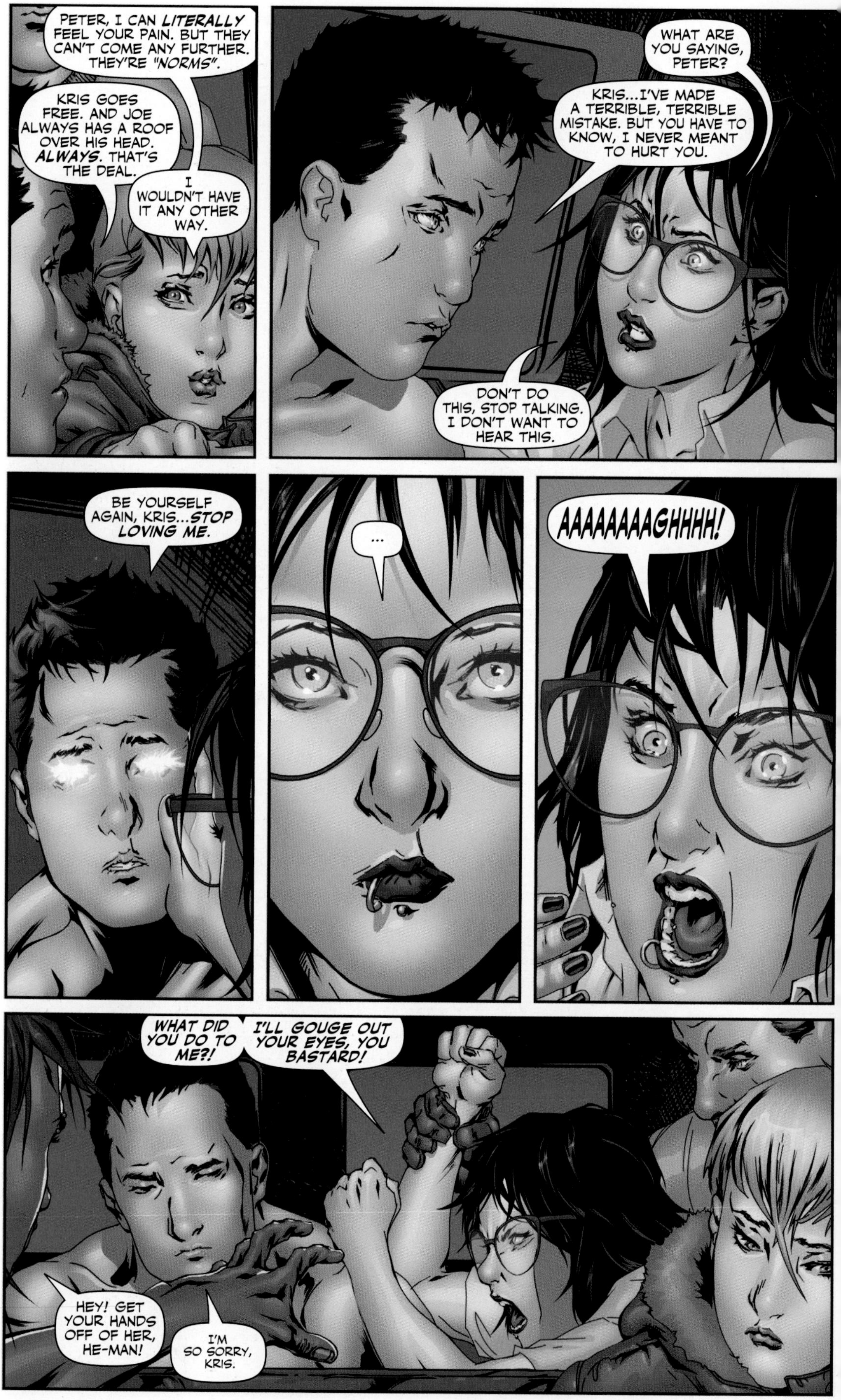
PETER, I CAN *LITERALLY* FEEL YOUR PAIN. BUT THEY CAN'T COME ANY FURTHER. THEY'RE *"NORMS"*.
KRIS GOES FREE. AND JOE ALWAYS HAS A ROOF OVER HIS HEAD. **ALWAYS**. THAT'S THE DEAL.
I WOULDN'T HAVE IT ANY OTHER WAY.
WHAT ARE YOU SAYING, PETER?
KRIS...I'VE MADE A TERRIBLE, TERRIBLE MISTAKE. BUT YOU HAVE TO KNOW, I NEVER MEANT TO HURT YOU.
DON'T DO THIS, STOP TALKING. I DON'T WANT TO HEAR THIS.
BE YOURSELF AGAIN, KRIS...*STOP LOVING ME*.
...
AAAAAAAAGHHHH!
WHAT DID YOU DO TO ME?!
I'LL GOUGE OUT YOUR EYES, YOU BASTARD!
HEY! GET YOUR HANDS OFF OF HER, HE-MAN!
I'M SO SORRY, KRIS.

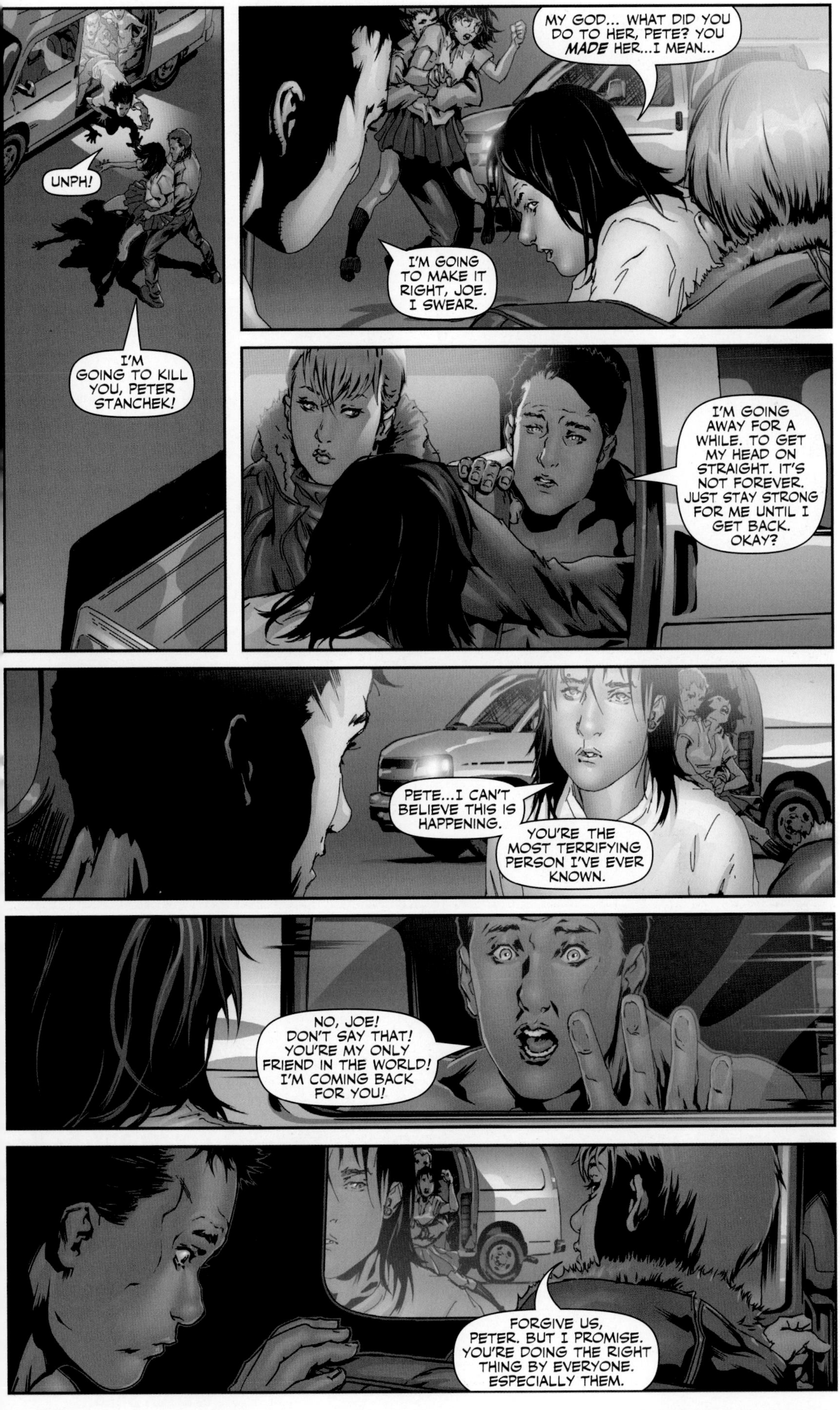
UNPH!
I'M GOING TO KILL YOU, PETER STANCHEK!
MY GOD... WHAT DID YOU DO TO HER, PETE? YOU *MADE* HER...I MEAN...
I'M GOING TO MAKE IT RIGHT, JOE. I SWEAR.
I'M GOING AWAY FOR A WHILE. TO GET MY HEAD ON STRAIGHT. IT'S NOT FOREVER. JUST STAY STRONG FOR ME UNTIL I GET BACK. OKAY?
PETE...I CAN'T BELIEVE THIS IS HAPPENING.
YOU'RE THE MOST TERRIFYING PERSON I'VE EVER KNOWN.
NO, JOE! DON'T SAY THAT! YOU'RE MY ONLY FRIEND IN THE WORLD! I'M COMING BACK FOR YOU!
FORGIVE US, PETER. BUT I PROMISE. YOU'RE DOING THE RIGHT THING BY EVERYONE. ESPECIALLY THEM.

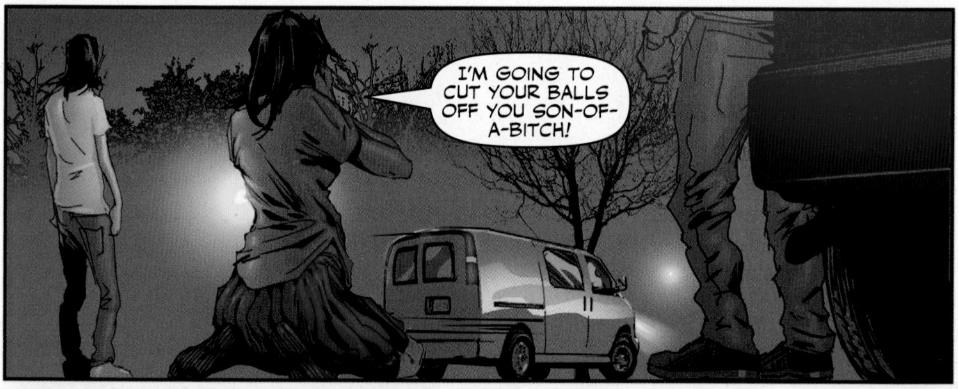
I'M GOING TO CUT YOUR BALLS OFF YOU SON-OF-A-BITCH!

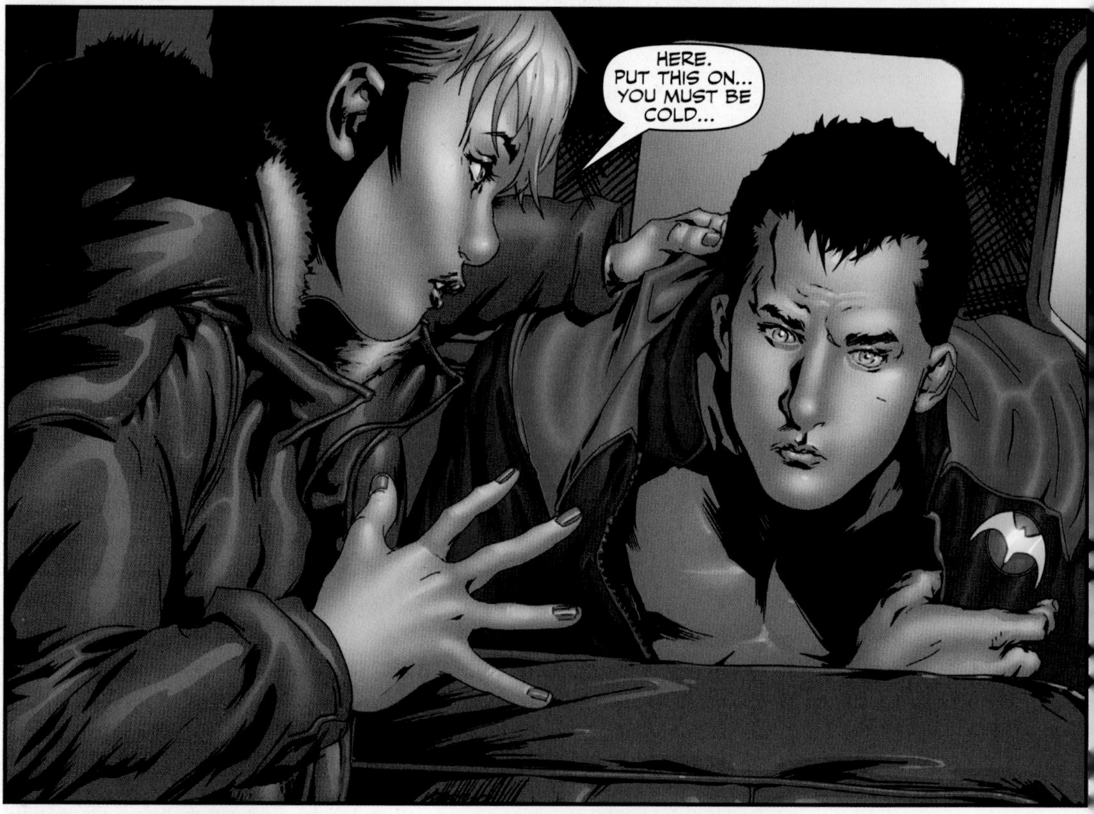
HERE. PUT THIS ON... YOU MUST BE COLD...

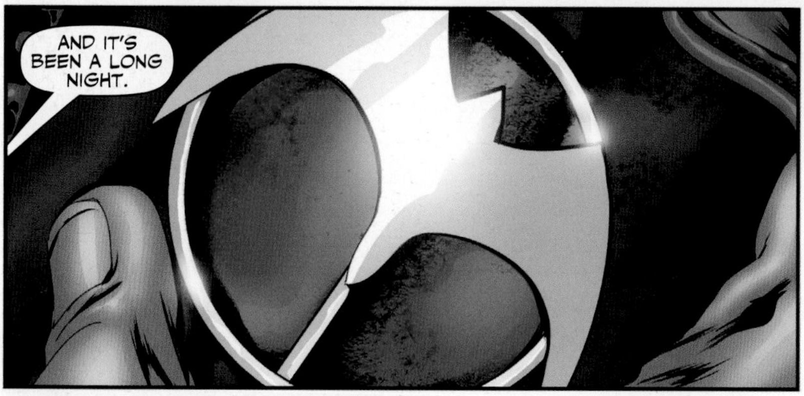
AND IT'S BEEN A LONG NIGHT.

OMEGA RISIN
PART 2

WRITER: Joshua Dysar
ARTIST: Khari Evans with Lewis LaRosa
COLOR ART: Ian Hann with Moose Baumann
LETTERS: Rob Steen
COVERS: Arturo Lozzi and Doug Braithwaite
ASSISTANT EDITOR: Josh Johns
ASSOCIATE EDITOR: Jody LeHeup
EXECUTIVE EDITOR: Warren Simons

NEXT: THE HARBINGER FOUNDATION...

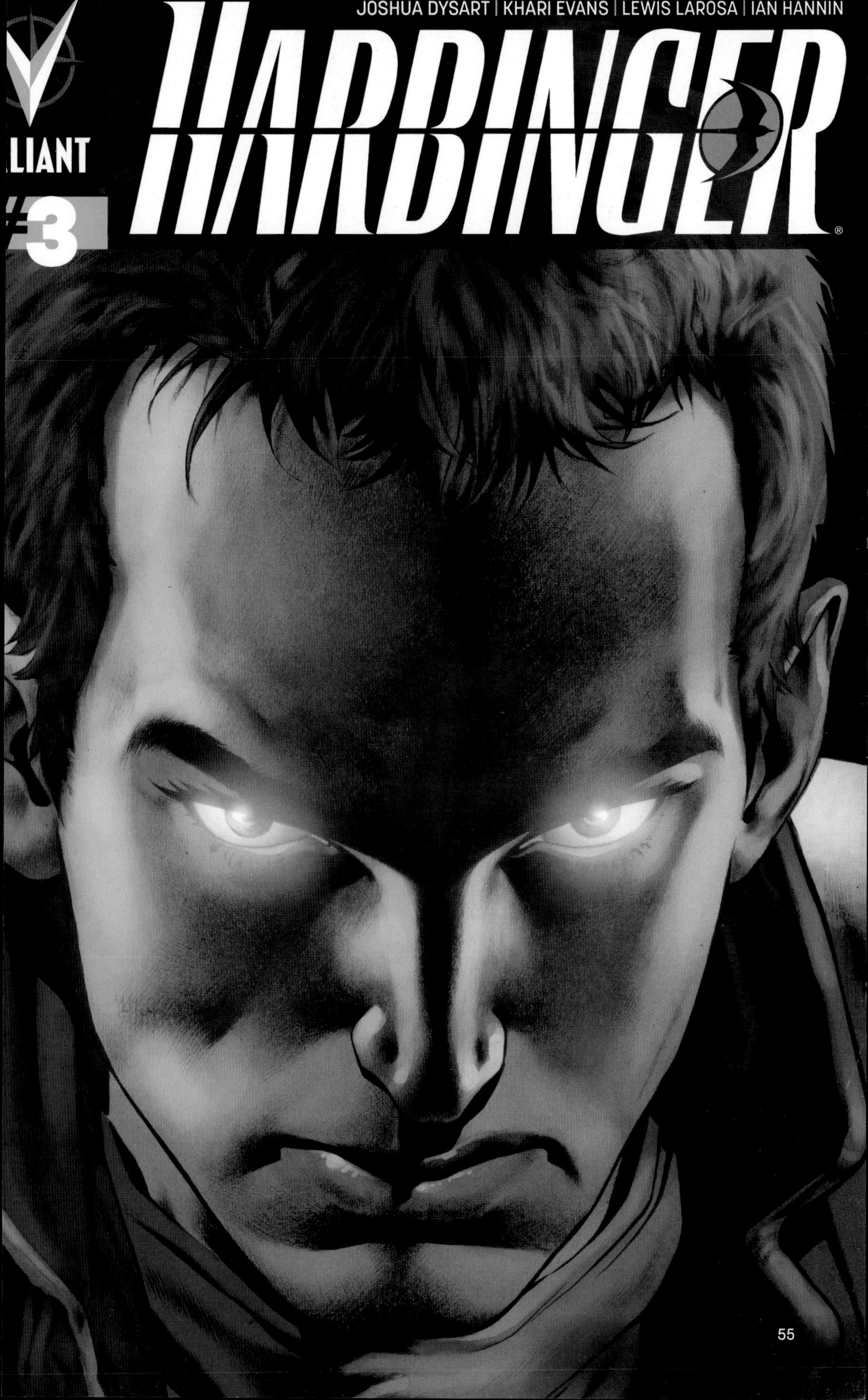
JOSHUA DYSART | KHARI EVANS | LEWIS LAROSA | IAN HANNIN
HARBINGER
#3

HARADA GLOBAL CONGLOMERATES. DOWNTOWN PITTSBURGH.

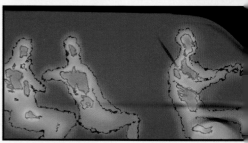

"GREAT..."

...MORE JACKASSES WITH GUNS.

IT'S OKAY, PETER. THEY'RE ON OUR SIDE. WE'RE EXPECTED.

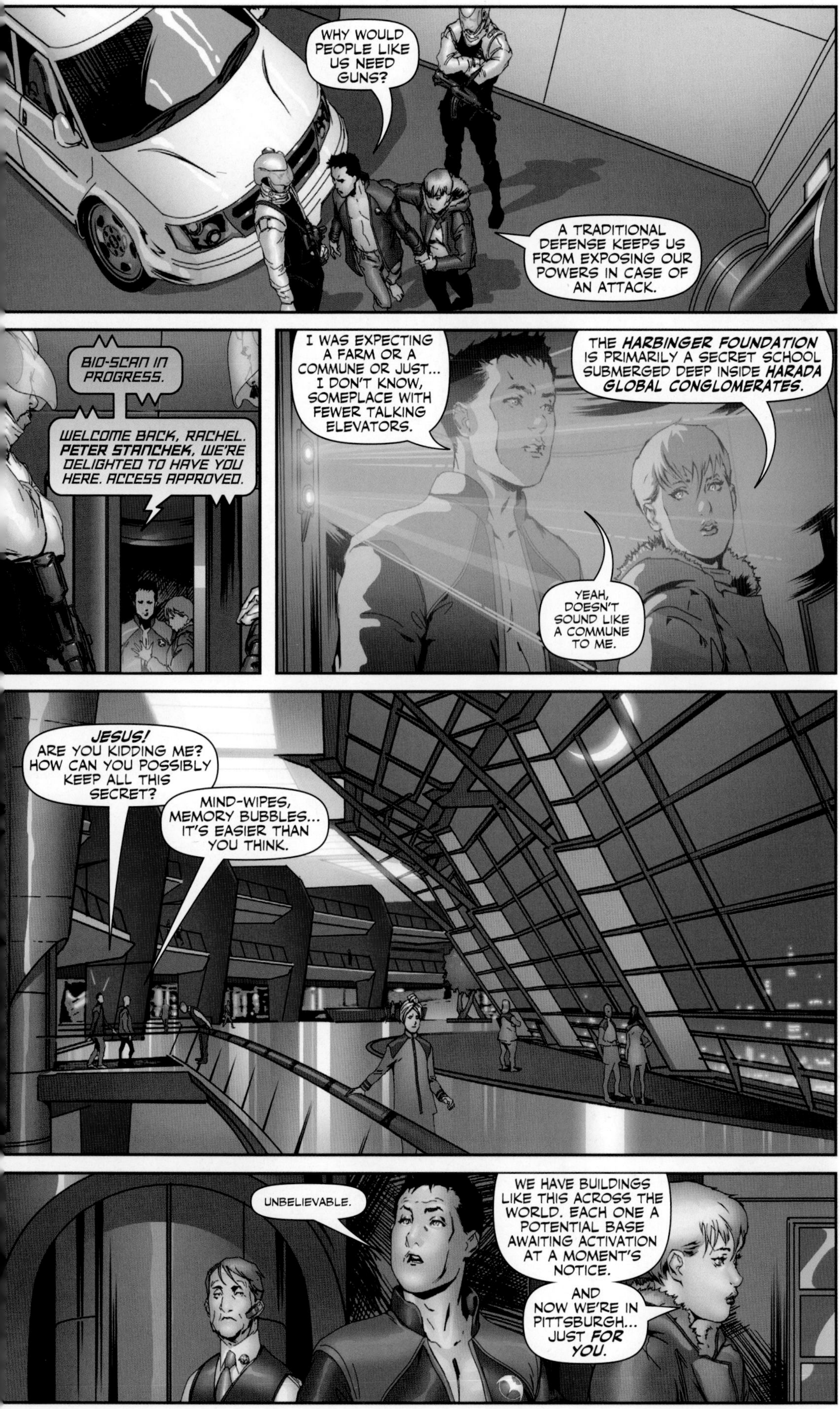
WHY WOULD PEOPLE LIKE US NEED GUNS?
A TRADITIONAL DEFENSE KEEPS US FROM EXPOSING OUR POWERS IN CASE OF AN ATTACK.
BIO-SCAN IN PROGRESS.
WELCOME BACK, RACHEL. PETER STANCHEK, WE'RE DELIGHTED TO HAVE YOU HERE. ACCESS APPROVED.
I WAS EXPECTING A FARM OR A COMMUNE OR JUST... I DON'T KNOW, SOMEPLACE WITH FEWER TALKING ELEVATORS.
THE HARBINGER FOUNDATION IS PRIMARILY A SECRET SCHOOL SUBMERGED DEEP INSIDE HARADA GLOBAL CONGLOMERATES.
YEAH, DOESN'T SOUND LIKE A COMMUNE TO ME.
JESUS! ARE YOU KIDDING ME? HOW CAN YOU POSSIBLY KEEP ALL THIS SECRET?
MIND-WIPES, MEMORY BUBBLES... IT'S EASIER THAN YOU THINK.
UNBELIEVABLE.
WE HAVE BUILDINGS LIKE THIS ACROSS THE WORLD. EACH ONE A POTENTIAL BASE AWAITING ACTIVATION AT A MOMENT'S NOTICE.
AND NOW WE'RE IN PITTSBURGH... JUST FOR YOU.

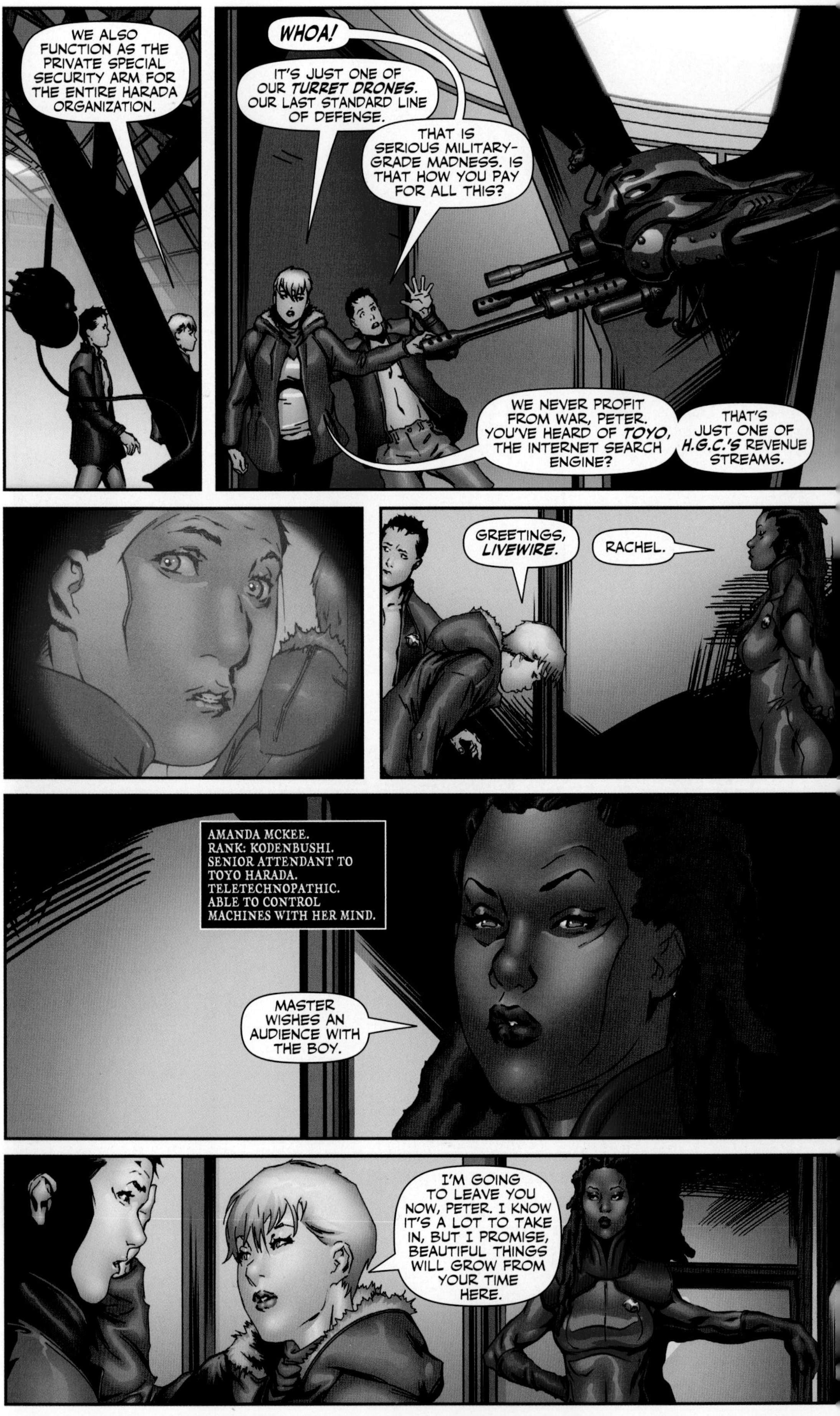
WE ALSO FUNCTION AS THE PRIVATE SPECIAL SECURITY ARM FOR THE ENTIRE HARADA ORGANIZATION.
WHOA!
IT'S JUST ONE OF OUR TURRET DRONES. OUR LAST STANDARD LINE OF DEFENSE.
THAT IS SERIOUS MILITARY-GRADE MADNESS. IS THAT HOW YOU PAY FOR ALL THIS?
WE NEVER PROFIT FROM WAR, PETER. YOU'VE HEARD OF TOYO, THE INTERNET SEARCH ENGINE?
THAT'S JUST ONE OF H.G.C.'S REVENUE STREAMS.
GREETINGS, LIVEWIRE.
RACHEL.
AMANDA MCKEE. RANK: KODENBUSHI. SENIOR ATTENDANT TO TOYO HARADA. TELETECHNOPATHIC. ABLE TO CONTROL MACHINES WITH HER MIND.
MASTER WISHES AN AUDIENCE WITH THE BOY.
I'M GOING TO LEAVE YOU NOW, PETER. I KNOW IT'S A LOT TO TAKE IN, BUT I PROMISE, BEAUTIFUL THINGS WILL GROW FROM YOUR TIME HERE.

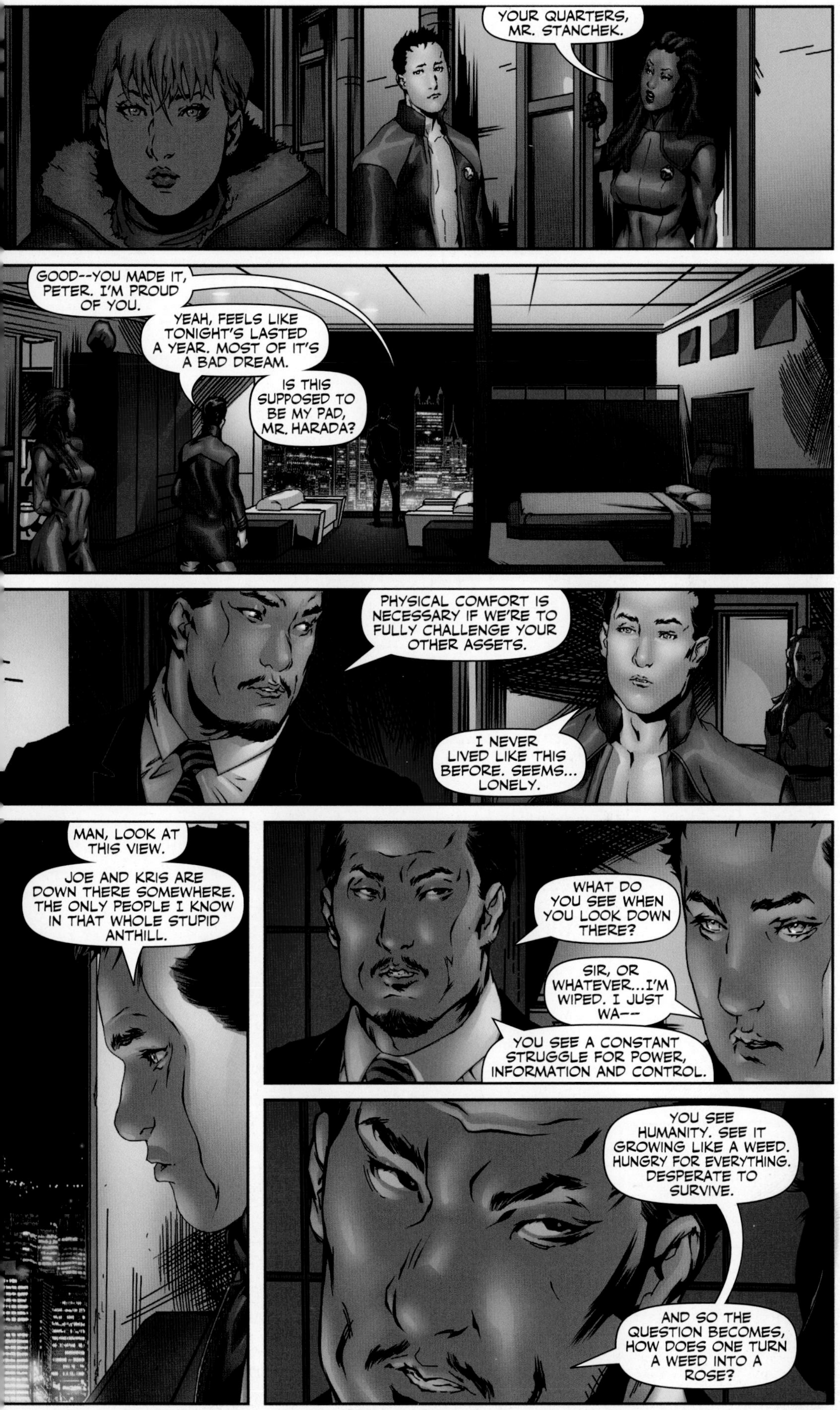
YOUR QUARTERS, MR. STANCHEK.
GOOD--YOU MADE IT, PETER. I'M PROUD OF YOU.
YEAH, FEELS LIKE TONIGHT'S LASTED A YEAR. MOST OF IT'S A BAD DREAM.
IS THIS SUPPOSED TO BE MY PAD, MR. HARADA?
PHYSICAL COMFORT IS NECESSARY IF WE'RE TO FULLY CHALLENGE YOUR OTHER ASSETS.
I NEVER LIVED LIKE THIS BEFORE. SEEMS... LONELY.
MAN, LOOK AT THIS VIEW.
JOE AND KRIS ARE DOWN THERE SOMEWHERE. THE ONLY PEOPLE I KNOW IN THAT WHOLE STUPID ANTHILL.
WHAT DO YOU SEE WHEN YOU LOOK DOWN THERE?
SIR, OR WHATEVER...I'M WIPED. I JUST WA--
YOU SEE A CONSTANT STRUGGLE FOR POWER, INFORMATION AND CONTROL.
YOU SEE HUMANITY. SEE IT GROWING LIKE A WEED. HUNGRY FOR EVERYTHING. DESPERATE TO SURVIVE.
AND SO THE QUESTION BECOMES, HOW DOES ONE TURN A WEED INTO A ROSE?

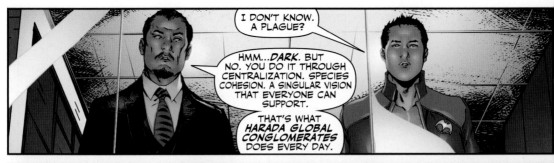

I DON'T KNOW. A PLAGUE?

HMM...*DARK.* BUT NO. YOU DO IT THROUGH CENTRALIZATION. SPECIES COHESION. A SINGULAR VISION THAT EVERYONE CAN SUPPORT.

THAT'S WHAT *HARADA GLOBAL CONGLOMERATES* DOES EVERY DAY.

"WE ARE THE LARGEST MULTINATIONAL CORPORATE GROUP IN THE HISTORY OF THE WORLD...

"WE SHELTER, FUND AND OPERATE HUNDREDS OF TECH, PHARM AND ENERGY CORPS, NGO'S AND ENDOWMENT GROUPS.

"WE STRENGTHEN ECONOMIES AND PROVIDE JOBS ON AN INTERNATIONAL LEVEL NEVER SEEN BEFORE.

"AND WE CENTRALIZE POWER AND INFORMATION ACROSS THE PLANET. HOLDING OUR ACTIONS TO THE STRICTEST *ETHICAL* SCRUTINY."

WE ARE THE SPEARHEAD IN THE STRUGGLE FOR SPECIES COHESION.

WITH RESPECT, I DIDN'T KNOW I WAS COMING TO WORK FOR A CORPORATION.

WE'RE A CULTURE, PETER. NOT A CORPORATION.

BUT WITH THESE POWERS, IT'D BE EASY TO MANIPULATE MARKETS...BILK THE SYSTEM, YOU KNOW?

YES. BUT THEN THE SYSTEM DOESN'T WORK, DOES IT?

FORGIVE ME FOR KEEPING YOU. GET PLENTY OF REST. TOMORROW YOU BEGIN...

"AND THE FIRST DAY CAN BE DIFFICULT."

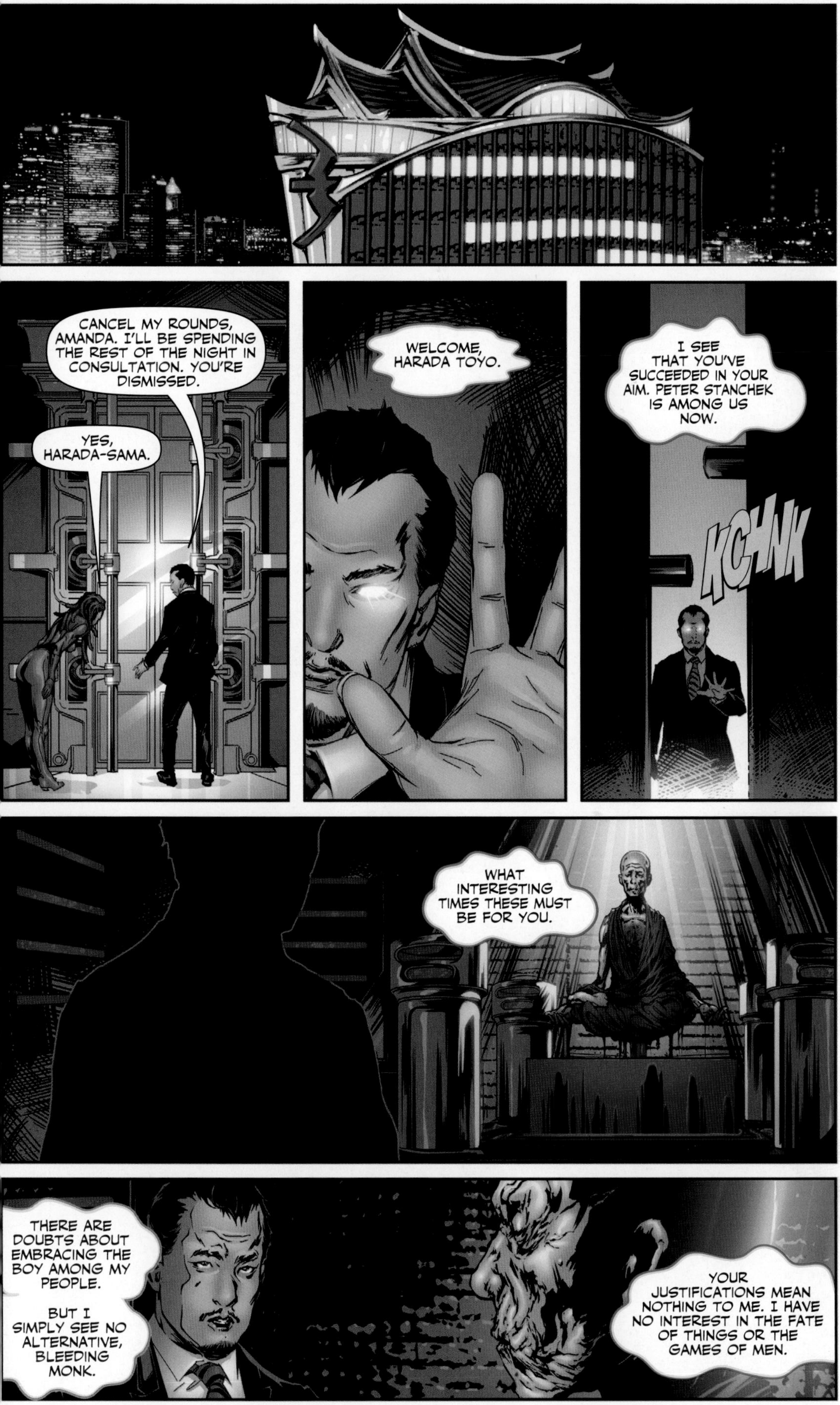
CANCEL MY ROUNDS, AMANDA. I'LL BE SPENDING THE REST OF THE NIGHT IN CONSULTATION. YOU'RE DISMISSED.
YES, HARADA-SAMA.
WELCOME, HARADA TOYO.
I SEE THAT YOU'VE SUCCEEDED IN YOUR AIM. PETER STANCHEK IS AMONG US NOW.
KCHNK
WHAT INTERESTING TIMES THESE MUST BE FOR YOU.
THERE ARE DOUBTS ABOUT EMBRACING THE BOY AMONG MY PEOPLE.
BUT I SIMPLY SEE NO ALTERNATIVE, BLEEDING MONK.
YOUR JUSTIFICATIONS MEAN NOTHING TO ME. I HAVE NO INTEREST IN THE FATE OF THINGS OR THE GAMES OF MEN.

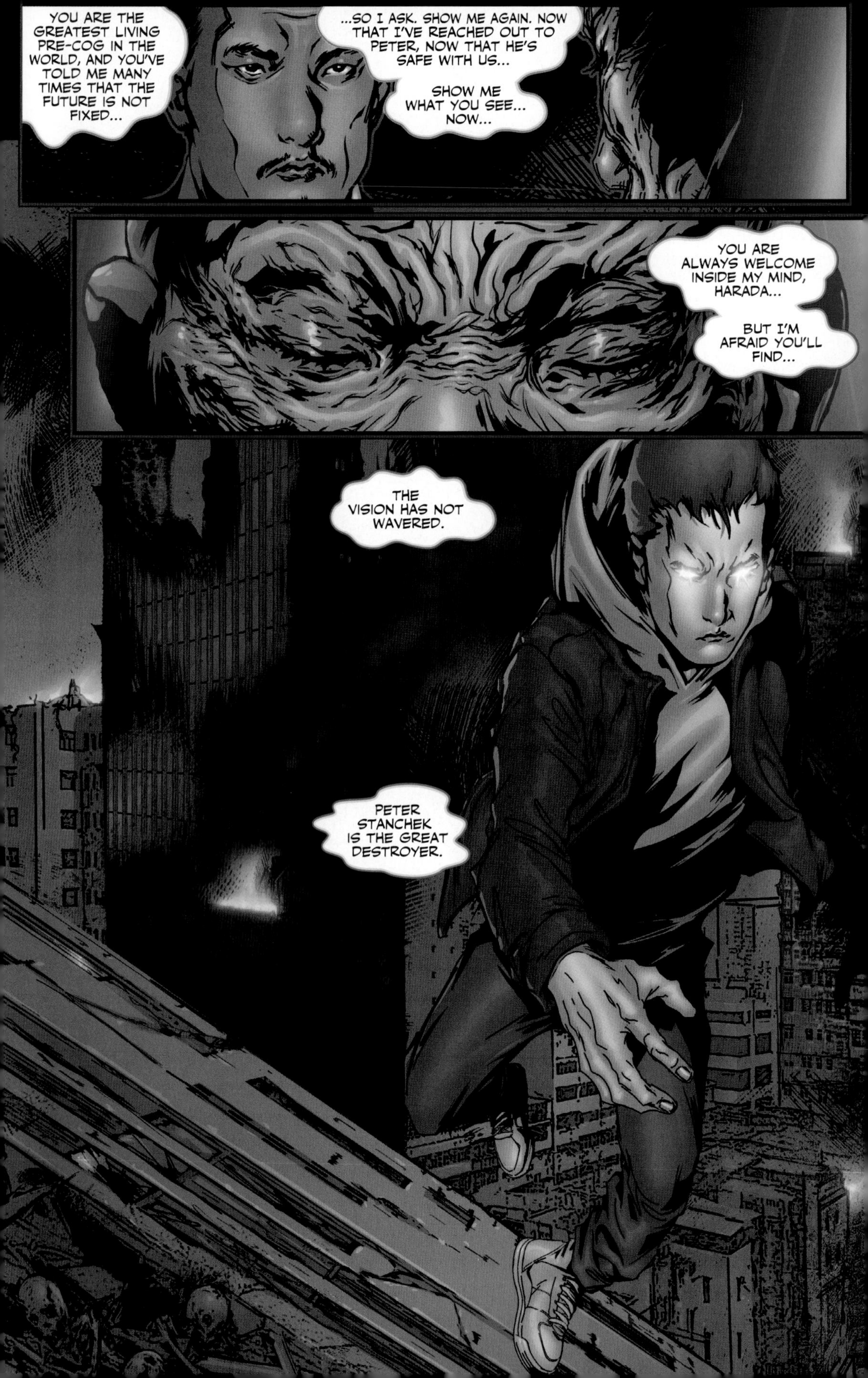
YOU ARE THE GREATEST LIVING PRE-COG IN THE WORLD, AND YOU'VE TOLD ME MANY TIMES THAT THE FUTURE IS NOT FIXED...
...SO I ASK. SHOW ME AGAIN. NOW THAT I'VE REACHED OUT TO PETER, NOW THAT HE'S SAFE WITH US...
SHOW ME WHAT YOU SEE... NOW...
YOU ARE ALWAYS WELCOME INSIDE MY MIND, HARADA...
BUT I'M AFRAID YOU'LL FIND...
THE VISION HAS NOT WAVERED.
PETER STANCHEK IS THE GREAT DESTROYER.

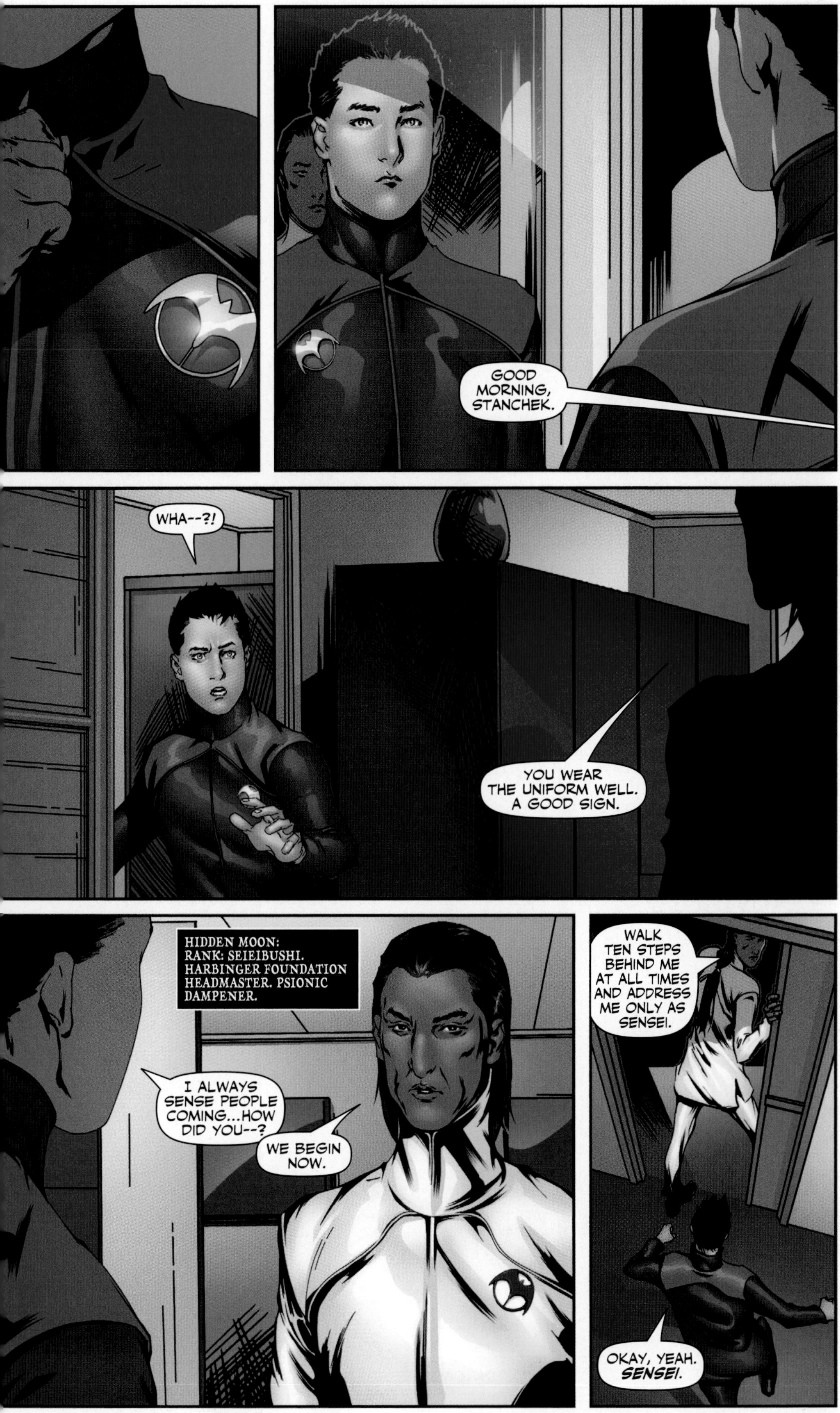
GOOD MORNING, STANCHEK.
WHA--?!
YOU WEAR THE UNIFORM WELL. A GOOD SIGN.
HIDDEN MOON: RANK: SEIEIBUSHI. HARBINGER FOUNDATION HEADMASTER. PSIONIC DAMPENER.
I ALWAYS SENSE PEOPLE COMING...HOW DID YOU--?
WE BEGIN NOW.
WALK TEN STEPS BEHIND ME AT ALL TIMES AND ADDRESS ME ONLY AS SENSEI.
OKAY, YEAH. *SENSEI*.

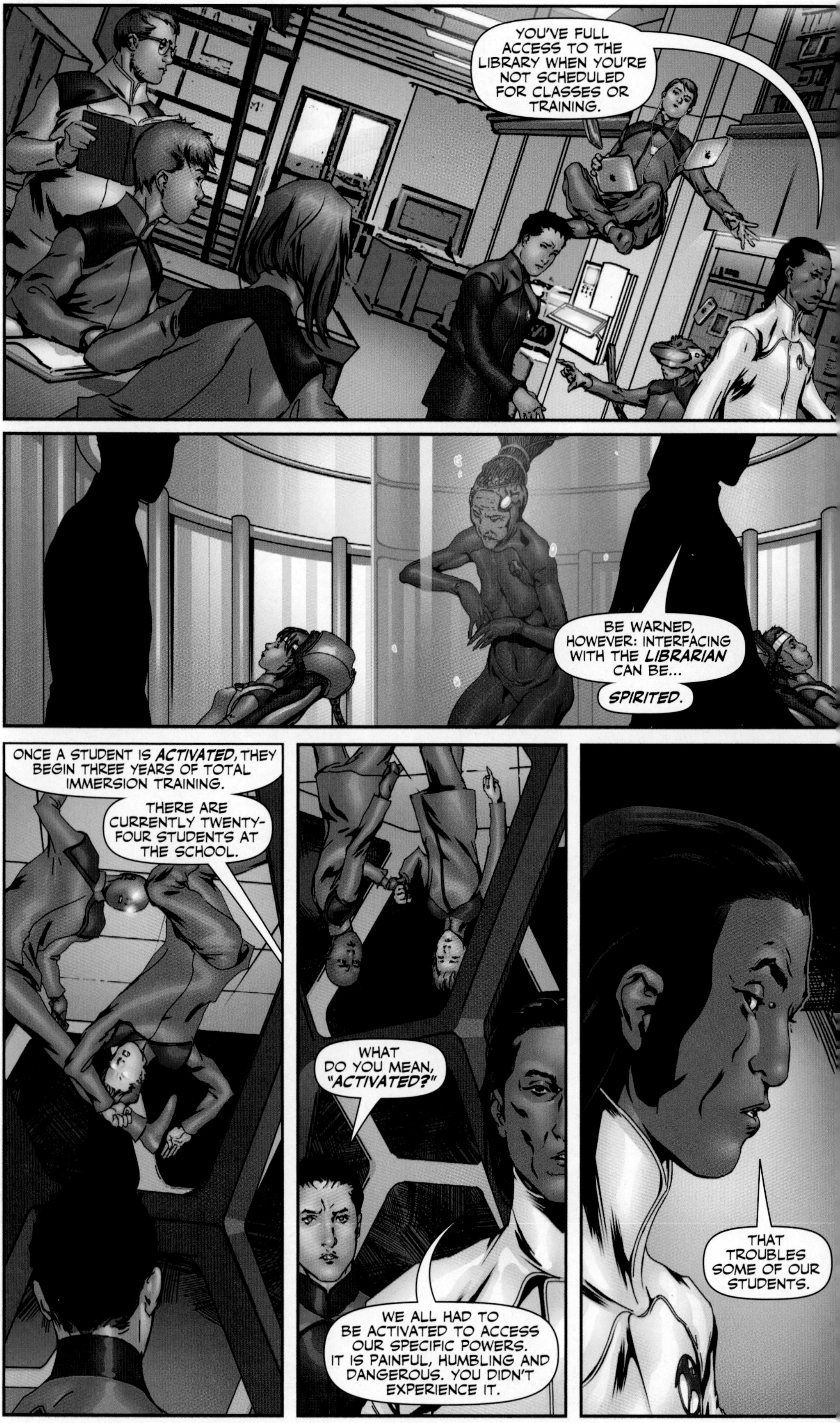
YOU'VE FULL ACCESS TO THE LIBRARY WHEN YOU'RE NOT SCHEDULED FOR CLASSES OR TRAINING.
BE WARNED, HOWEVER: INTERFACING WITH THE *LIBRARIAN* CAN BE...
SPIRITED.
ONCE A STUDENT IS *ACTIVATED*, THEY BEGIN THREE YEARS OF TOTAL IMMERSION TRAINING.
THERE ARE CURRENTLY TWENTY-FOUR STUDENTS AT THE SCHOOL.
WHAT DO YOU MEAN, "*ACTIVATED?*"
WE ALL HAD TO BE ACTIVATED TO ACCESS OUR SPECIFIC POWERS. IT IS PAINFUL, HUMBLING AND DANGEROUS. YOU DIDN'T EXPERIENCE IT.
THAT TROUBLES SOME OF OUR STUDENTS.

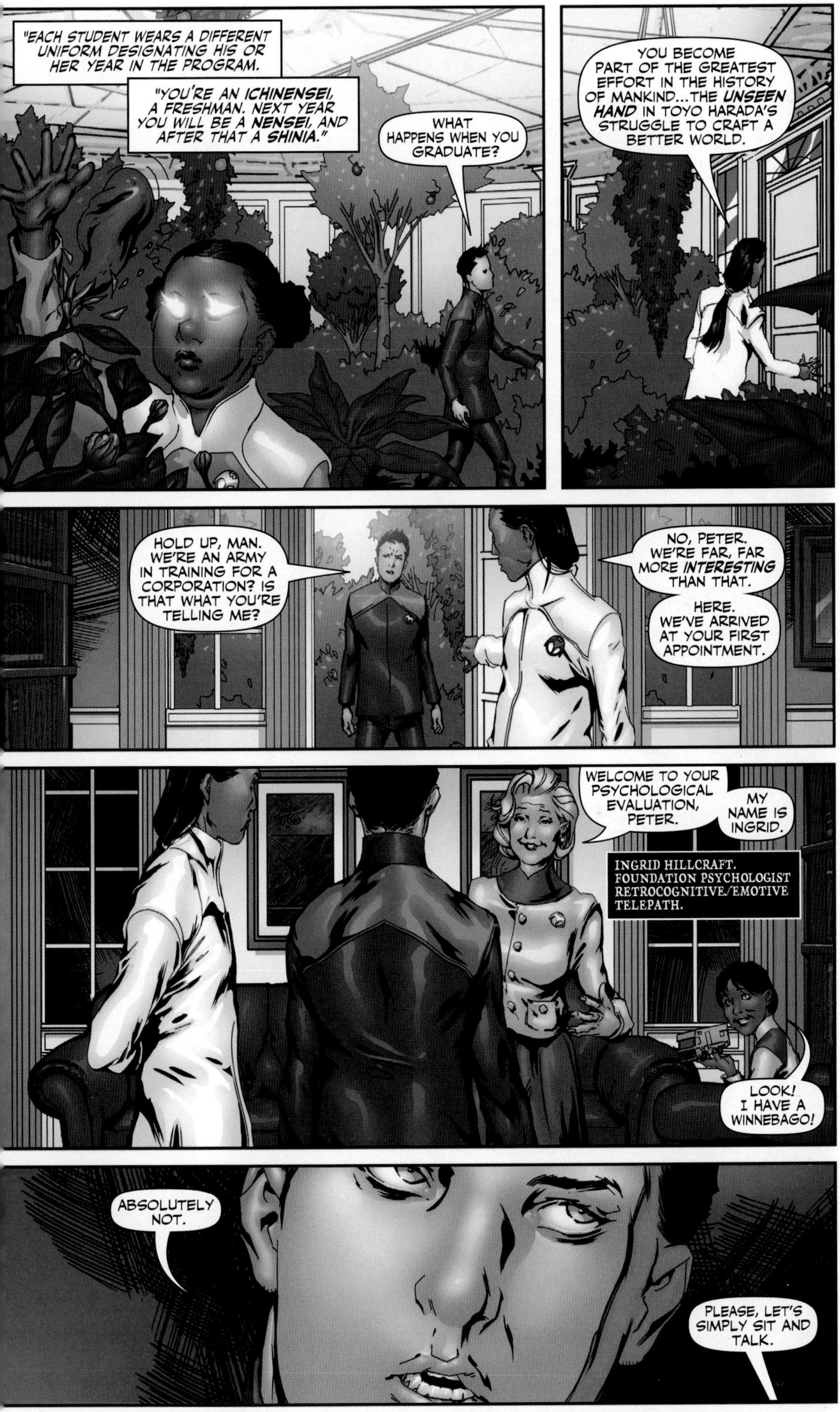
"EACH STUDENT WEARS A DIFFERENT UNIFORM DESIGNATING HIS OR HER YEAR IN THE PROGRAM.
"YOU'RE AN ICHINENSEI, A FRESHMAN. NEXT YEAR YOU WILL BE A NENSEI, AND AFTER THAT A SHINIA."
WHAT HAPPENS WHEN YOU GRADUATE?
YOU BECOME PART OF THE GREATEST EFFORT IN THE HISTORY OF MANKIND...THE UNSEEN HAND IN TOYO HARADA'S STRUGGLE TO CRAFT A BETTER WORLD.
HOLD UP, MAN. WE'RE AN ARMY IN TRAINING FOR A CORPORATION? IS THAT WHAT YOU'RE TELLING ME?
NO, PETER. WE'RE FAR, FAR MORE INTERESTING THAN THAT.
HERE. WE'VE ARRIVED AT YOUR FIRST APPOINTMENT.
WELCOME TO YOUR PSYCHOLOGICAL EVALUATION, PETER.
MY NAME IS INGRID.
INGRID HILLCRAFT. FOUNDATION PSYCHOLOGIST RETROCOGNITIVE/EMOTIVE TELEPATH.
LOOK! I HAVE A WINNEBAGO!
ABSOLUTELY NOT.
PLEASE, LET'S SIMPLY SIT AND TALK.

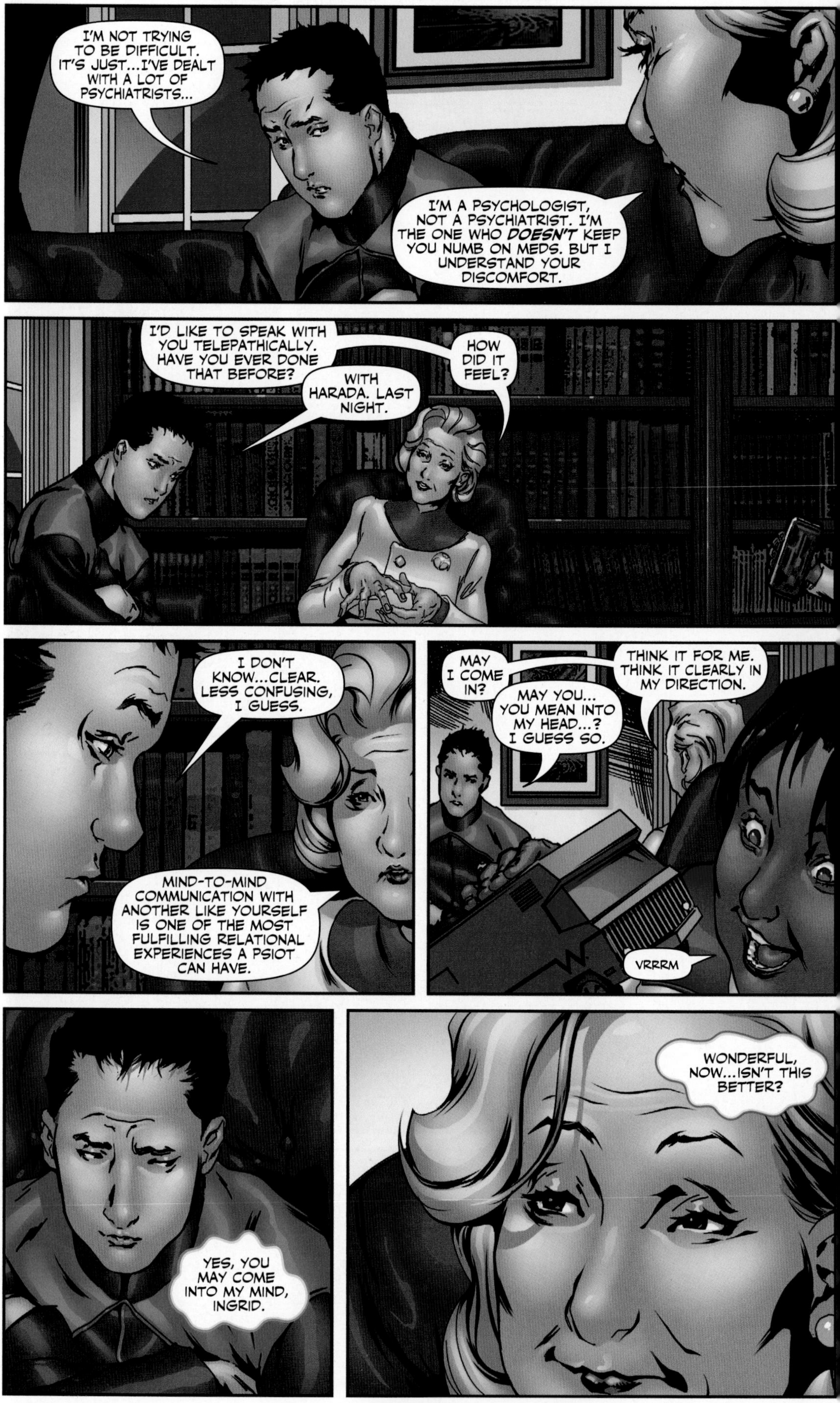
I'M NOT TRYING TO BE DIFFICULT. IT'S JUST...I'VE DEALT WITH A LOT OF PSYCHIATRISTS...
I'M A PSYCHOLOGIST, NOT A PSYCHIATRIST. I'M THE ONE WHO *DOESN'T* KEEP YOU NUMB ON MEDS. BUT I UNDERSTAND YOUR DISCOMFORT.
I'D LIKE TO SPEAK WITH YOU TELEPATHICALLY. HAVE YOU EVER DONE THAT BEFORE?
WITH HARADA. LAST NIGHT.
HOW DID IT FEEL?
I DON'T KNOW...CLEAR. LESS CONFUSING, I GUESS.
MIND-TO-MIND COMMUNICATION WITH ANOTHER LIKE YOURSELF IS ONE OF THE MOST FULFILLING RELATIONAL EXPERIENCES A PSIOT CAN HAVE.
MAY I COME IN?
MAY YOU... YOU MEAN INTO MY HEAD...? I GUESS SO.
THINK IT FOR ME. THINK IT CLEARLY IN MY DIRECTION.
VRRRM
YES, YOU MAY COME INTO MY MIND, INGRID.
WONDERFUL, NOW...ISN'T THIS BETTER?

I WANT YOU TO MEET SOMEONE. A WARD OF THE FOUNDATION. LIKE YOU, HE WAS BORN ACTIVATED.

AS FAR AS WE KNOW YOU'RE ONLY TWO OF THREE IN THE WHOLE WORLD THAT WERE BORN THAT WAY.

THIS IS DARPAN.

HI, PETER!

PETER, THINGS ARE GOING TO GET A BIT INTENSE FOR A MOMENT. BUT I KNOW YOU'LL BE STRONG.

INTENSE? LIKE HOW?

YOU'LL BE FINE. DARPAN...

SHOW US.

♪ STUPID STANCHEK IS WEIRD! STUPID STANCHEK IS WEIRD! ♪

♪ STUPID STANCHEK IS WEIRD! ♪
♪ STUPID STANCHEK IS WEIRD! ♪

WAIT... WHAT'S HAPPENING? INGRID?!

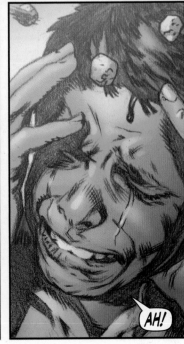

AH!

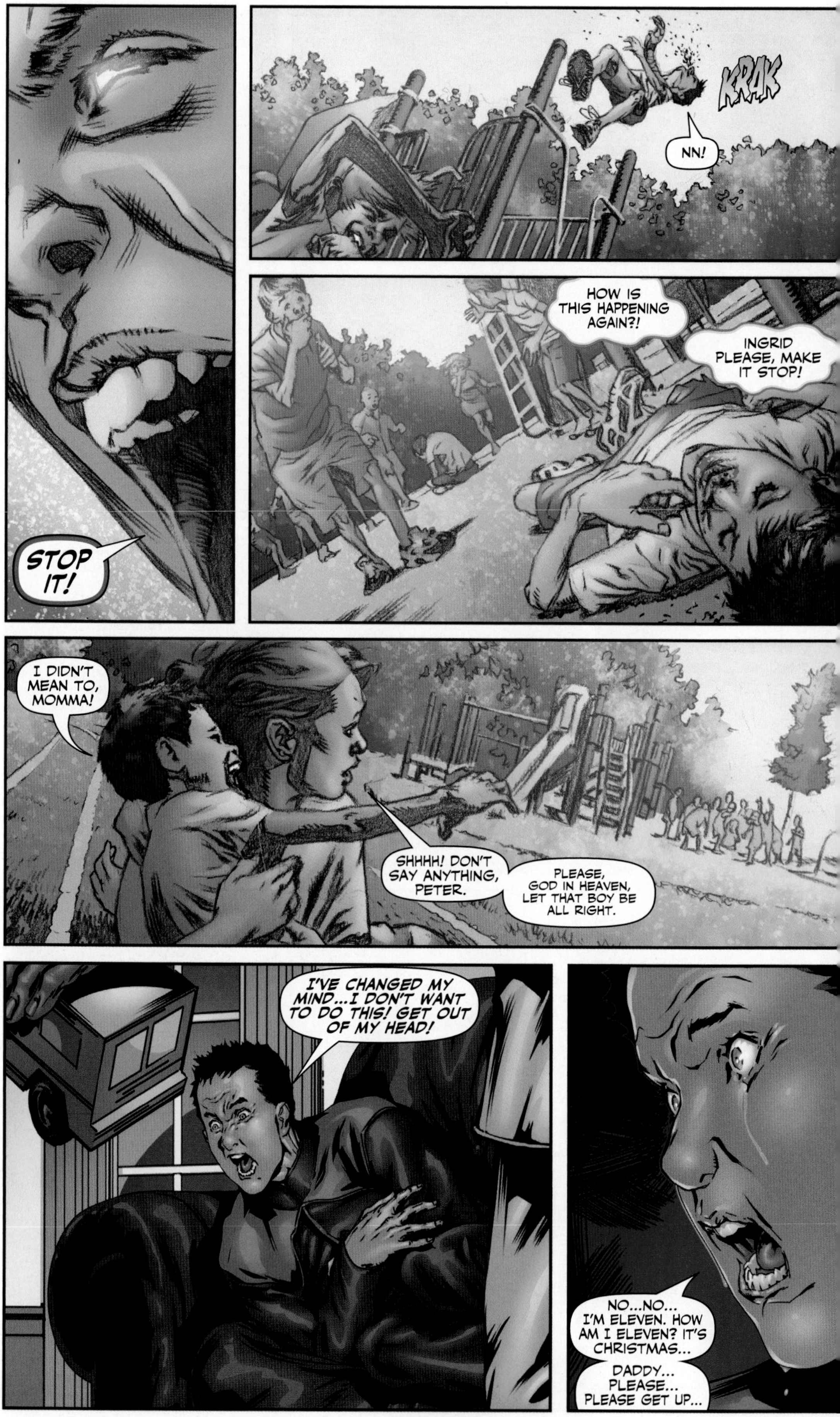
STOP IT!
KRAK
NN!
HOW IS THIS HAPPENING AGAIN?!
INGRID PLEASE, MAKE IT STOP!
I DIDN'T MEAN TO, MOMMA!
SHHHH! DON'T SAY ANYTHING, PETER.
PLEASE, GOD IN HEAVEN, LET THAT BOY BE ALL RIGHT.
I'VE CHANGED MY MIND...I DON'T WANT TO DO THIS! GET OUT OF MY HEAD!
NO...NO... I'M ELEVEN. HOW AM I ELEVEN? IT'S CHRISTMAS...
DADDY... PLEASE... PLEASE GET UP...

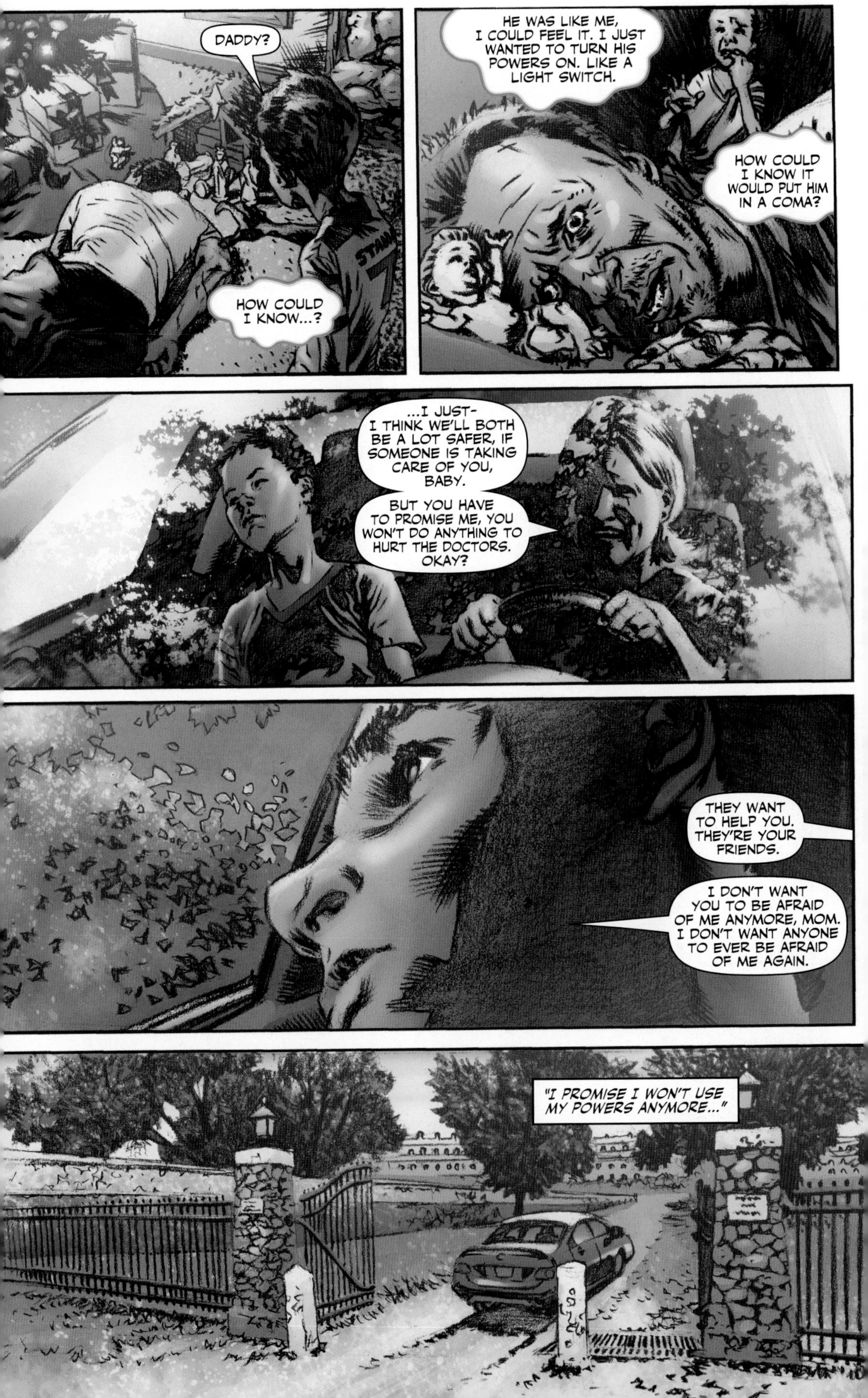
DADDY?
HOW COULD I KNOW...?
HE WAS LIKE ME, I COULD FEEL IT. I JUST WANTED TO TURN HIS POWERS ON. LIKE A LIGHT SWITCH.
HOW COULD I KNOW IT WOULD PUT HIM IN A COMA?
...I JUST- I THINK WE'LL BOTH BE A LOT SAFER, IF SOMEONE IS TAKING CARE OF YOU, BABY.
BUT YOU HAVE TO PROMISE ME, YOU WON'T DO ANYTHING TO HURT THE DOCTORS. OKAY?
THEY WANT TO HELP YOU. THEY'RE YOUR FRIENDS.
I DON'T WANT YOU TO BE AFRAID OF ME ANYMORE, MOM. I DON'T WANT ANYONE TO EVER BE AFRAID OF ME AGAIN.
"I PROMISE I WON'T USE MY POWERS ANYMORE..."

"I'LL LET THEM DO ANYTHING THEY WANT TO ME. YOU'LL SEE..."

NNNNNAAAAGH!

"I CAN BE GOOD."

FFZKOK

PLEASE MAKE IT STOP, INGRID, PLEASE...

IT'S OKAY, PETER.

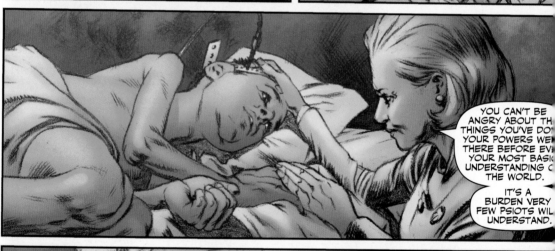

YOU CAN'T BE ANGRY ABOUT TH' THINGS YOU'VE DO' YOUR POWERS WE' THERE BEFORE EV' YOUR MOST BASIC UNDERSTANDING (THE WORLD.

IT'S A BURDEN VERY FEW PSIOTS WIL' UNDERSTAND.

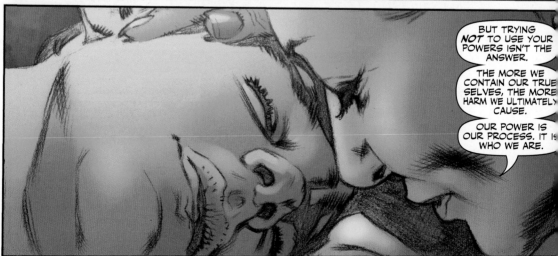

BUT TRYING *NOT* TO USE YOUR POWERS ISN'T THE ANSWER.

THE MORE WE CONTAIN OUR TRUE SELVES, THE MORE HARM WE ULTIMATELY CAUSE.

OUR POWER IS OUR PROCESS. IT I' WHO WE ARE.

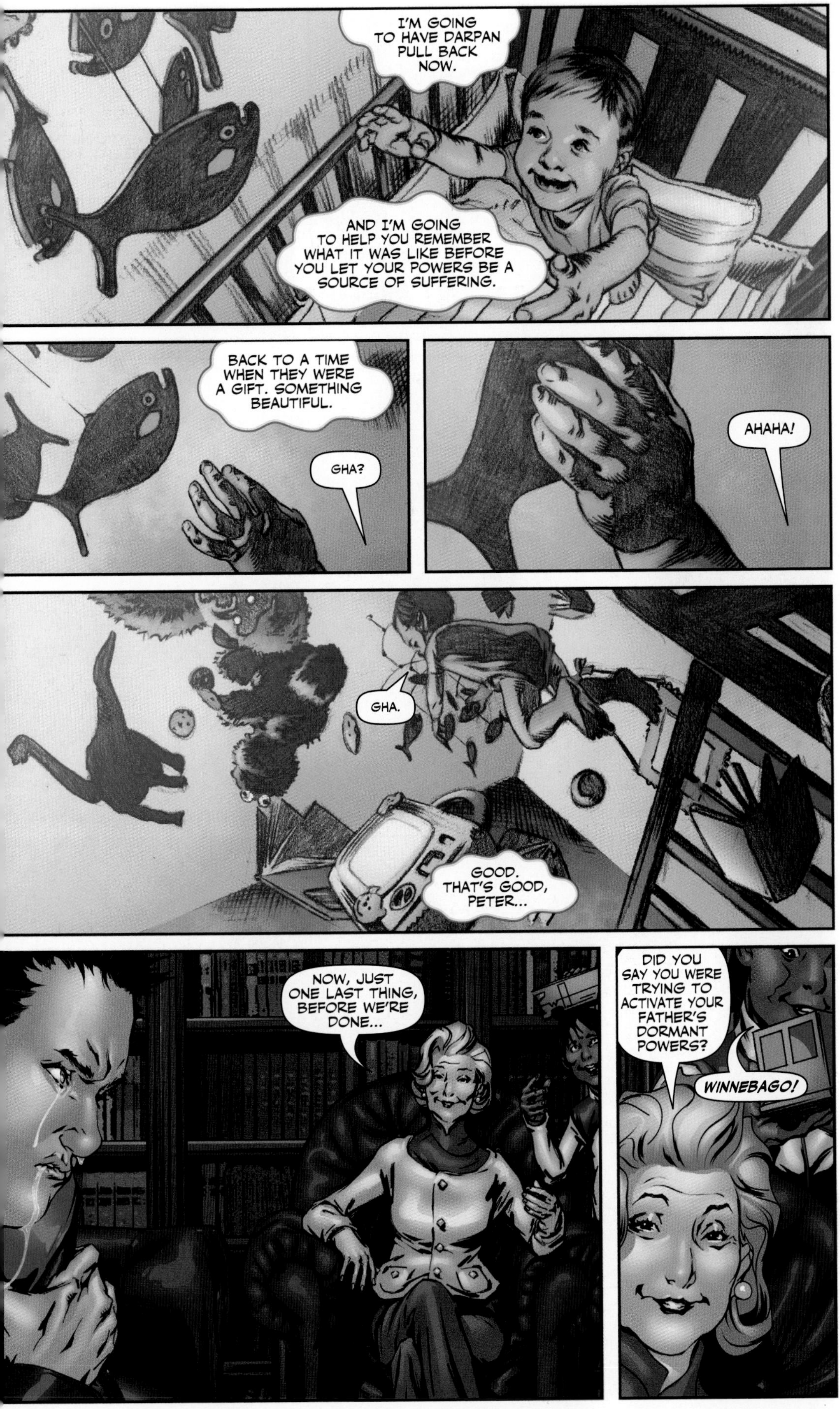
I'M GOING TO HAVE DARPAN PULL BACK NOW.
AND I'M GOING TO HELP YOU REMEMBER WHAT IT WAS LIKE BEFORE YOU LET YOUR POWERS BE A SOURCE OF SUFFERING.
BACK TO A TIME WHEN THEY WERE A GIFT. SOMETHING BEAUTIFUL.
GHA?
AHAHA!
GHA.
GOOD. THAT'S GOOD, PETER...
NOW, JUST ONE LAST THING, BEFORE WE'RE DONE...
DID YOU SAY YOU WERE TRYING TO ACTIVATE YOUR FATHER'S DORMANT POWERS?
WINNEBAGO!

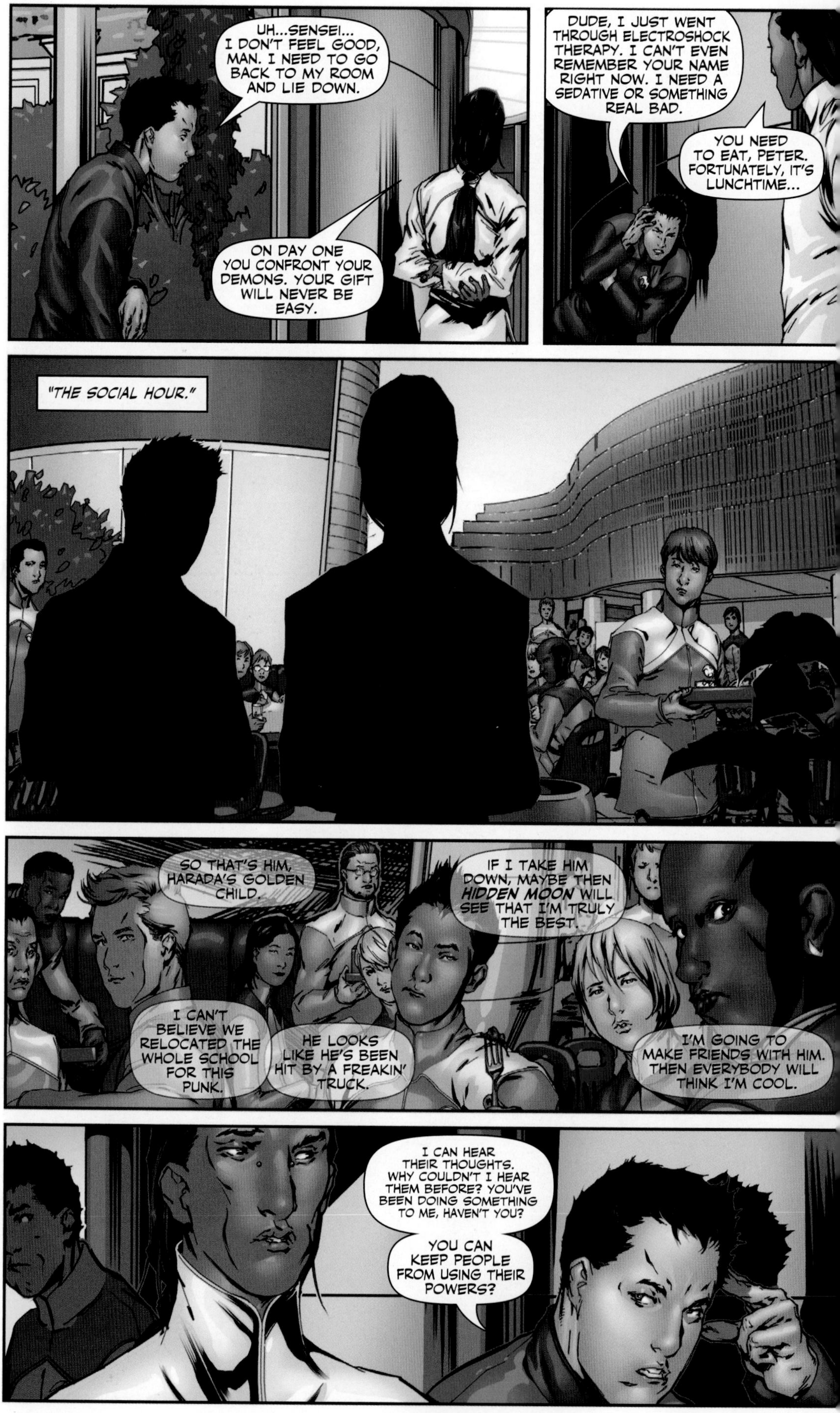
UH...SENSEI... I DON'T FEEL GOOD, MAN. I NEED TO GO BACK TO MY ROOM AND LIE DOWN.
ON DAY ONE YOU CONFRONT YOUR DEMONS. YOUR GIFT WILL NEVER BE EASY.
DUDE, I JUST WENT THROUGH ELECTROSHOCK THERAPY. I CAN'T EVEN REMEMBER YOUR NAME RIGHT NOW. I NEED A SEDATIVE OR SOMETHING REAL BAD.
YOU NEED TO EAT, PETER. FORTUNATELY, IT'S LUNCHTIME...
"THE SOCIAL HOUR."
SO THAT'S HIM, HARADA'S GOLDEN CHILD.
IF I TAKE HIM DOWN, MAYBE THEN HIDDEN MOON WILL SEE THAT I'M TRULY THE BEST.
I CAN'T BELIEVE WE RELOCATED THE WHOLE SCHOOL FOR THIS PUNK.
HE LOOKS LIKE HE'S BEEN HIT BY A FREAKIN' TRUCK.
I'M GOING TO MAKE FRIENDS WITH HIM. THEN EVERYBODY WILL THINK I'M COOL.
I CAN HEAR THEIR THOUGHTS. WHY COULDN'T I HEAR THEM BEFORE? YOU'VE BEEN DOING SOMETHING TO ME, HAVEN'T YOU?
YOU CAN KEEP PEOPLE FROM USING THEIR POWERS?

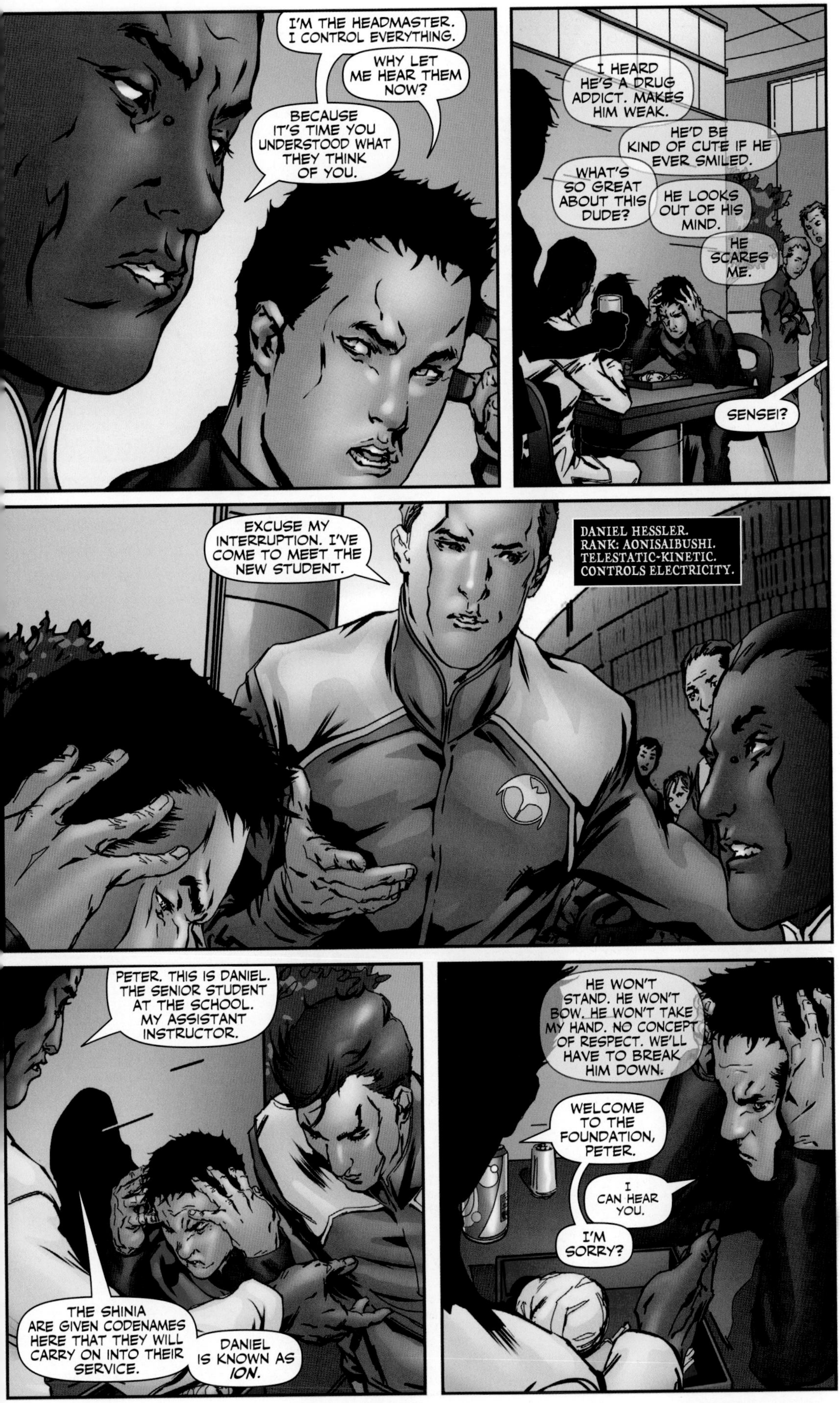

I'M THE HEADMASTER. I CONTROL EVERYTHING.
WHY LET ME HEAR THEM NOW?
BECAUSE IT'S TIME YOU UNDERSTOOD WHAT THEY THINK OF YOU.
I HEARD HE'S A DRUG ADDICT. MAKES HIM WEAK.
HE'D BE KIND OF CUTE IF HE EVER SMILED.
WHAT'S SO GREAT ABOUT THIS DUDE?
HE LOOKS OUT OF HIS MIND.
HE SCARES ME.
SENSEI?
EXCUSE MY INTERRUPTION. I'VE COME TO MEET THE NEW STUDENT.
DANIEL HESSLER.
RANK: AONISAIBUSHI.
TELESTATIC-KINETIC.
CONTROLS ELECTRICITY.
PETER. THIS IS DANIEL. THE SENIOR STUDENT AT THE SCHOOL. MY ASSISTANT INSTRUCTOR.
THE SHINIA ARE GIVEN CODENAMES HERE THAT THEY WILL CARRY ON INTO THEIR SERVICE.
DANIEL IS KNOWN AS *ION*.
HE WON'T STAND. HE WON'T BOW. HE WON'T TAKE MY HAND. NO CONCEPT OF RESPECT. WE'LL HAVE TO BREAK HIM DOWN.
WELCOME TO THE FOUNDATION, PETER.
I CAN HEAR YOU.
I'M SORRY?

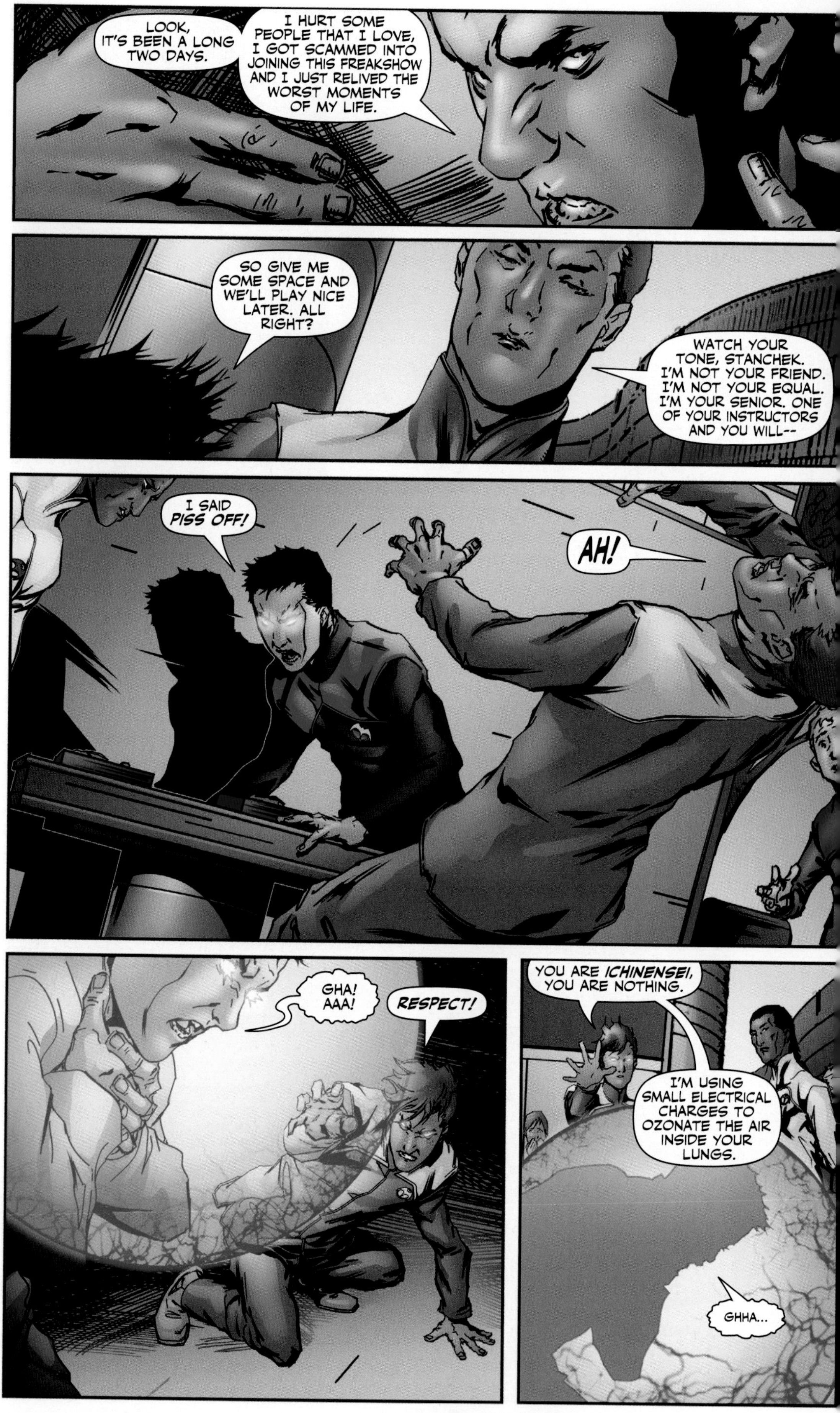
LOOK, IT'S BEEN A LONG TWO DAYS.
I HURT SOME PEOPLE THAT I LOVE, I GOT SCAMMED INTO JOINING THIS FREAKSHOW AND I JUST RELIVED THE WORST MOMENTS OF MY LIFE.
SO GIVE ME SOME SPACE AND WE'LL PLAY NICE LATER. ALL RIGHT?
WATCH YOUR TONE, STANCHEK. I'M NOT YOUR FRIEND. I'M NOT YOUR EQUAL. I'M YOUR SENIOR. ONE OF YOUR INSTRUCTORS AND YOU WILL--
I SAID *PISS OFF!*
AH!
GHA! AAA!
RESPECT!
YOU ARE *ICHINENSEI*, YOU ARE NOTHING.
I'M USING SMALL ELECTRICAL CHARGES TO OZONATE THE AIR INSIDE YOUR LUNGS.
GHHA...

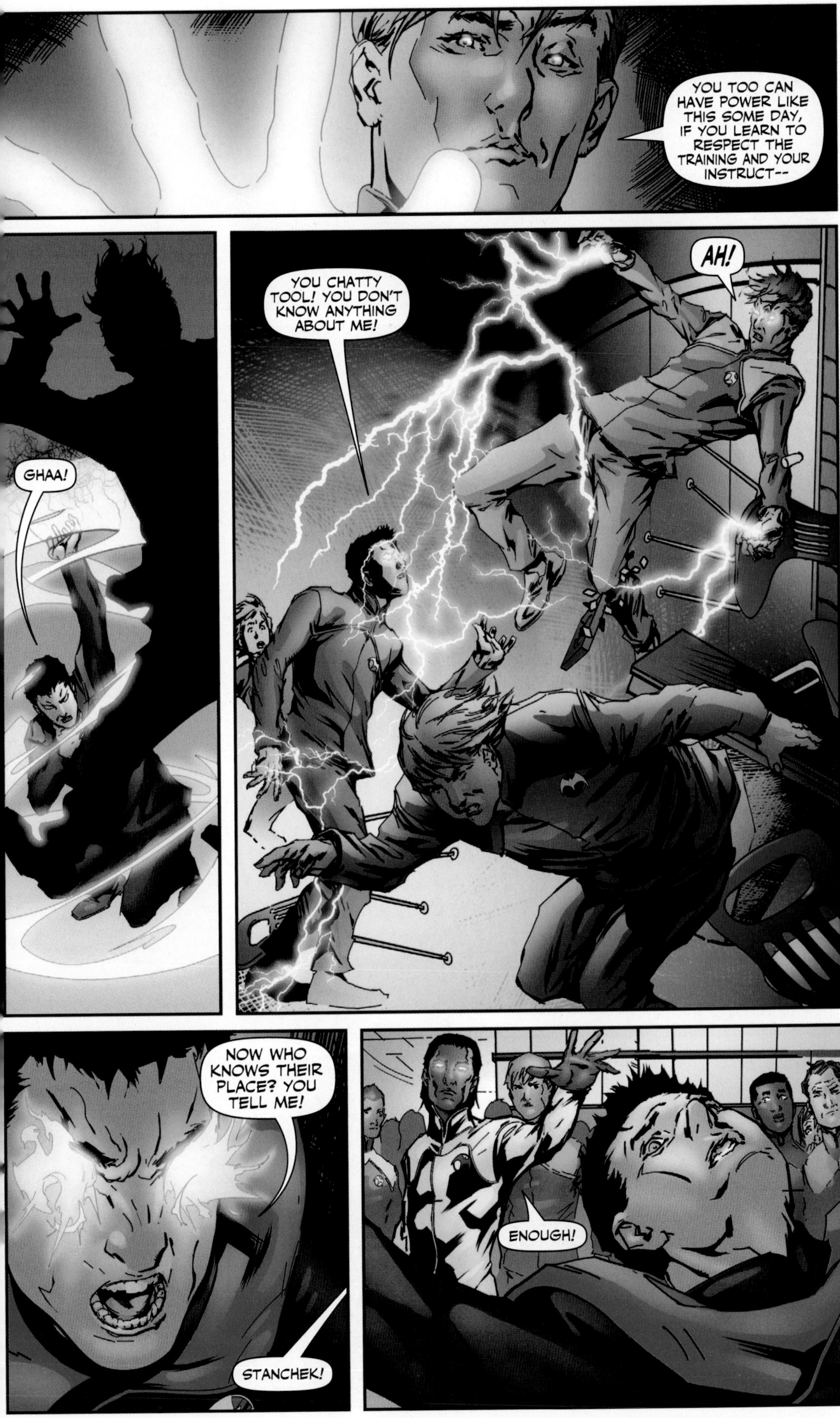
YOU TOO CAN HAVE POWER LIKE THIS SOME DAY, IF YOU LEARN TO RESPECT THE TRAINING AND YOUR INSTRUCT--
GHAA!
YOU CHATTY TOOL! YOU DON'T KNOW ANYTHING ABOUT ME!
AH!
NOW WHO KNOWS THEIR PLACE? YOU TELL ME!
STANCHEK!
ENOUGH!

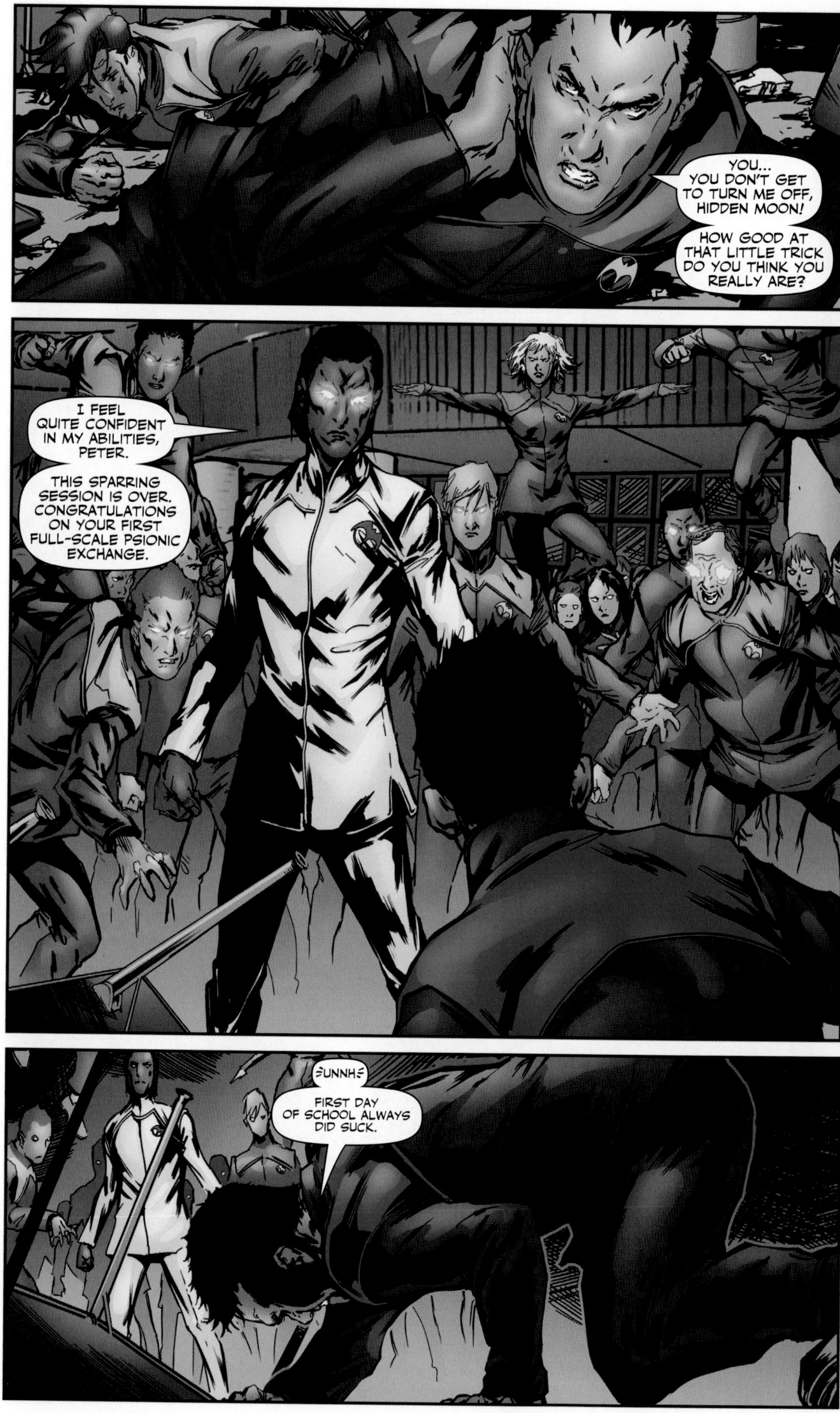
YOU... YOU DON'T GET TO TURN ME OFF, HIDDEN MOON!
HOW GOOD AT THAT LITTLE TRICK DO YOU THINK YOU REALLY ARE?
I FEEL QUITE CONFIDENT IN MY ABILITIES, PETER.
THIS SPARRING SESSION IS OVER. CONGRATULATIONS ON YOUR FIRST FULL-SCALE PSIONIC EXCHANGE.
UNNH
FIRST DAY OF SCHOOL ALWAYS DID SUCK.

RICHMOND, VIRGINIA

HEROGRL08: LEVEL 47 COUGAR ON GUARD! I'M ON A PVE SERVER SO IT'S COOL.

HEROGRL08: ANYWAY, I **TOTALLY** THINK FOXFACE KILLED HERSELF!

HEROGRL08: LIKE, WHY COULDN'T SHE WAIT FOR PEETA TO EAT THE NIGHT-LOCK BERRIES FIRST?!

FA_TIGER: DO YOU THINK WE COULD TALK ABOUT SOMETHING OTHER THAN THE HUNGER GAMES?

HEROGRL08: GEEZE! YOU'RE TOTALLY RIGHT! I'M SO SORRY! UHM… DO YOU LIKE FIREFLY?

FA_TIGER: NO, LIKE, WHEN CAN WE MEET? FOR REAL?

HEROGRL08: UHM…IT'S HARD, YOU KNOW?

FA_TIGER: YES IT IS!

HEROGRL08: NO, PERV! :-) IT'S HARD TO BELIEVE THAT SOMEONE WHO LOOKS LIKE YOU COULD THINK SOMEONE LIKE ME IS PRETTY.

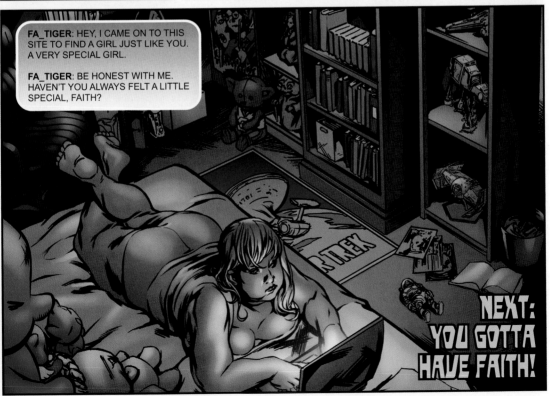

FA_TIGER: HEY, I CAME ON TO THIS SITE TO FIND A GIRL JUST LIKE YOU. A VERY SPECIAL GIRL.

FA_TIGER: BE HONEST WITH ME. HAVEN'T YOU ALWAYS FELT A LITTLE SPECIAL, FAITH?

NEXT:
YOU GOTTA
HAVE FAITH!

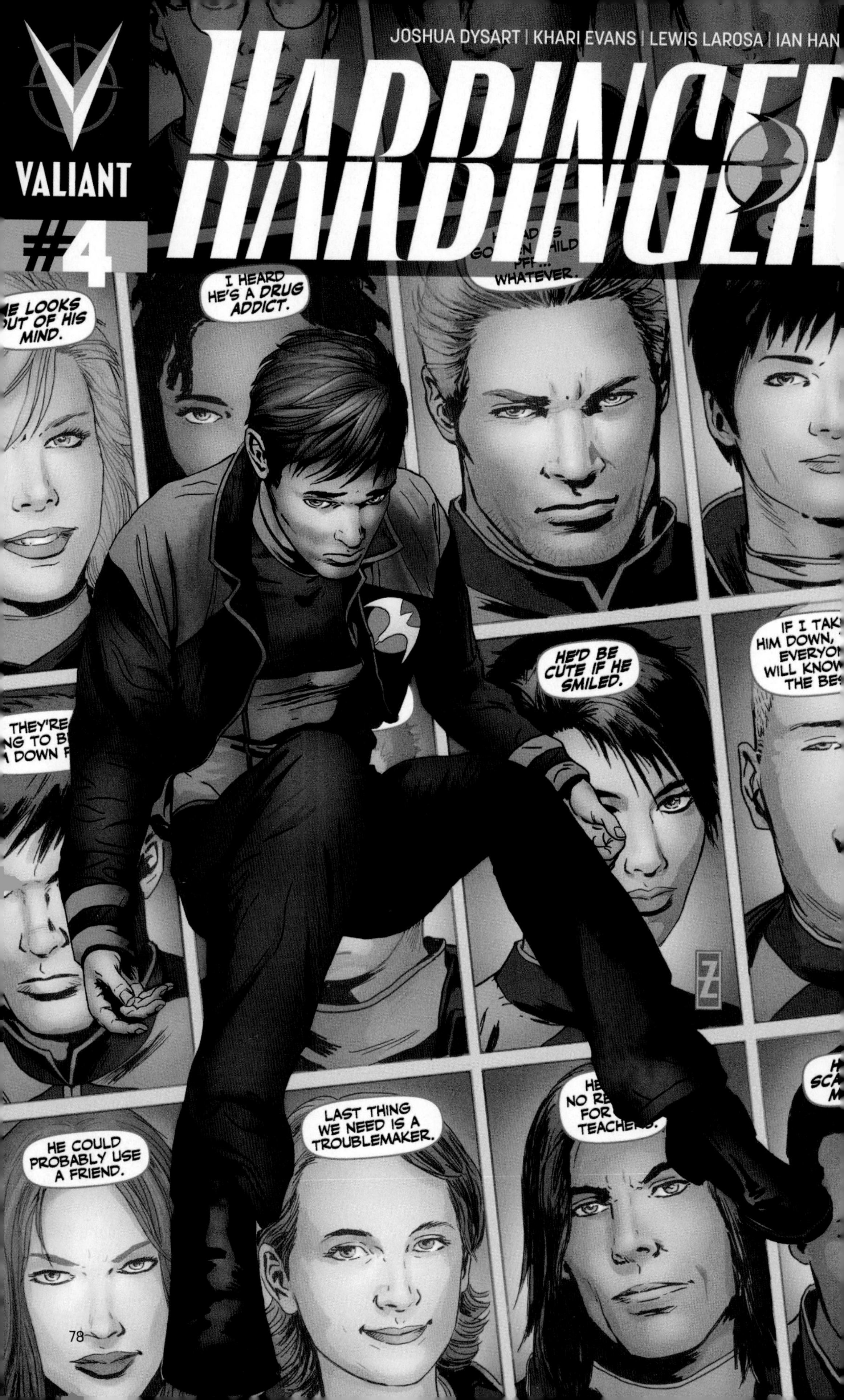

VALIANT
#4
JOSHUA DYSART | KHARI EVANS | LEWIS LAROSA
I HEARD HE'S A DRUG ADDICT.
HE'D BE CUTE IF HE SMILED.
HE COULD PROBABLY USE A FRIEND.
LAST THING WE NEED IS A TROUBLEMAKER.

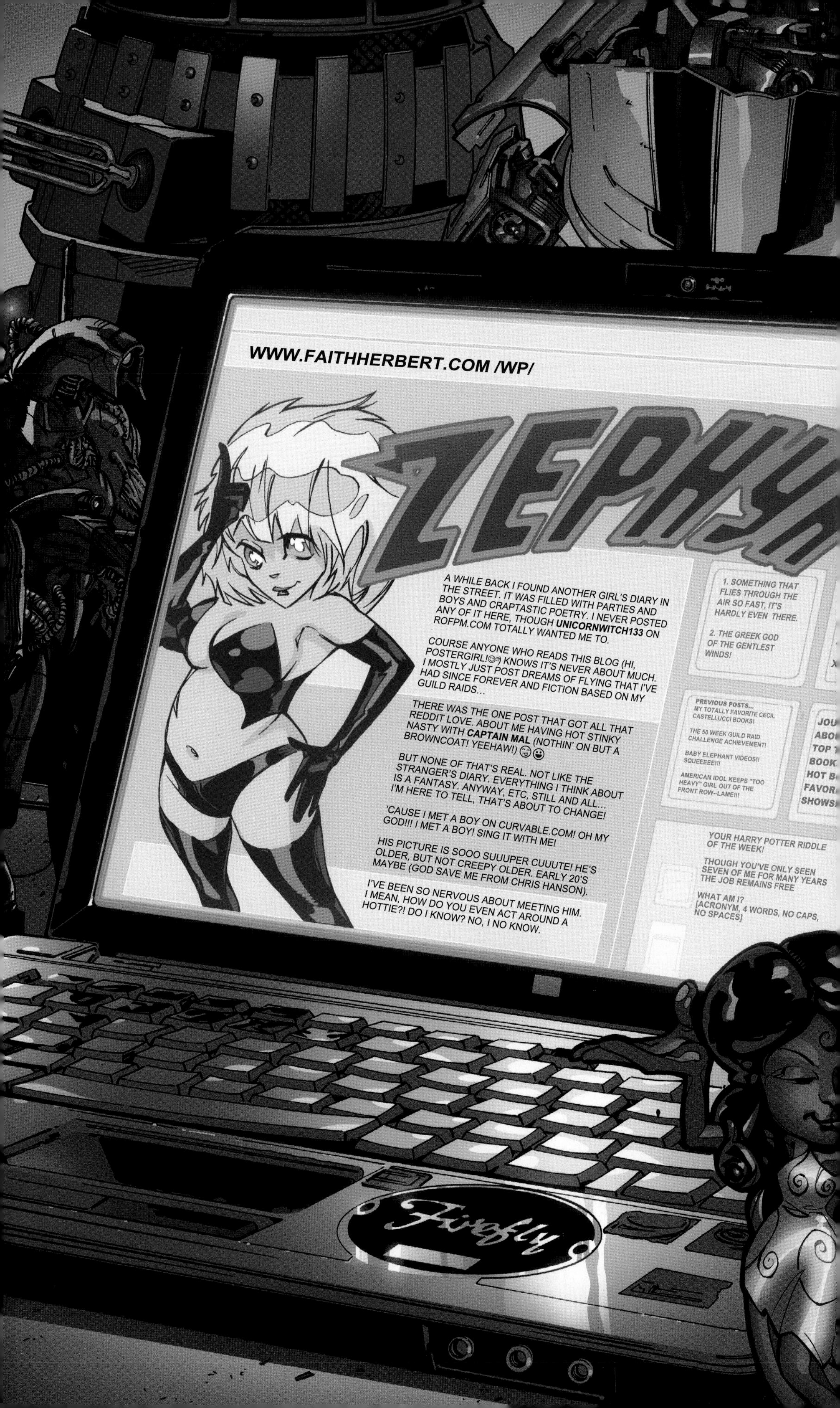

WWW.FAITHHERBERT.COM /WP/
A WHILE BACK I FOUND ANOTHER GIRL'S DIARY IN THE STREET. IT WAS FILLED WITH PARTIES AND BOYS AND CRAPTASTIC POETRY. I NEVER POSTED ANY OF IT HERE, THOUGH UNICORNWITCH133 ON ROFPM.COM TOTALLY WANTED ME TO.
COURSE ANYONE WHO READS THIS BLOG (HI, POSTERGIRL!) KNOWS IT'S NEVER ABOUT MUCH. I MOSTLY JUST POST DREAMS OF FLYING THAT I'VE HAD SINCE FOREVER AND FICTION BASED ON MY GUILD RAIDS...
THERE WAS THE ONE POST THAT GOT ALL THAT REDDIT LOVE. ABOUT ME HAVING HOT STINKY NASTY WITH CAPTAIN MAL (NOTHIN' ON BUT A BROWNCOAT! YEEHAW!)
BUT NONE OF THAT'S REAL. NOT LIKE THE STRANGER'S DIARY. EVERYTHING I THINK ABOUT IS A FANTASY. ANYWAY, ETC, STILL AND ALL... I'M HERE TO TELL, THAT'S ABOUT TO CHANGE!
'CAUSE I MET A BOY ON CURVABLE.COM! OH MY GOD!!! I MET A BOY! SING IT WITH ME!
HIS PICTURE IS SOOO SUUUPER CUUUTE! HE'S OLDER, BUT NOT CREEPY OLDER. EARLY 20'S MAYBE (GOD SAVE ME FROM CHRIS HANSON).
I'VE BEEN SO NERVOUS ABOUT MEETING HIM. I MEAN, HOW DO YOU EVEN ACT AROUND A HOTTIE?! DO I KNOW? NO, I NO KNOW.
1. SOMETHING THAT FLIES THROUGH THE AIR SO FAST, IT'S HARDLY EVEN THERE.
2. THE GREEK GOD OF THE GENTLEST WINDS!
PREVIOUS POSTS...
MY TOTALLY FAVORITE CECIL CASTELLUCCI BOOKS!
THE 50 WEEK GUILD RAID CHALLENGE ACHIEVEMENT!
BABY ELEPHANT VIDEOS!! SQUEEEEE!!!
AMERICAN IDOL KEEPS "TOO HEAVY" GIRL OUT OF THE FRONT ROW--LAME!!!
YOUR HARRY POTTER RIDDLE OF THE WEEK!
THOUGH YOU'VE ONLY SEEN SEVEN OF ME FOR MANY YEARS THE JOB REMAINS FREE
WHAT AM I?
[ACRONYM, 4 WORDS, NO CAPS, NO SPACES]
Firefly

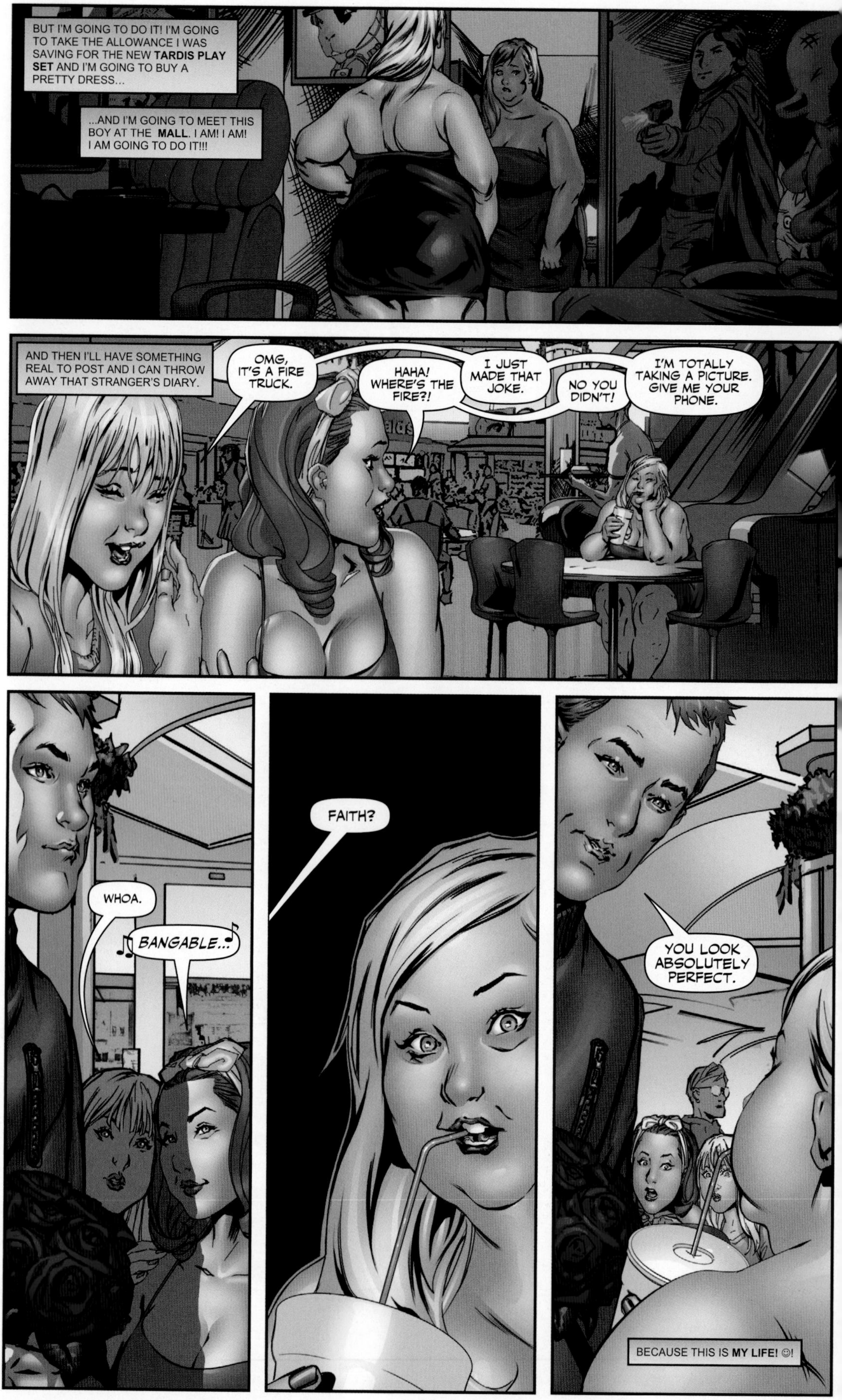
BUT I'M GOING TO DO IT! I'M GOING TO TAKE THE ALLOWANCE I WAS SAVING FOR THE NEW **TARDIS PLAY SET** AND I'M GOING TO BUY A PRETTY DRESS...
...AND I'M GOING TO MEET THIS BOY AT THE **MALL**. I AM! I AM! I AM GOING TO DO IT!!!
AND THEN I'LL HAVE SOMETHING REAL TO POST AND I CAN THROW AWAY THAT STRANGER'S DIARY.
OMG, IT'S A FIRE TRUCK.
HAHA! WHERE'S THE FIRE?!
I JUST MADE THAT JOKE.
NO YOU DIDN'T!
I'M TOTALLY TAKING A PICTURE. GIVE ME YOUR PHONE.
WHOA.
BANGABLE...
FAITH?
YOU LOOK ABSOLUTELY PERFECT.
BECAUSE THIS IS **MY LIFE**! ☺!

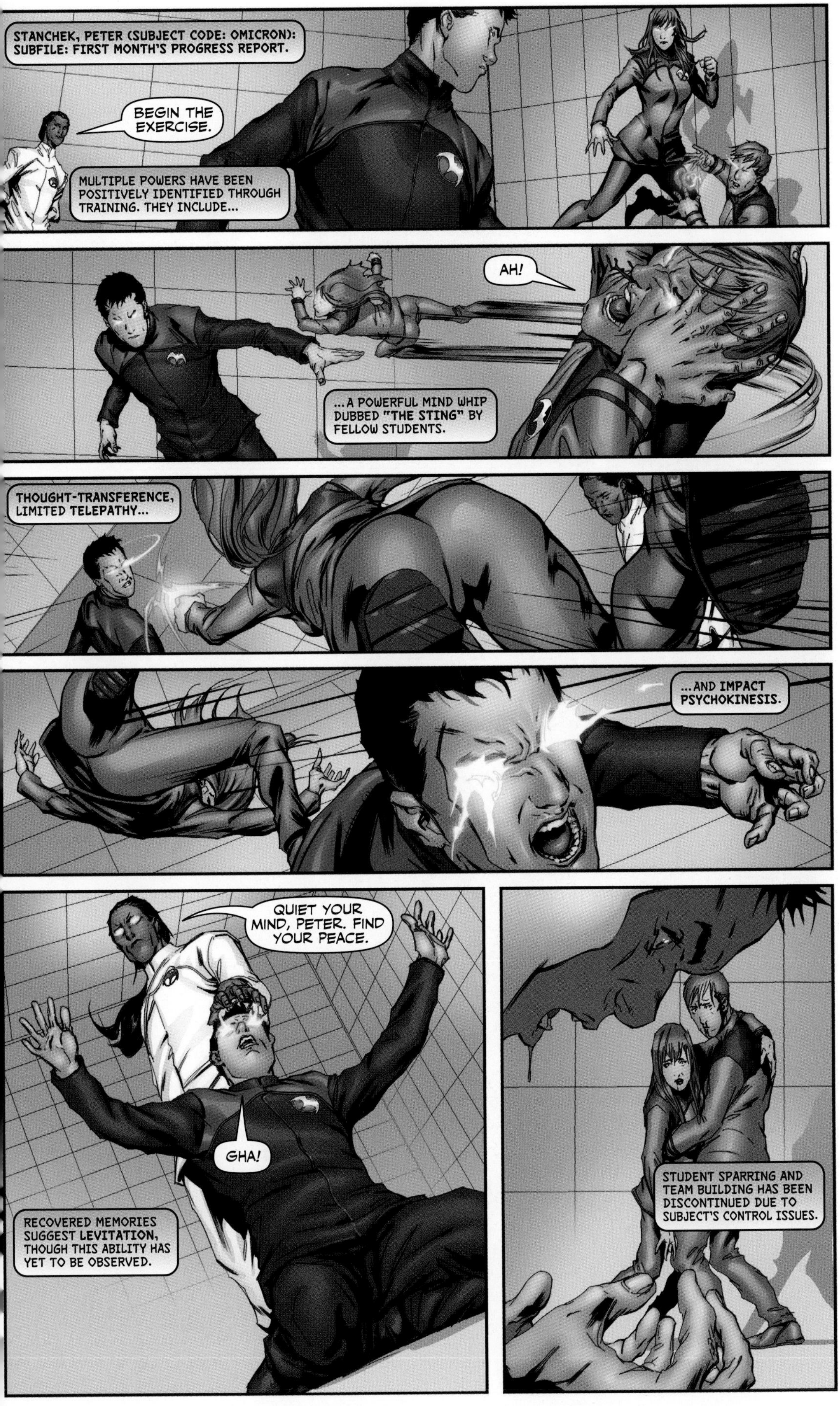
STANCHEK, PETER (SUBJECT CODE: OMICRON): SUBFILE: FIRST MONTH'S PROGRESS REPORT.
BEGIN THE EXERCISE.
MULTIPLE POWERS HAVE BEEN POSITIVELY IDENTIFIED THROUGH TRAINING. THEY INCLUDE...
AH!
...A POWERFUL MIND WHIP DUBBED "THE STING" BY FELLOW STUDENTS.
THOUGHT-TRANSFERENCE, LIMITED TELEPATHY...
...AND IMPACT PSYCHOKINESIS.
QUIET YOUR MIND, PETER. FIND YOUR PEACE.
GHA!
RECOVERED MEMORIES SUGGEST LEVITATION, THOUGH THIS ABILITY HAS YET TO BE OBSERVED.
STUDENT SPARRING AND TEAM BUILDING HAS BEEN DISCONTINUED DUE TO SUBJECT'S CONTROL ISSUES.

SUBJECT SCORES 130 IN VERBAL IQ EXAMINATIONS...

...THOUGH INTEREST IN ACADEMIC STUDIES CONTINUES TO BE MINIMAL.

?

JOE?

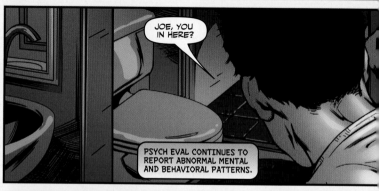

JOE, YOU IN HERE?

PSYCH EVAL CONTINUES TO REPORT ABNORMAL MENTAL AND BEHAVIORAL PATTERNS.

KRIS?

I'M SORRY.

END REPORT OVERVIEW.

DISPLAYING NEUROIMAGING FILES.

NOW TO ORAL ARGUMENTS.

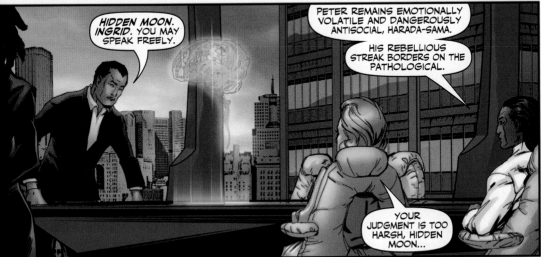

HIDDEN MOON. INGRID. YOU MAY SPEAK FREELY.

PETER REMAINS EMOTIONALLY VOLATILE AND DANGEROUSLY ANTISOCIAL, HARADA-SAMA.

HIS REBELLIOUS STREAK BORDERS ON THE PATHOLOGICAL.

YOUR JUDGMENT IS TOO HARSH, HIDDEN MOON...

HIS CONTROL IS IMPROVING. HE'S OFF THE DRUGS AND ABLE TO FILTER OUT THE THOUGHT CLOUD.

HIS INCREASING CONTROL IS MY GREATEST CONCERN. IT'S MORE PRUDENT TO KILL HIM THAN TRAIN HIM.

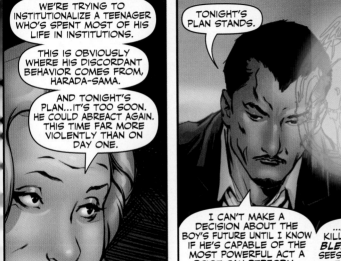

WE'RE TRYING TO INSTITUTIONALIZE A TEENAGER WHO'S SPENT MOST OF HIS LIFE IN INSTITUTIONS.

THIS IS OBVIOUSLY WHERE HIS DISCORDANT BEHAVIOR COMES FROM, HARADA-SAMA.

AND TONIGHT'S PLAN...IT'S TOO SOON. HE COULD ABREACT AGAIN. THIS TIME FAR MORE VIOLENTLY THAN ON DAY ONE.

TONIGHT'S PLAN STANDS.

I CAN'T MAKE A DECISION ABOUT THE BOY'S FUTURE UNTIL I KNOW IF HE'S CAPABLE OF THE MOST POWERFUL ACT A PSIOT CAN PERFORM...

...AND AS FOR KILLING HIM: THE BLEEDING MONK SEES GREAT THINGS FOR PETER...

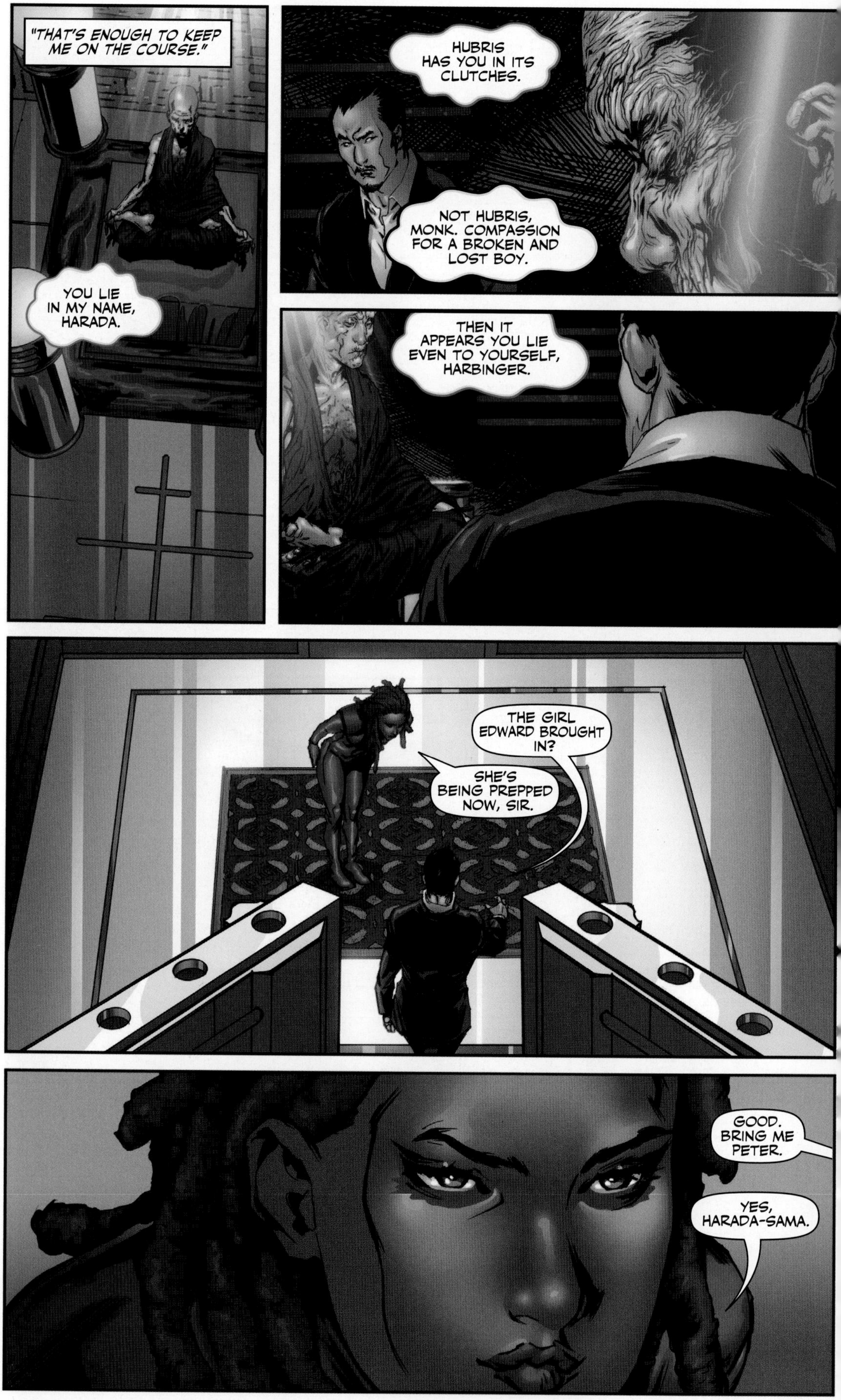
"THAT'S ENOUGH TO KEEP ME ON THE COURSE."
HUBRIS HAS YOU IN ITS CLUTCHES.
NOT HUBRIS, MONK. COMPASSION FOR A BROKEN AND LOST BOY.
YOU LIE IN MY NAME, HARADA.
THEN IT APPEARS YOU LIE EVEN TO YOURSELF, HARBINGER.
THE GIRL EDWARD BROUGHT IN?
SHE'S BEING PREPPED NOW, SIR.
GOOD. BRING ME PETER.
YES, HARADA-SAMA.

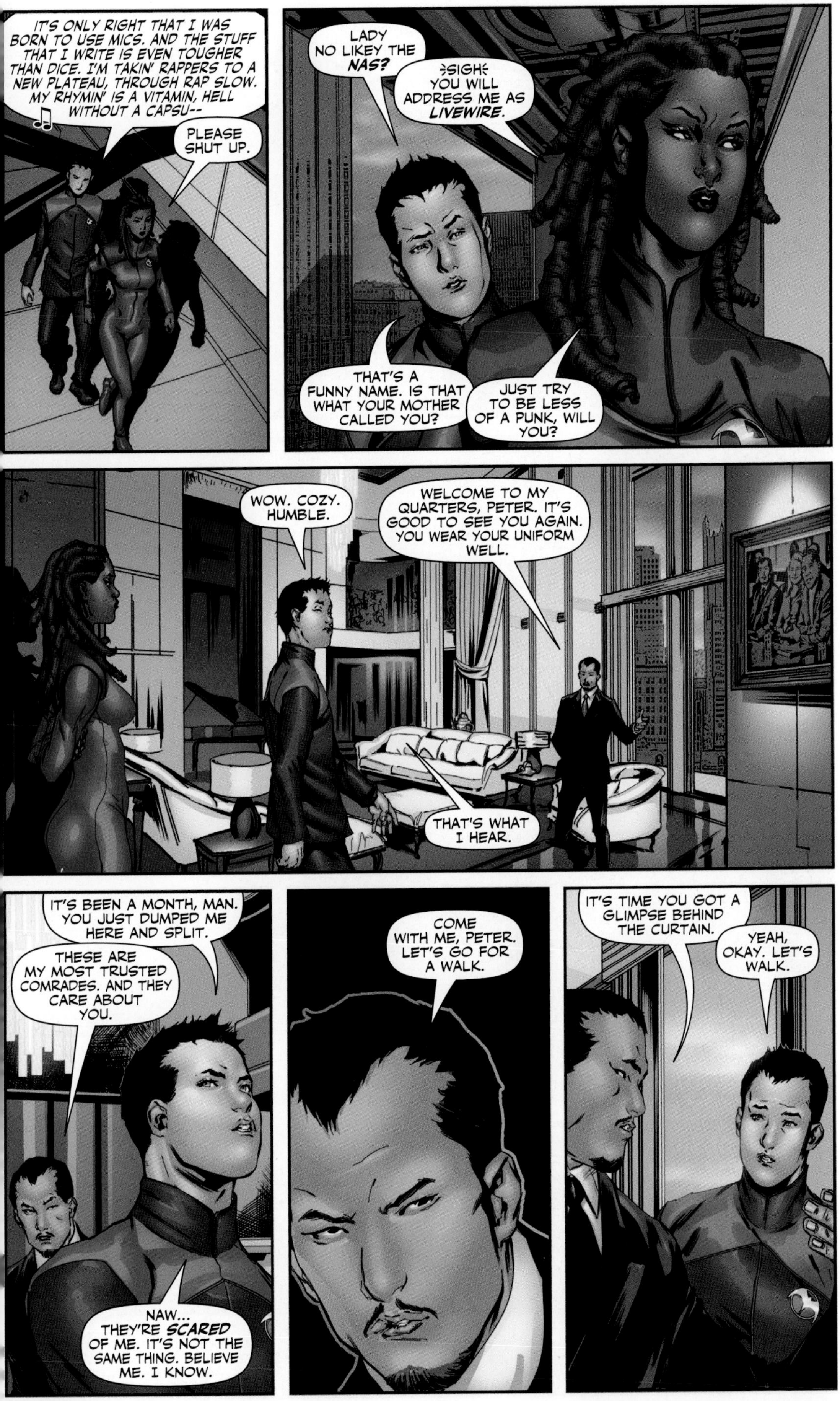
IT'S ONLY RIGHT THAT I WAS BORN TO USE MICS. AND THE STUFF THAT I WRITE IS EVEN TOUGHER THAN DICE. I'M TAKIN' RAPPERS TO A NEW PLATEAU, THROUGH RAP SLOW. MY RHYMIN' IS A VITAMIN, HELL WITHOUT A CAPSU--
PLEASE SHUT UP.
LADY NO LIKEY THE NAS?
SIGH YOU WILL ADDRESS ME AS LIVEWIRE.
THAT'S A FUNNY NAME. IS THAT WHAT YOUR MOTHER CALLED YOU?
JUST TRY TO BE LESS OF A PUNK, WILL YOU?
WOW. COZY. HUMBLE.
WELCOME TO MY QUARTERS, PETER. IT'S GOOD TO SEE YOU AGAIN. YOU WEAR YOUR UNIFORM WELL.
THAT'S WHAT I HEAR.
IT'S BEEN A MONTH, MAN. YOU JUST DUMPED ME HERE AND SPLIT.
THESE ARE MY MOST TRUSTED COMRADES. AND THEY CARE ABOUT YOU.
NAW... THEY'RE SCARED OF ME. IT'S NOT THE SAME THING. BELIEVE ME. I KNOW.
COME WITH ME, PETER. LET'S GO FOR A WALK.
IT'S TIME YOU GOT A GLIMPSE BEHIND THE CURTAIN.
YEAH, OKAY. LET'S WALK.

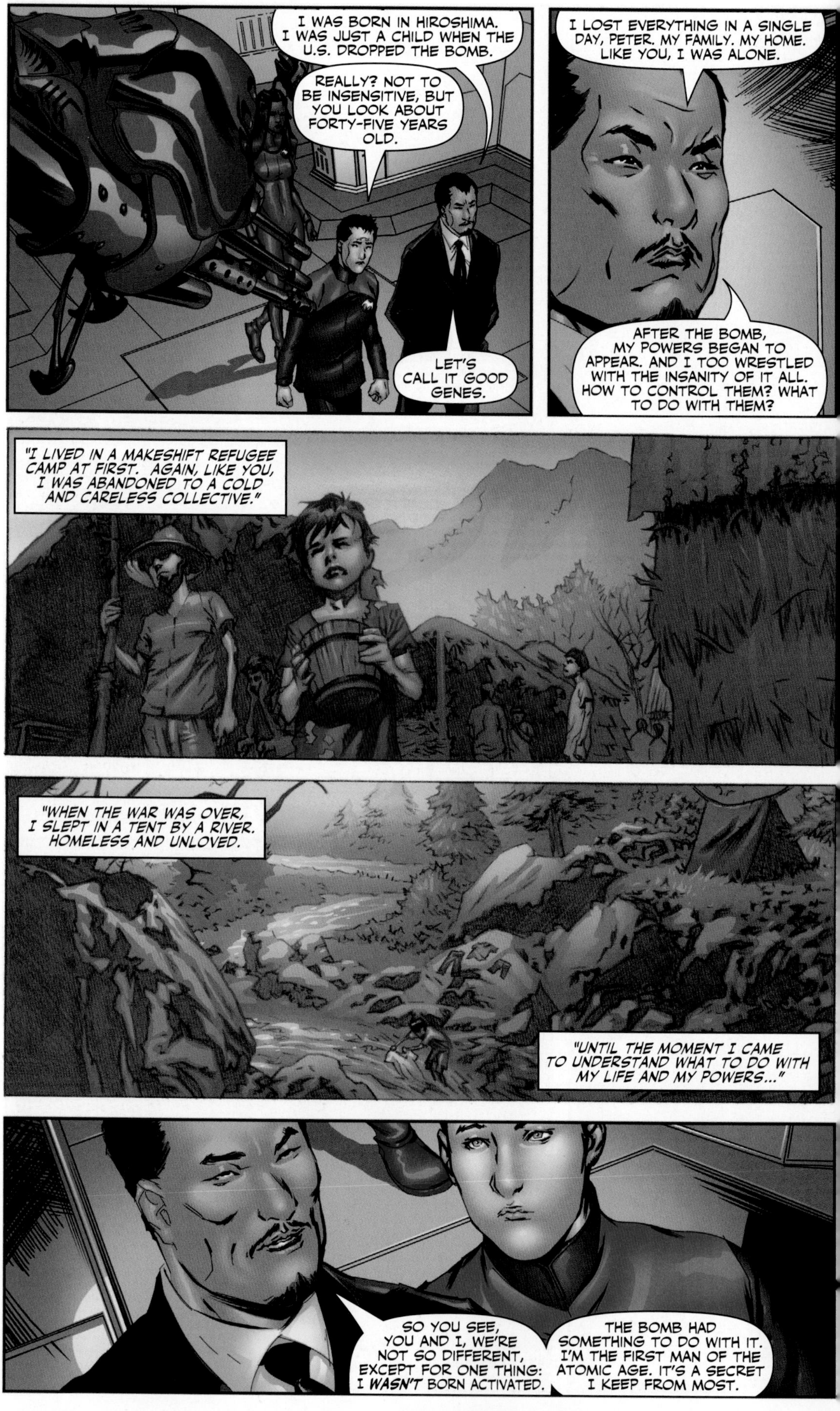
I WAS BORN IN HIROSHIMA. I WAS JUST A CHILD WHEN THE U.S. DROPPED THE BOMB.
REALLY? NOT TO BE INSENSITIVE, BUT YOU LOOK ABOUT FORTY-FIVE YEARS OLD.
LET'S CALL IT GOOD GENES.
I LOST EVERYTHING IN A SINGLE DAY, PETER. MY FAMILY. MY HOME. LIKE YOU, I WAS ALONE.
AFTER THE BOMB, MY POWERS BEGAN TO APPEAR. AND I TOO WRESTLED WITH THE INSANITY OF IT ALL. HOW TO CONTROL THEM? WHAT TO DO WITH THEM?
"I LIVED IN A MAKESHIFT REFUGEE CAMP AT FIRST. AGAIN, LIKE YOU, I WAS ABANDONED TO A COLD AND CARELESS COLLECTIVE."
"WHEN THE WAR WAS OVER, I SLEPT IN A TENT BY A RIVER. HOMELESS AND UNLOVED.
"UNTIL THE MOMENT I CAME TO UNDERSTAND WHAT TO DO WITH MY LIFE AND MY POWERS..."
SO YOU SEE, YOU AND I, WE'RE NOT SO DIFFERENT, EXCEPT FOR ONE THING: I *WASN'T* BORN ACTIVATED.
THE BOMB HAD SOMETHING TO DO WITH IT. I'M THE FIRST MAN OF THE ATOMIC AGE. IT'S A SECRET I KEEP FROM MOST.

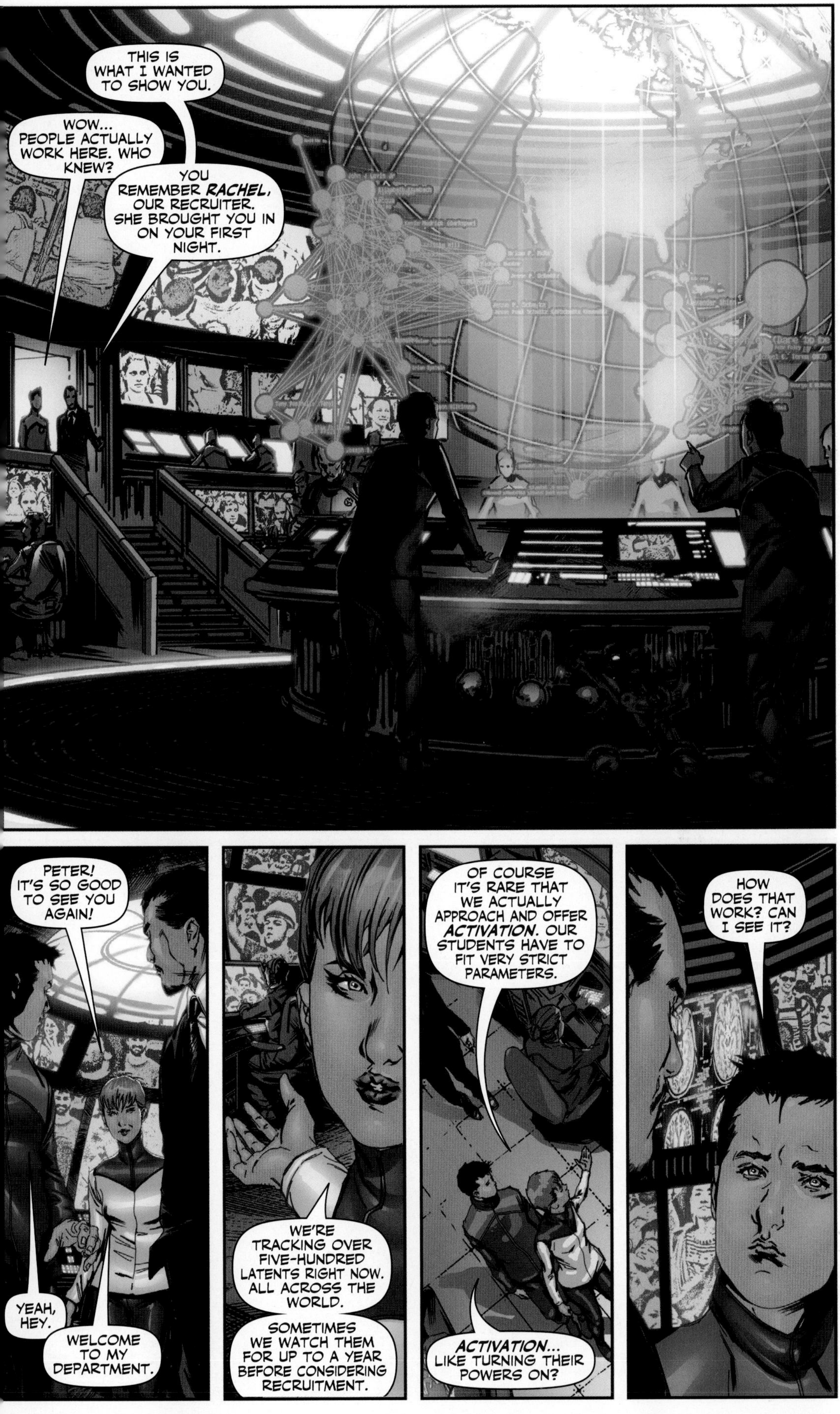
THIS IS WHAT I WANTED TO SHOW YOU.
WOW... PEOPLE ACTUALLY WORK HERE. WHO KNEW?
YOU REMEMBER *RACHEL*, OUR RECRUITER. SHE BROUGHT YOU IN ON YOUR FIRST NIGHT.
PETER! IT'S SO GOOD TO SEE YOU AGAIN!
YEAH, HEY.
WELCOME TO MY DEPARTMENT.
WE'RE TRACKING OVER FIVE-HUNDRED LATENTS RIGHT NOW. ALL ACROSS THE WORLD.
SOMETIMES WE WATCH THEM FOR UP TO A YEAR BEFORE CONSIDERING RECRUITMENT.
OF COURSE IT'S RARE THAT WE ACTUALLY APPROACH AND OFFER *ACTIVATION*. OUR STUDENTS HAVE TO FIT VERY STRICT PARAMETERS.
ACTIVATION... LIKE TURNING THEIR POWERS ON?
HOW DOES THAT WORK? CAN I SEE IT?

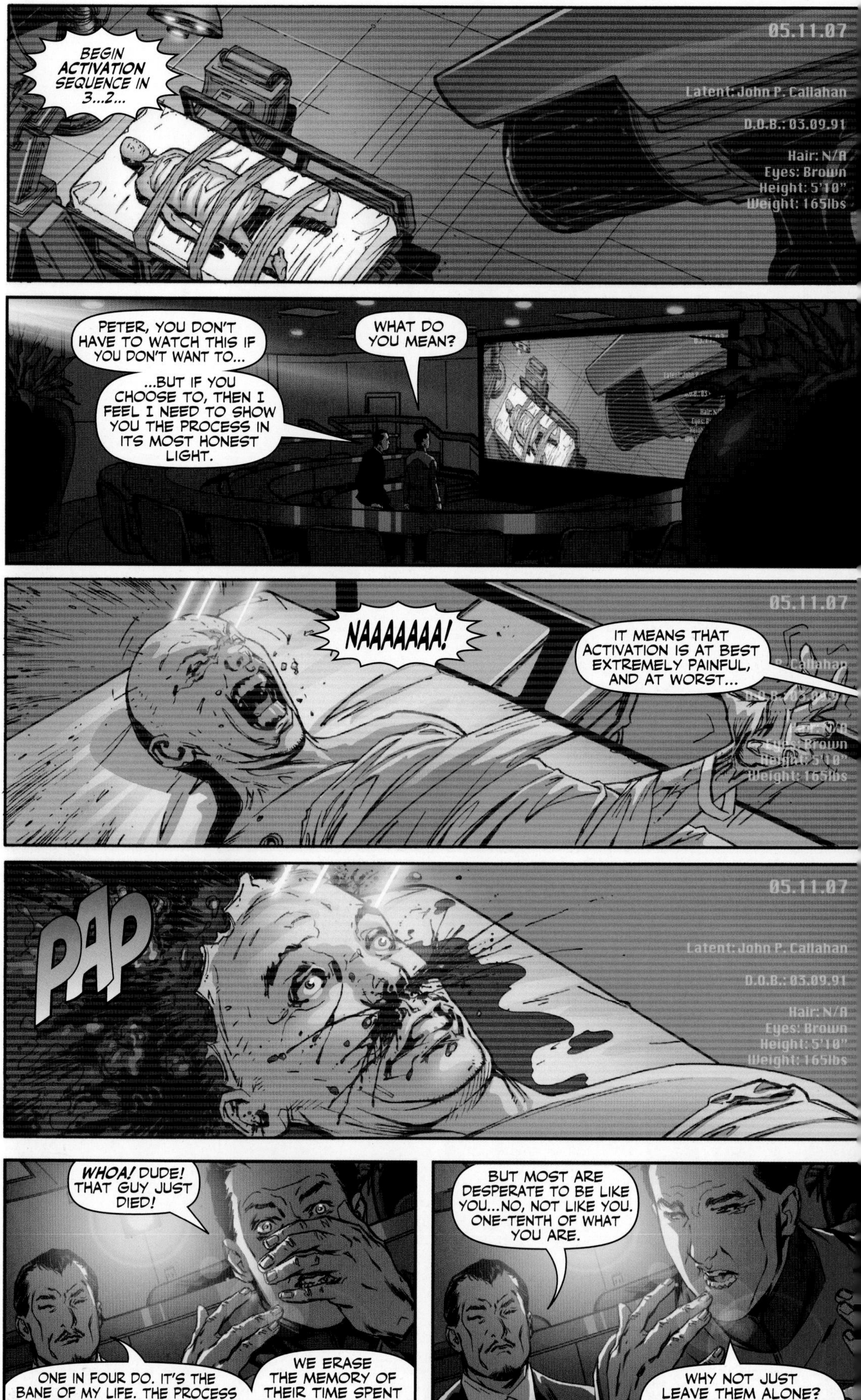
BEGIN ACTIVATION SEQUENCE IN 3...2...
05.11.07
Latent: John P. Callahan
D.O.B.: 03.09.91
Hair: N/A
Eyes: Brown
Height: 5'10"
Weight: 165lbs
PETER, YOU DON'T HAVE TO WATCH THIS IF YOU DON'T WANT TO...
WHAT DO YOU MEAN?
...BUT IF YOU CHOOSE TO, THEN I FEEL I NEED TO SHOW YOU THE PROCESS IN ITS MOST HONEST LIGHT.
05.11.07
NAAAAAAA!
IT MEANS THAT ACTIVATION IS AT BEST EXTREMELY PAINFUL, AND AT WORST...
PAP
05.11.07
Latent: John P. Callahan
D.O.B.: 03.09.91
Hair: N/A
Eyes: Brown
Height: 5'10"
Weight: 165lbs
WHOA! DUDE! THAT GUY JUST DIED!
ONE IN FOUR DO. IT'S THE BANE OF MY LIFE. THE PROCESS IS VOLUNTARY, OF COURSE. SOME CHOOSE NOT TO TRY.
WE ERASE THE MEMORY OF THEIR TIME SPENT HERE AND SEND THEM BACK TO THEIR LIVES.
BUT MOST ARE DESPERATE TO BE LIKE YOU...NO, NOT LIKE YOU. ONE-TENTH OF WHAT YOU ARE.
WHY NOT JUST LEAVE THEM ALONE? LET PEOPLE LIVE THEIR LIVES? WHAT'S THE POINT?!

LOOK AT THE WORLD, PETER. AT THE WARS WE WAGE AND THE BOMBS WE DROP...

WITHOUT ACTIVATED PSIOTS AND STRONG LEADERSHIP HUMANITY WON'T SURVIVE ITSELF, MUCH LESS THE EXTERIOR THREAT THAT'S COMING.

YOU TALK LIKE A CULT LEADER, YOU KNOW THAT? YOU WANT FOLLOWERS? BE GANDHI! BE JESUS!

NOT SOME SUPER CAPITALIST WITH A GOD COMPLEX HAND-PICKING PEOPLE YOU THINK DESERVE POWER AND THEN TORTURING THEM.

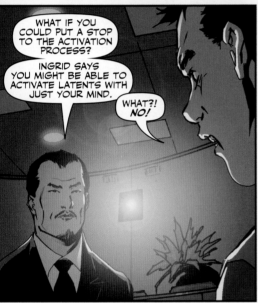

WHAT IF YOU COULD PUT A STOP TO THE ACTIVATION PROCESS?

INGRID SAYS YOU MIGHT BE ABLE TO ACTIVATE LATENTS WITH JUST YOUR MIND.

WHAT?! NO!

I KNOW THIS IS HARD. I KNOW ABOUT YOUR FATHER. BUT YOU WERE JUST A CHILD THEN.

THERE'S NO LIVING PSIOT, NOR ANY IN MEMORY, THAT HAS BEEN ABLE TO ACTIVATE OTHERS.

IT IS A GIFT BEYOND YOUR UNDERSTANDING.

I HAVE A LATENT GIRL HERE. SHE'LL DO ANYTHING TO BE MORE THAN WHAT SHE IS. HELP ME HELP HER.

ABSOLUTELY NOT. SEND HER HOME. MIND-WIPE HER, WHATEVER IT IS YOU DO. NO WAY. I'M NOT DOING IT.

IT'S HER CHOICE, PETER. AT THIS POINT, I'M AFRAID TO SAY, IT'S *YOU* OR THE *MACHINE*. AT LEAST MEET WITH HER.

HER NAME IS *FAITH*.

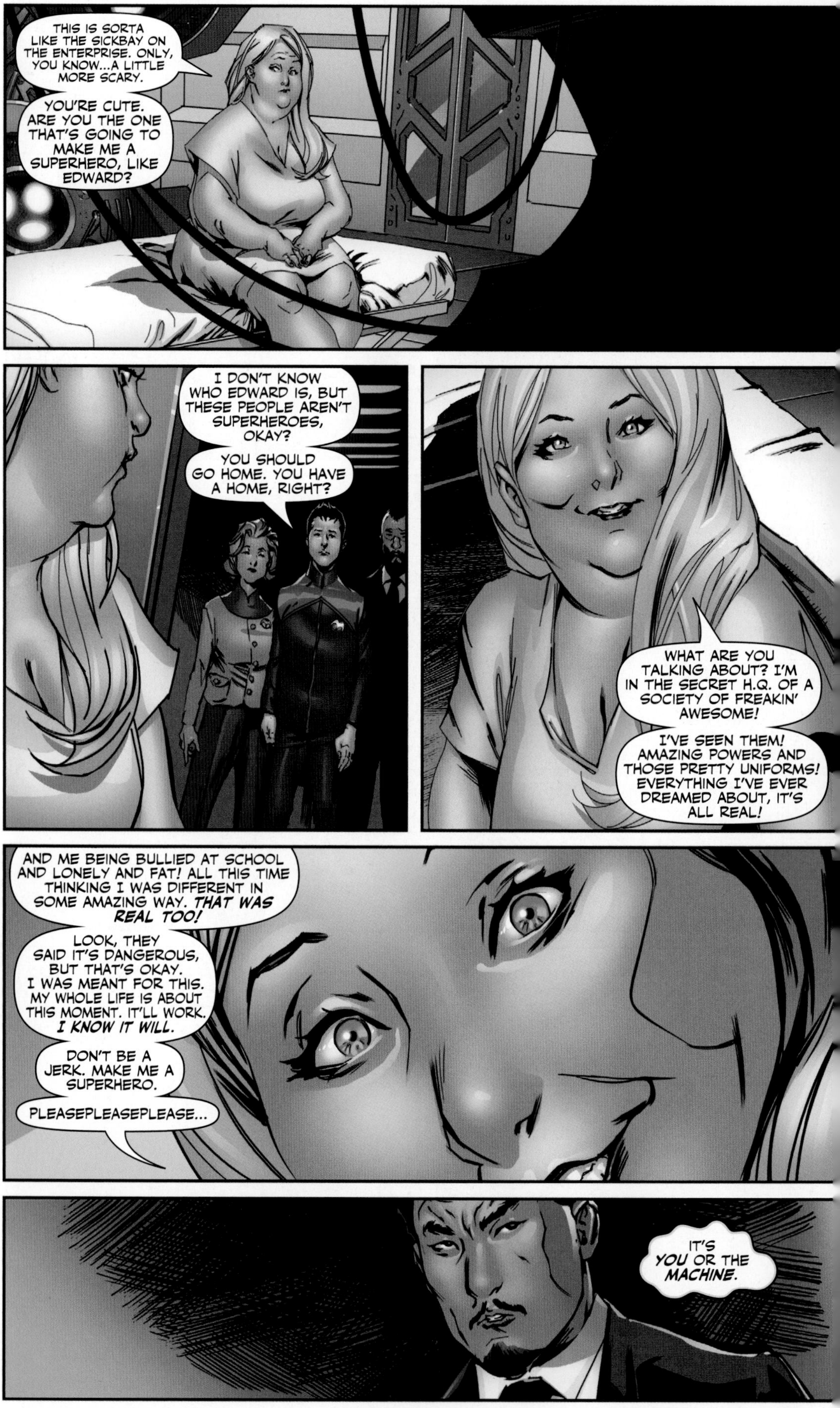
THIS IS SORTA LIKE THE SICKBAY ON THE ENTERPRISE. ONLY, YOU KNOW...A LITTLE MORE SCARY.
YOU'RE CUTE. ARE YOU THE ONE THAT'S GOING TO MAKE ME A SUPERHERO, LIKE EDWARD?
I DON'T KNOW WHO EDWARD IS, BUT THESE PEOPLE AREN'T SUPERHEROES, OKAY?
YOU SHOULD GO HOME. YOU HAVE A HOME, RIGHT?
WHAT ARE YOU TALKING ABOUT? I'M IN THE SECRET H.Q. OF A SOCIETY OF FREAKIN' AWESOME!
I'VE SEEN THEM! AMAZING POWERS AND THOSE PRETTY UNIFORMS! EVERYTHING I'VE EVER DREAMED ABOUT, IT'S ALL REAL!
AND ME BEING BULLIED AT SCHOOL AND LONELY AND FAT! ALL THIS TIME THINKING I WAS DIFFERENT IN SOME AMAZING WAY. *THAT WAS REAL TOO!*
LOOK, THEY SAID IT'S DANGEROUS, BUT THAT'S OKAY. I WAS MEANT FOR THIS. MY WHOLE LIFE IS ABOUT THIS MOMENT. IT'LL WORK. *I KNOW IT WILL.*
DON'T BE A JERK. MAKE ME A SUPERHERO.
PLEASEPLEASEPLEASE...
IT'S *YOU* OR THE *MACHINE*.

PLEASEPLEASEPLEASE-- STOP HUGGING ME, OKAY? I'LL... I'LL TRY.

I'M NOT PROMISING ANYTHING. JUST LEAN BACK AND CLOSE YOUR EYES...

KINKY!

SHHH...

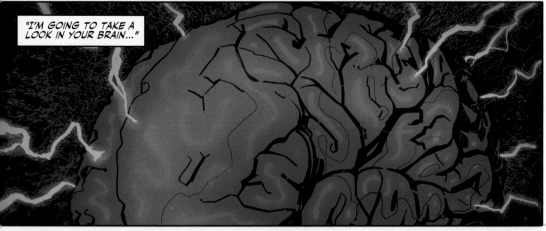

"I'M GOING TO TAKE A LOOK IN YOUR BRAIN..."

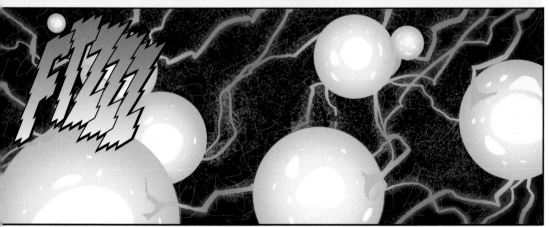

FTZZ

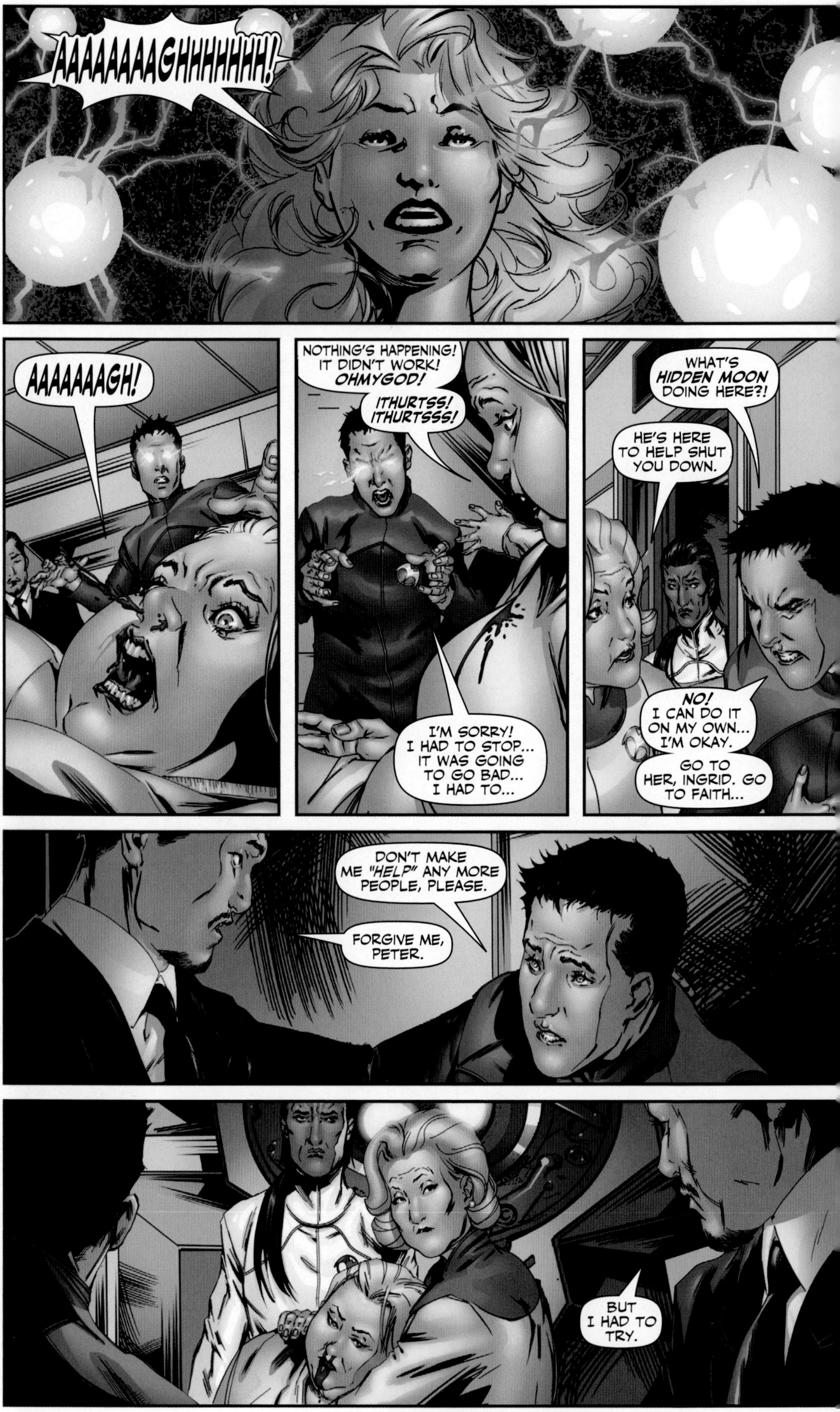
AAAAAAAAGHHHHHHH!
AAAAAAAGH!
NOTHING'S HAPPENING! IT DIDN'T WORK! OHMYGOD!
ITHURTSS! ITHURTSSS!
I'M SORRY! I HAD TO STOP... IT WAS GOING TO GO BAD... I HAD TO...
WHAT'S HIDDEN MOON DOING HERE?!
HE'S HERE TO HELP SHUT YOU DOWN.
NO! I CAN DO IT ON MY OWN... I'M OKAY.
GO TO HER, INGRID. GO TO FAITH...
DON'T MAKE ME "HELP" ANY MORE PEOPLE, PLEASE.
FORGIVE ME, PETER.
BUT I HAD TO TRY.

THAT SUCKED...

YEAH, IT'S CRAZY, PETE...

I ALWAYS WANTED US TO LIVE LIKE THIS. BUT YOU WERE ALL ABOUT THE LOW PROFILE.

JESUS, JOE. *WHAT THE HELL?!*

DON'T KNOW, MAN. I'M JUST HERE. IT'S A WEIRD TRIP.

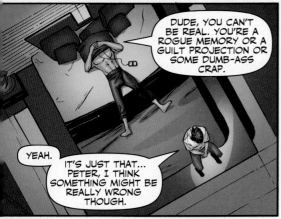

DUDE, YOU CAN'T BE REAL. YOU'RE A ROGUE MEMORY OR A GUILT PROJECTION OR SOME DUMB-ASS CRAP.

YEAH.

IT'S JUST THAT... PETER, I THINK SOMETHING MIGHT BE REALLY WRONG THOUGH.

I THINK JOE'S BEEN TRYING TO REACH OUT TO YOU... AND I THINK THEY'RE KEEPING IT FROM YOU SOMEHOW. BLOCKING YOUR POWERS, YOU KNOW?

I MEAN, AREN'T YOU DONE FUSSIN' OVER THIS LAME PLACE ANYWAY?

YEAH, I AM. CAN YOU...CAN YOU TAKE ME TO HIM? TO THE REAL JOE?

I'M PRETTY SURE THAT'S THE WHOLE REASON WHY I'M HERE, AMIGO.

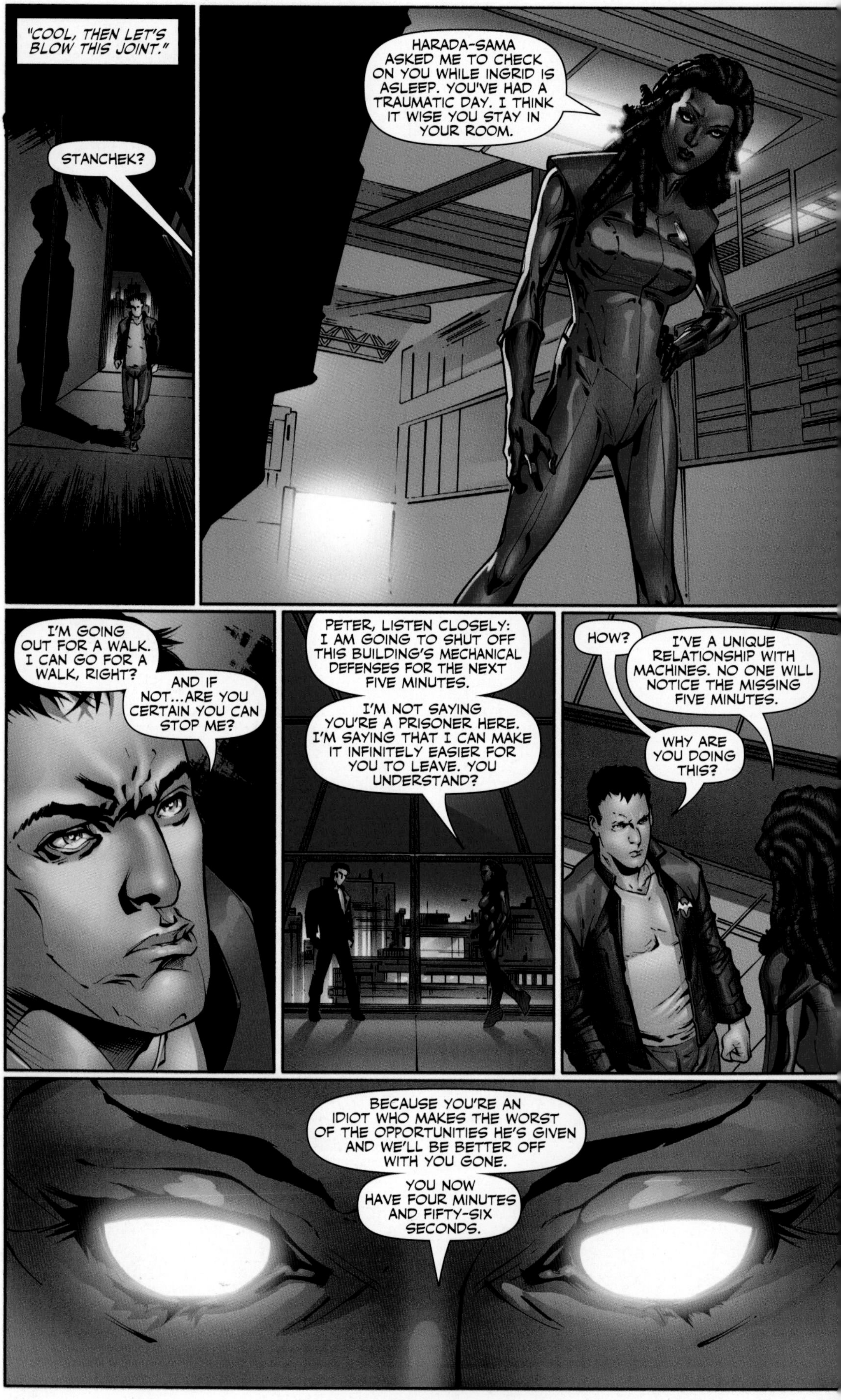
"COOL, THEN LET'S BLOW THIS JOINT."
STANCHEK?
HARADA-SAMA ASKED ME TO CHECK ON YOU WHILE INGRID IS ASLEEP. YOU'VE HAD A TRAUMATIC DAY. I THINK IT WISE YOU STAY IN YOUR ROOM.
I'M GOING OUT FOR A WALK. I CAN GO FOR A WALK, RIGHT?
AND IF NOT...ARE YOU CERTAIN YOU CAN STOP ME?
PETER, LISTEN CLOSELY: I AM GOING TO SHUT OFF THIS BUILDING'S MECHANICAL DEFENSES FOR THE NEXT FIVE MINUTES.
I'M NOT SAYING YOU'RE A PRISONER HERE. I'M SAYING THAT I CAN MAKE IT INFINITELY EASIER FOR YOU TO LEAVE. YOU UNDERSTAND?
HOW?
I'VE A UNIQUE RELATIONSHIP WITH MACHINES. NO ONE WILL NOTICE THE MISSING FIVE MINUTES.
WHY ARE YOU DOING THIS?
BECAUSE YOU'RE AN IDIOT WHO MAKES THE WORST OF THE OPPORTUNITIES HE'S GIVEN AND WE'LL BE BETTER OFF WITH YOU GONE.
YOU NOW HAVE FOUR MINUTES AND FIFTY-SIX SECONDS.

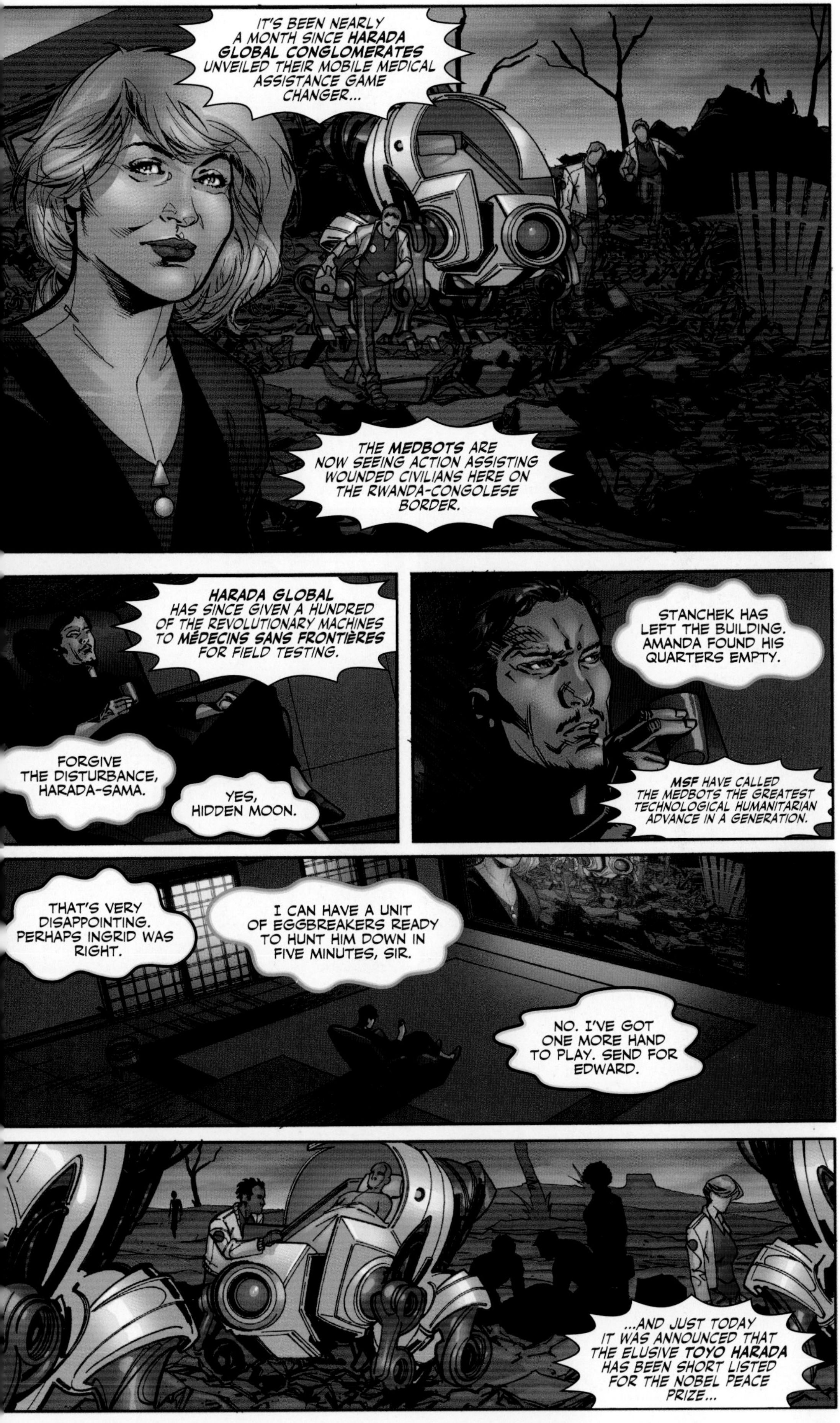
IT'S BEEN NEARLY A MONTH SINCE HARADA GLOBAL CONGLOMERATES UNVEILED THEIR MOBILE MEDICAL ASSISTANCE GAME CHANGER...
THE MEDBOTS ARE NOW SEEING ACTION ASSISTING WOUNDED CIVILIANS HERE ON THE RWANDA-CONGOLESE BORDER.
HARADA GLOBAL HAS SINCE GIVEN A HUNDRED OF THE REVOLUTIONARY MACHINES TO MÉDECINS SANS FRONTIÈRES FOR FIELD TESTING.
FORGIVE THE DISTURBANCE, HARADA-SAMA.
YES, HIDDEN MOON.
STANCHEK HAS LEFT THE BUILDING. AMANDA FOUND HIS QUARTERS EMPTY.
MSF HAVE CALLED THE MEDBOTS THE GREATEST TECHNOLOGICAL HUMANITARIAN ADVANCE IN A GENERATION.
THAT'S VERY DISAPPOINTING. PERHAPS INGRID WAS RIGHT.
I CAN HAVE A UNIT OF EGGBREAKERS READY TO HUNT HIM DOWN IN FIVE MINUTES, SIR.
NO. I'VE GOT ONE MORE HAND TO PLAY. SEND FOR EDWARD.
...AND JUST TODAY IT WAS ANNOUNCED THAT THE ELUSIVE TOYO HARADA HAS BEEN SHORT LISTED FOR THE NOBEL PEACE PRIZE...

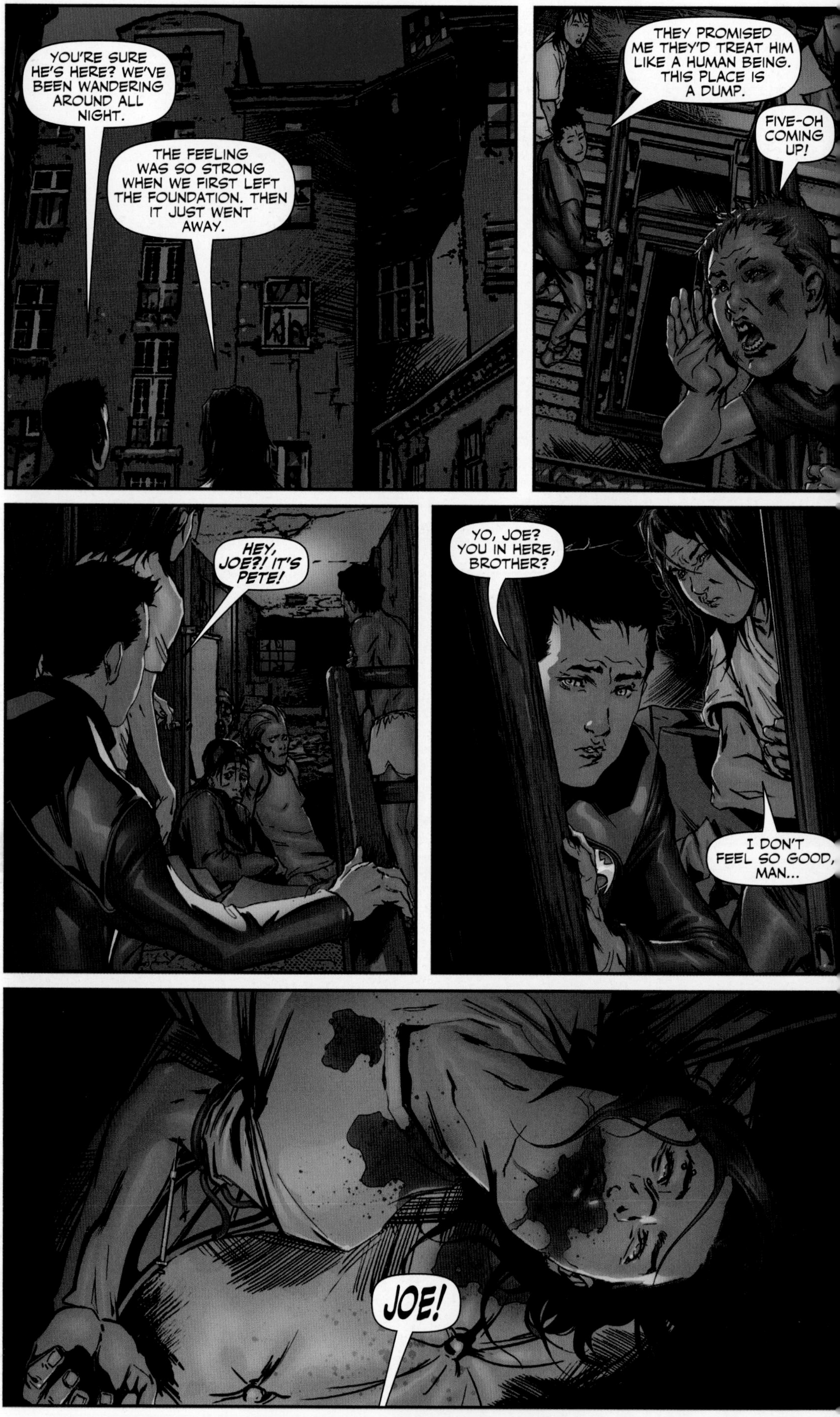
YOU'RE SURE HE'S HERE? WE'VE BEEN WANDERING AROUND ALL NIGHT.
THE FEELING WAS SO STRONG WHEN WE FIRST LEFT THE FOUNDATION. THEN IT JUST WENT AWAY.
THEY PROMISED ME THEY'D TREAT HIM LIKE A HUMAN BEING. THIS PLACE IS A DUMP.
FIVE-OH COMING UP!
HEY, JOE?! IT'S PETE!
YO, JOE? YOU IN HERE, BROTHER?
I DON'T FEEL SO GOOD, MAN...
JOE!

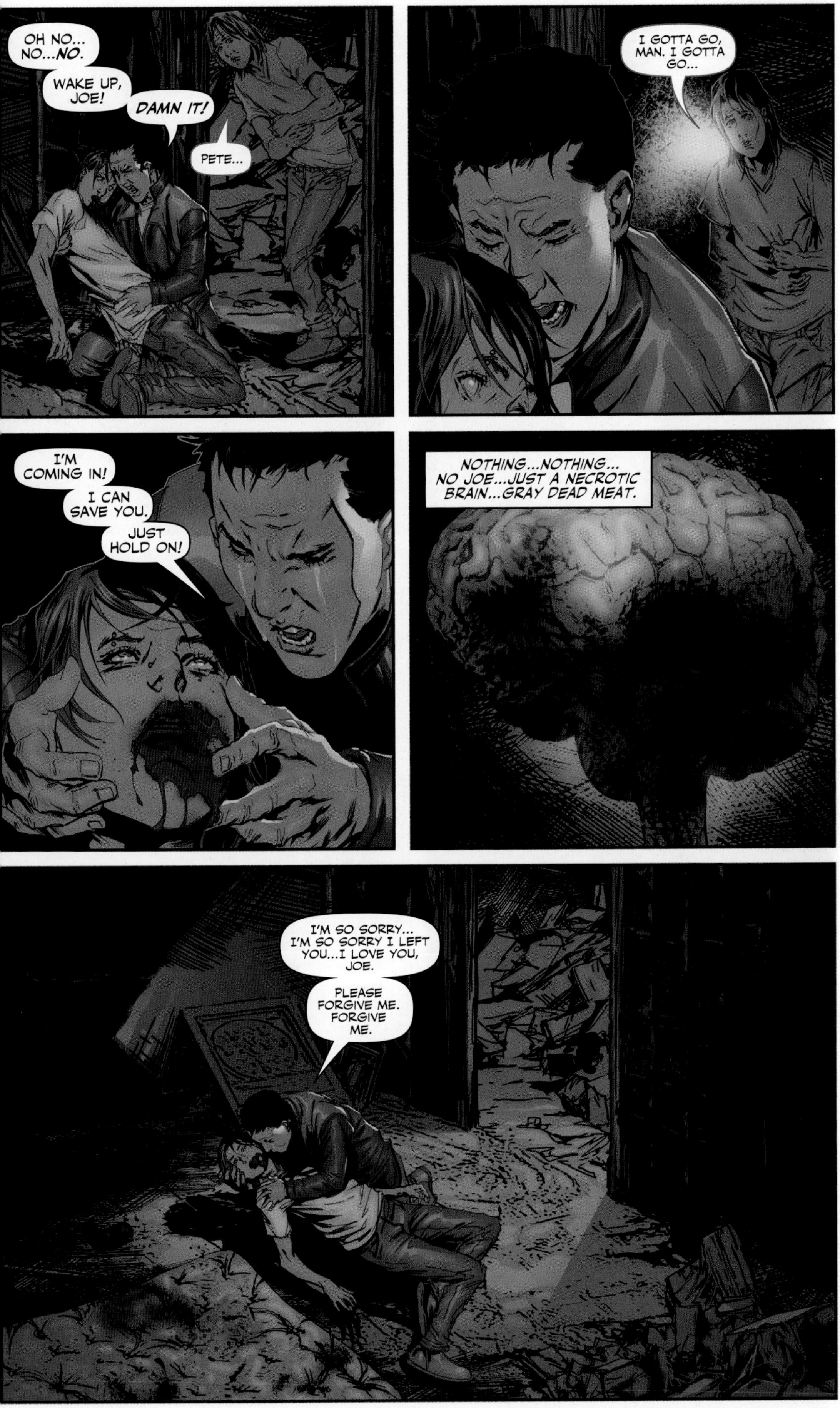
OH NO... NO...NO.
WAKE UP, JOE!
DAMN IT!
PETE...
I GOTTA GO, MAN. I GOTTA GO...
I'M COMING IN!
I CAN SAVE YOU.
JUST HOLD ON!
NOTHING...NOTHING... NO JOE...JUST A NECROTIC BRAIN...GRAY DEAD MEAT.
I'M SO SORRY... I'M SO SORRY I LEFT YOU...I LOVE YOU, JOE.
PLEASE FORGIVE ME. FORGIVE ME.

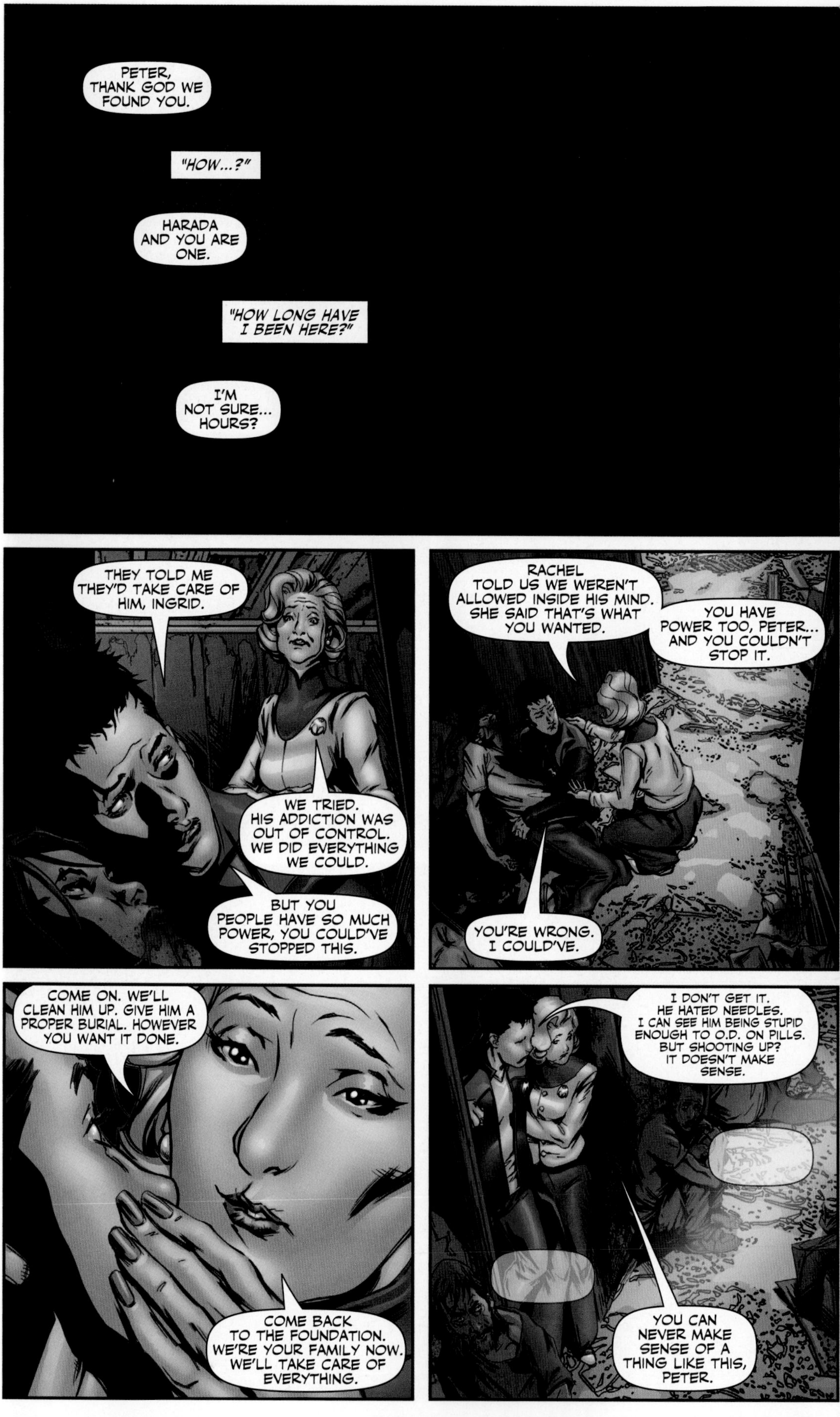
PETER, THANK GOD WE FOUND YOU.
"HOW...?"
HARADA AND YOU ARE ONE.
"HOW LONG HAVE I BEEN HERE?"
I'M NOT SURE... HOURS?
THEY TOLD ME THEY'D TAKE CARE OF HIM, INGRID.
WE TRIED. HIS ADDICTION WAS OUT OF CONTROL. WE DID EVERYTHING WE COULD.
BUT YOU PEOPLE HAVE SO MUCH POWER, YOU COULD'VE STOPPED THIS.
RACHEL TOLD US WE WEREN'T ALLOWED INSIDE HIS MIND. SHE SAID THAT'S WHAT YOU WANTED.
YOU HAVE POWER TOO, PETER... AND YOU COULDN'T STOP IT.
YOU'RE WRONG. I COULD'VE.
COME ON. WE'LL CLEAN HIM UP. GIVE HIM A PROPER BURIAL. HOWEVER YOU WANT IT DONE.
COME BACK TO THE FOUNDATION. WE'RE YOUR FAMILY NOW. WE'LL TAKE CARE OF EVERYTHING.
I DON'T GET IT. HE HATED NEEDLES. I CAN SEE HIM BEING STUPID ENOUGH TO O.D. ON PILLS. BUT SHOOTING UP? IT DOESN'T MAKE SENSE.
YOU CAN NEVER MAKE SENSE OF A THING LIKE THIS, PETER.

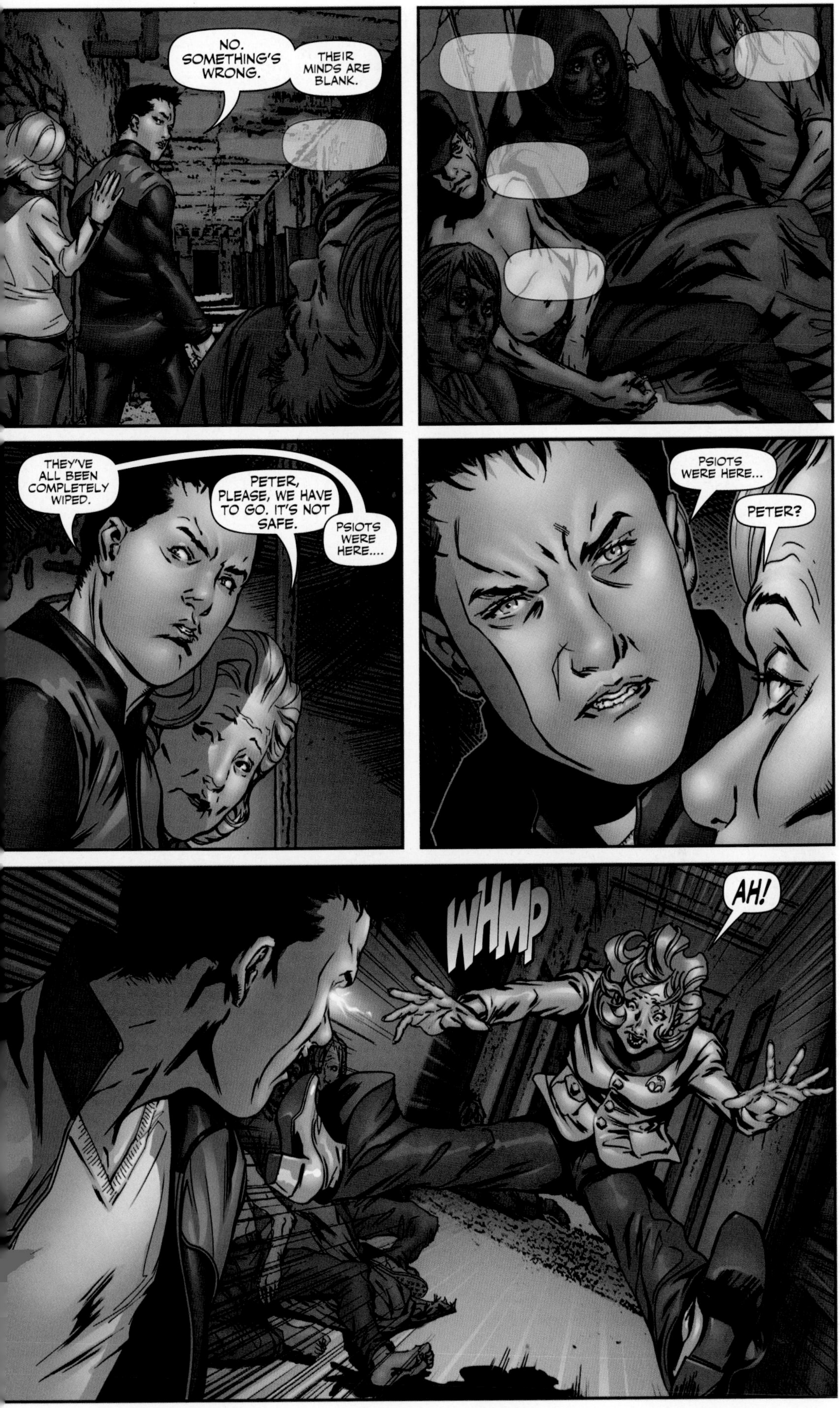
NO. SOMETHING'S WRONG.
THEIR MINDS ARE BLANK.
THEY'VE ALL BEEN COMPLETELY WIPED.
PETER, PLEASE, WE HAVE TO GO. IT'S NOT SAFE.
PSIOTS WERE HERE....
PSIOTS WERE HERE...
PETER?
WHMP
AH!

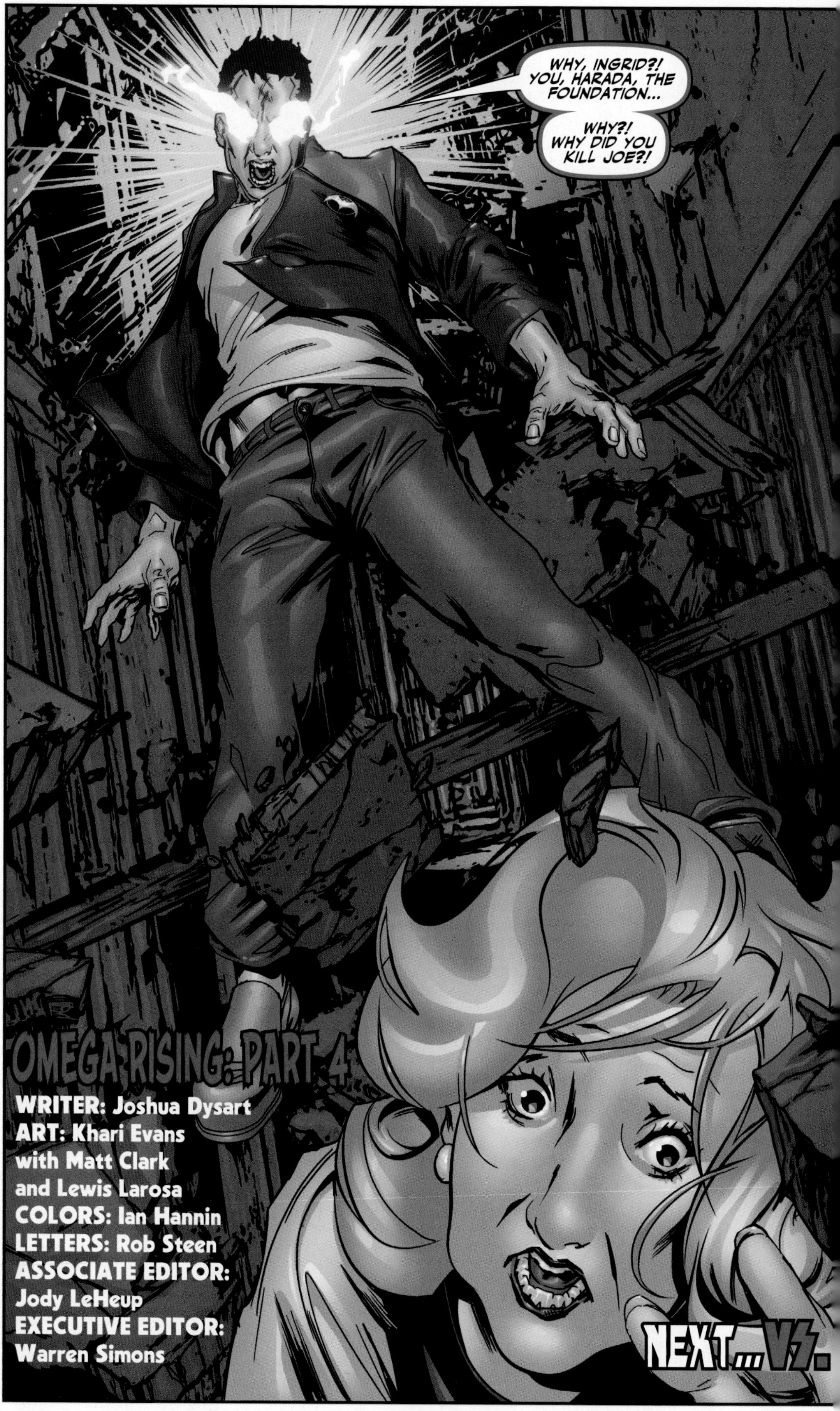
WHY, INGRID?! YOU, HARADA, THE FOUNDATION...
WHY?! WHY DID YOU KILL JOE?!
OMEGA RISING: PART 4
WRITER: Joshua Dysart
ART: Khari Evans
with Matt Clark
and Lewis Larosa
COLORS: Ian Hannin
LETTERS: Rob Steen
ASSOCIATE EDITOR:
Jody LeHeup
EXECUTIVE EDITOR:
Warren Simons
NEXT...VS.

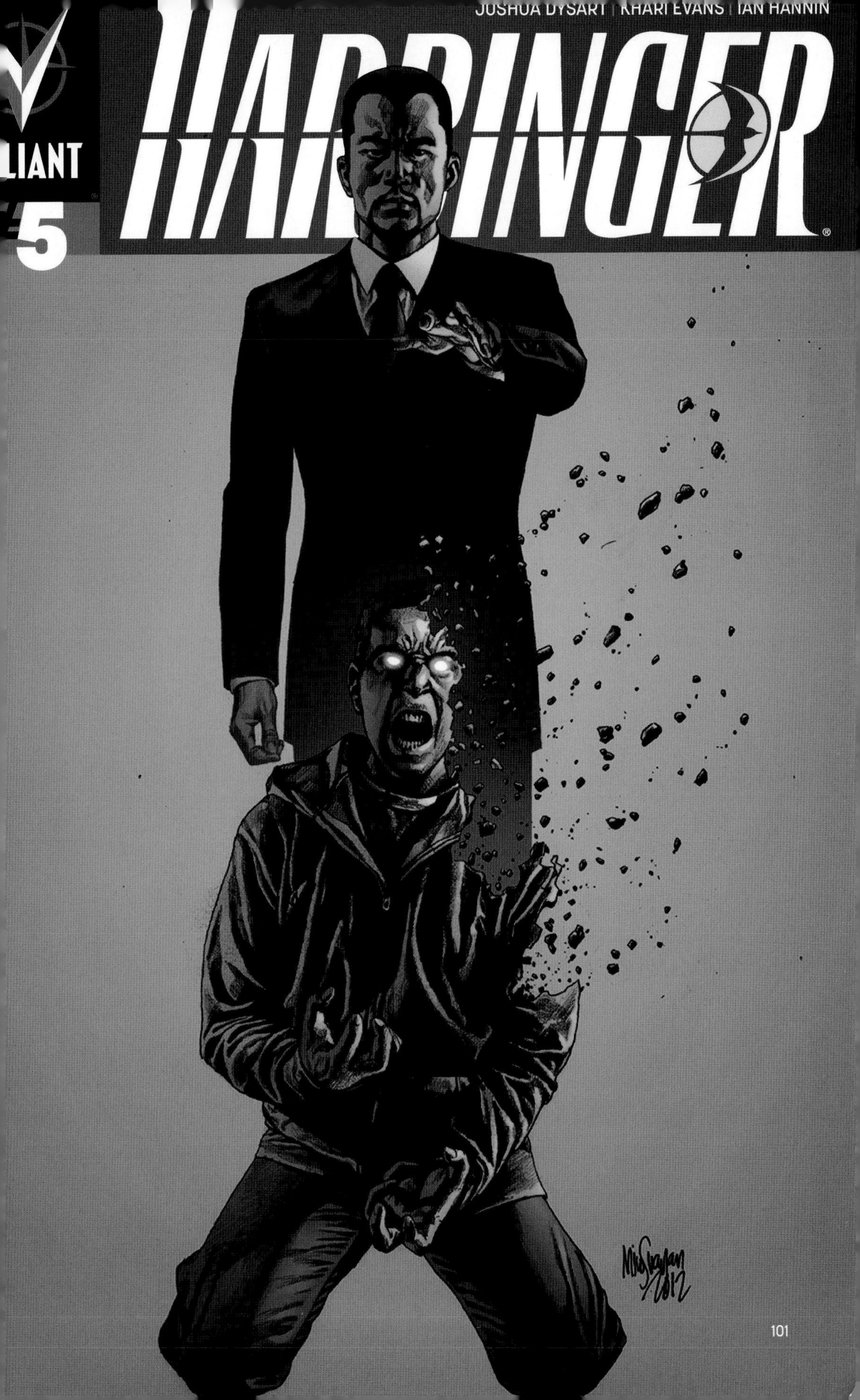
JOSHUA DYSART | KHARI EVANS | IAN HANNIN
LIANT
HARBINGER
#5

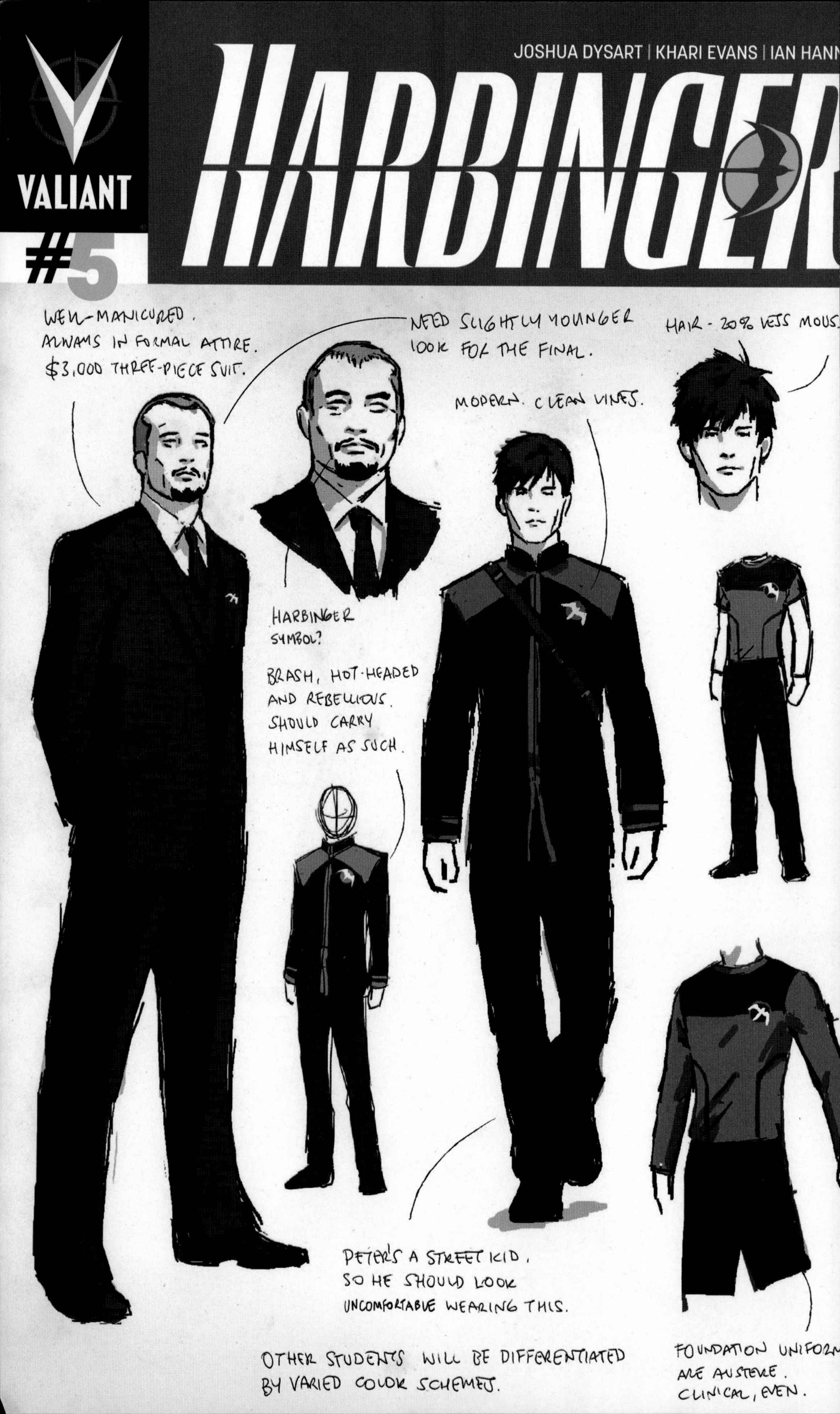
VALIANT
#5
JOSHUA DYSART | KHARI EVANS | IAN HANN
HARBINGER
WELL-MANICURED.
ALWAYS IN FORMAL ATTIRE.
$3,000 THREE-PIECE SUIT.
NEED SLIGHTLY YOUNGER
LOOK FOR THE FINAL.
HAIR - 20% LESS MOUS
MODERN. CLEAN LINES.
HARBINGER
SYMBOL?
BRASH, HOT-HEADED
AND REBELLIOUS.
SHOULD CARRY
HIMSELF AS SUCH.
PETER'S A STREET KID.
SO HE SHOULD LOOK
UNCOMFORTABLE WEARING THIS.
OTHER STUDENTS WILL BE DIFFERENTIATED
BY VARIED COLOR SCHEMES.
FOUNDATION UNIFORM
ARE AUSTERE.
CLINICAL, EVEN.

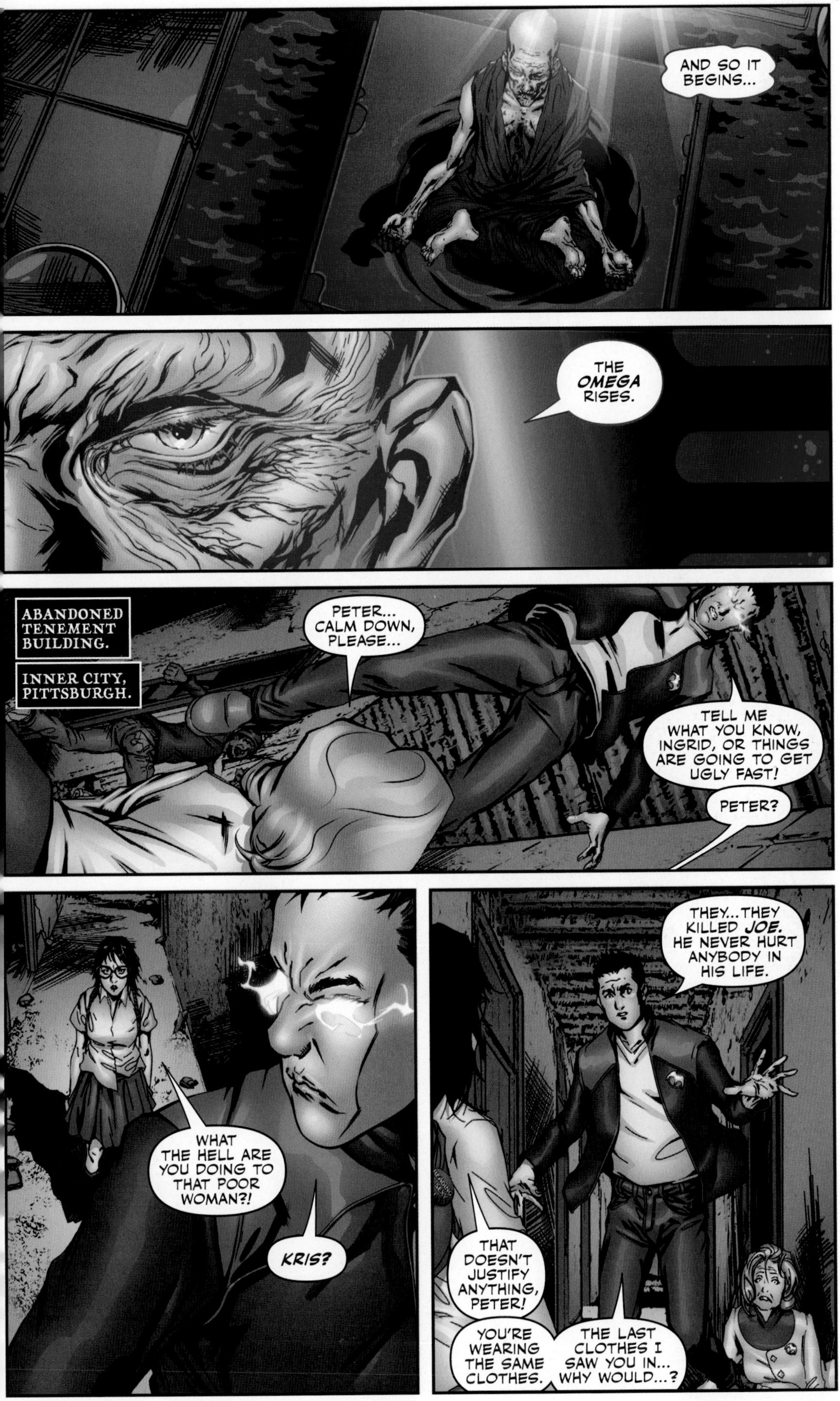
AND SO IT BEGINS...
THE OMEGA RISES.
ABANDONED TENEMENT BUILDING.
INNER CITY, PITTSBURGH.
PETER... CALM DOWN, PLEASE...
TELL ME WHAT YOU KNOW, INGRID, OR THINGS ARE GOING TO GET UGLY FAST!
PETER?
WHAT THE HELL ARE YOU DOING TO THAT POOR WOMAN?!
KRIS?
THEY...THEY KILLED JOE. HE NEVER HURT ANYBODY IN HIS LIFE.
THAT DOESN'T JUSTIFY ANYTHING, PETER!
YOU'RE WEARING THE SAME CLOTHES.
THE LAST CLOTHES I SAW YOU IN... WHY WOULD...?

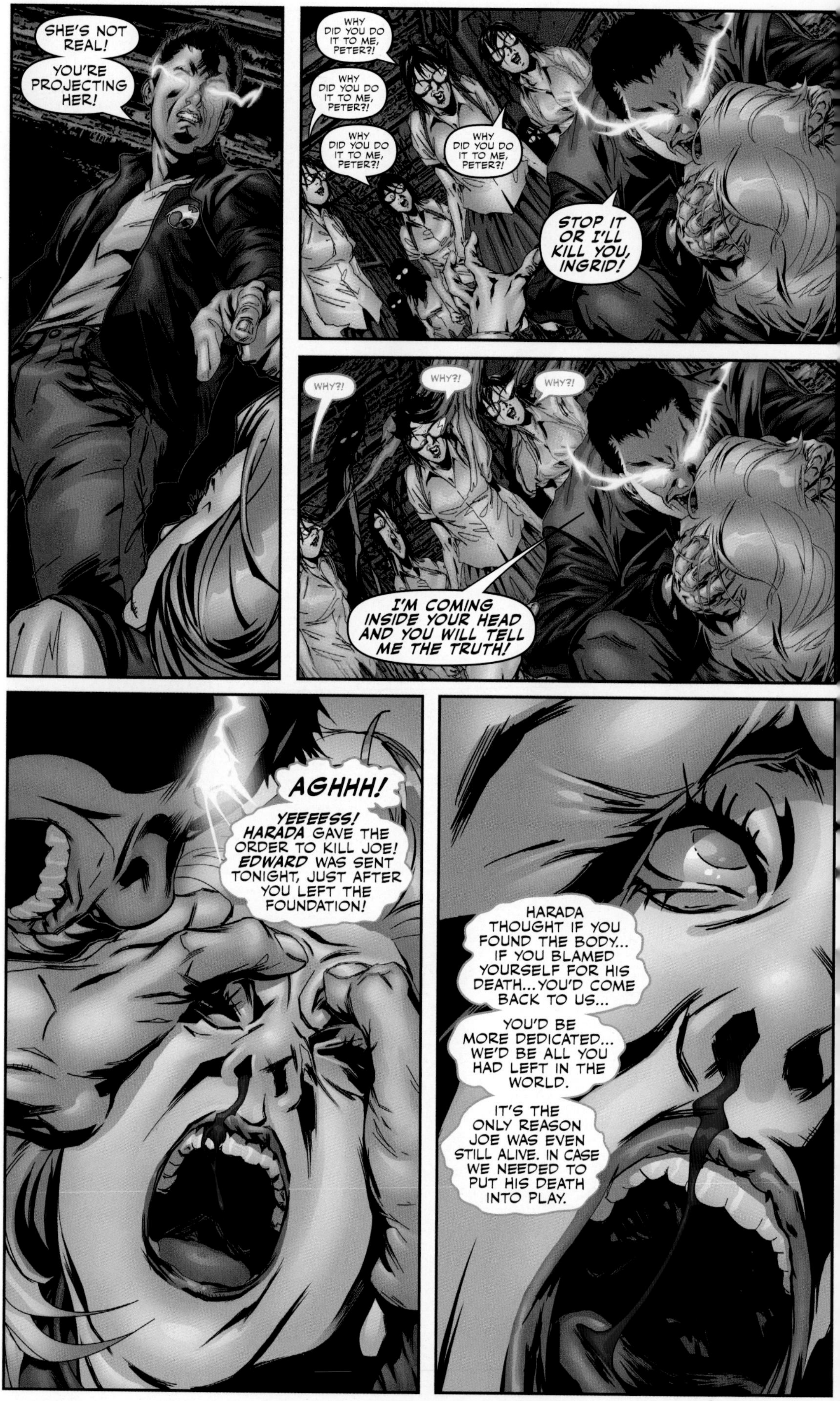

SHE'S NOT REAL!
YOU'RE PROJECTING HER!
WHY DID YOU DO IT TO ME, PETER?!
WHY DID YOU DO IT TO ME, PETER?!
WHY DID YOU DO IT TO ME, PETER?!
WHY DID YOU DO IT TO ME, PETER?!
STOP IT OR I'LL KILL YOU, INGRID!
WHY?!
WHY?!
WHY?!
I'M COMING INSIDE YOUR HEAD AND YOU WILL TELL ME THE TRUTH!
AGHHH!
YEEEESS! HARADA GAVE THE ORDER TO KILL JOE! EDWARD WAS SENT TONIGHT, JUST AFTER YOU LEFT THE FOUNDATION!
HARADA THOUGHT IF YOU FOUND THE BODY... IF YOU BLAMED YOURSELF FOR HIS DEATH...YOU'D COME BACK TO US...
YOU'D BE MORE DEDICATED... WE'D BE ALL YOU HAD LEFT IN THE WORLD.
IT'S THE ONLY REASON JOE WAS EVEN STILL ALIVE. IN CASE WE NEEDED TO PUT HIS DEATH INTO PLAY.

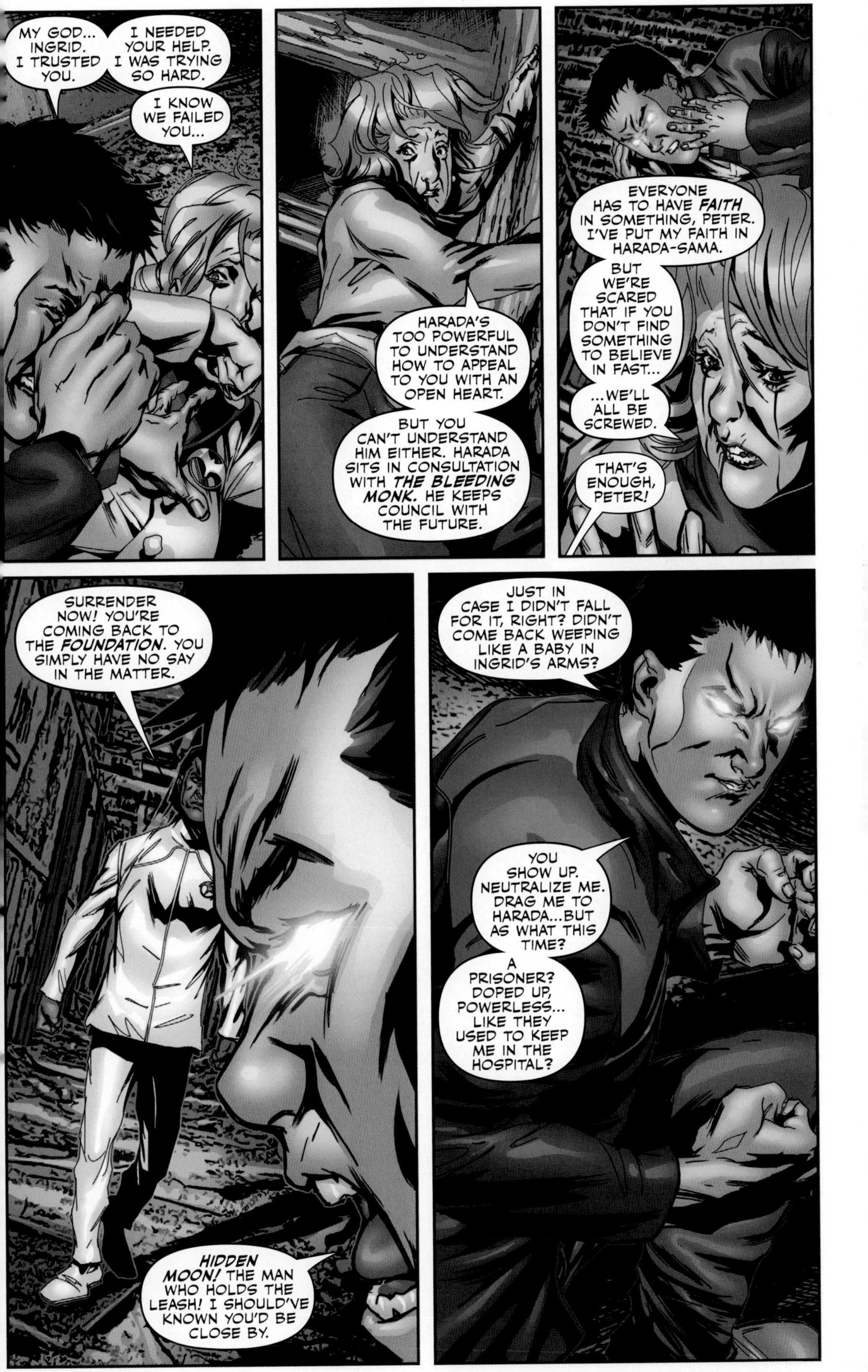
MY GOD... INGRID. I TRUSTED YOU.
I NEEDED YOUR HELP. I WAS TRYING SO HARD.
I KNOW WE FAILED YOU...
HARADA'S TOO POWERFUL TO UNDERSTAND HOW TO APPEAL TO YOU WITH AN OPEN HEART.
BUT YOU CAN'T UNDERSTAND HIM EITHER. HARADA SITS IN CONSULTATION WITH THE BLEEDING MONK. HE KEEPS COUNCIL WITH THE FUTURE.
EVERYONE HAS TO HAVE FAITH IN SOMETHING, PETER. I'VE PUT MY FAITH IN HARADA-SAMA.
BUT WE'RE SCARED THAT IF YOU DON'T FIND SOMETHING TO BELIEVE IN FAST...
...WE'LL ALL BE SCREWED.
THAT'S ENOUGH, PETER!
SURRENDER NOW! YOU'RE COMING BACK TO THE FOUNDATION. YOU SIMPLY HAVE NO SAY IN THE MATTER.
HIDDEN MOON! THE MAN WHO HOLDS THE LEASH! I SHOULD'VE KNOWN YOU'D BE CLOSE BY.
JUST IN CASE I DIDN'T FALL FOR IT, RIGHT? DIDN'T COME BACK WEEPING LIKE A BABY IN INGRID'S ARMS?
YOU SHOW UP. NEUTRALIZE ME. DRAG ME TO HARADA...BUT AS WHAT THIS TIME?
A PRISONER? DOPED UP, POWERLESS... LIKE THEY USED TO KEEP ME IN THE HOSPITAL?

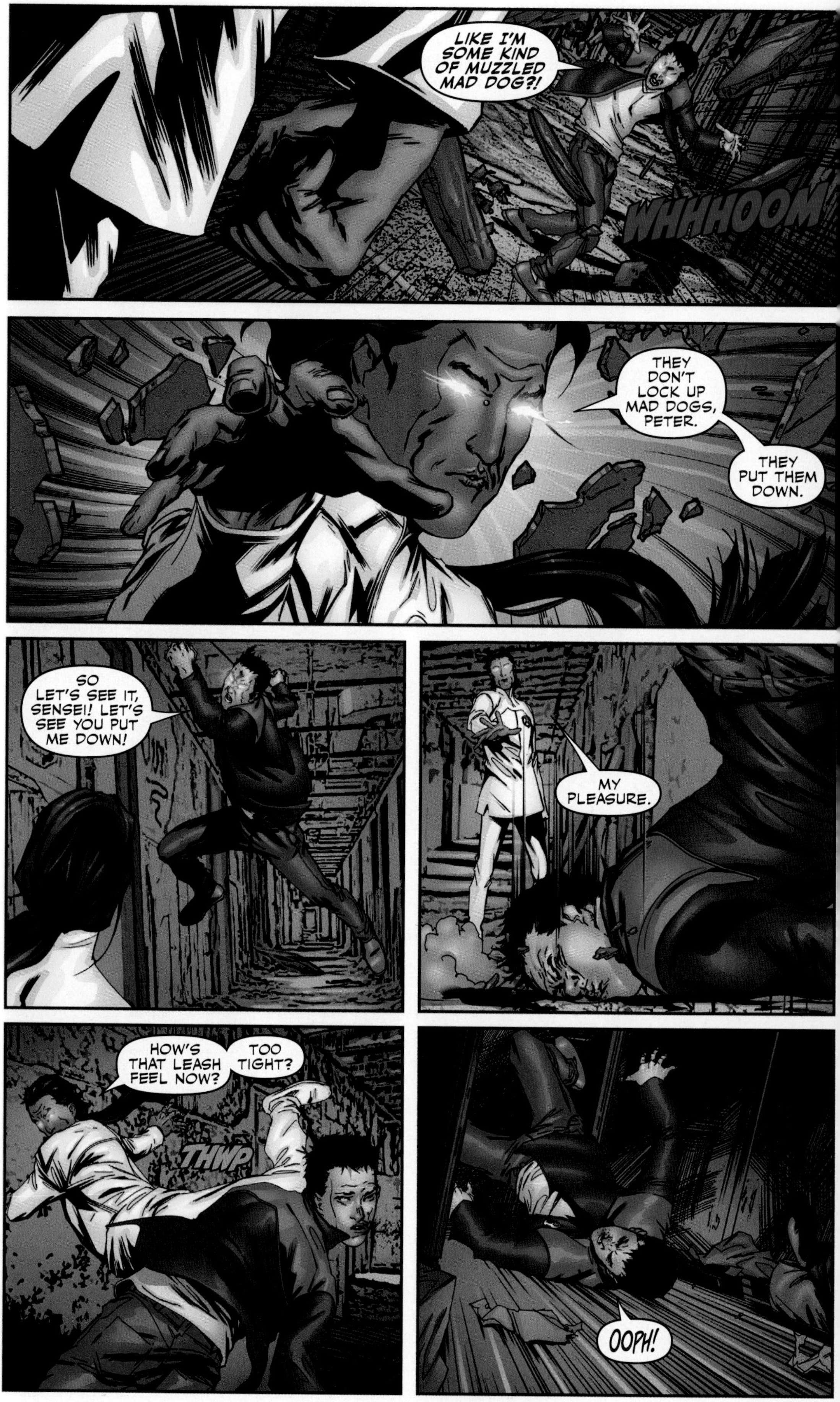
LIKE I'M SOME KIND OF MUZZLED MAD DOG?!
WHHHOOM
THEY DON'T LOCK UP MAD DOGS, PETER.
THEY PUT THEM DOWN.
SO LET'S SEE IT, SENSEI! LET'S SEE YOU PUT ME DOWN!
MY PLEASURE.
HOW'S THAT LEASH FEEL NOW?
TOO TIGHT?
THWP
OOPH!

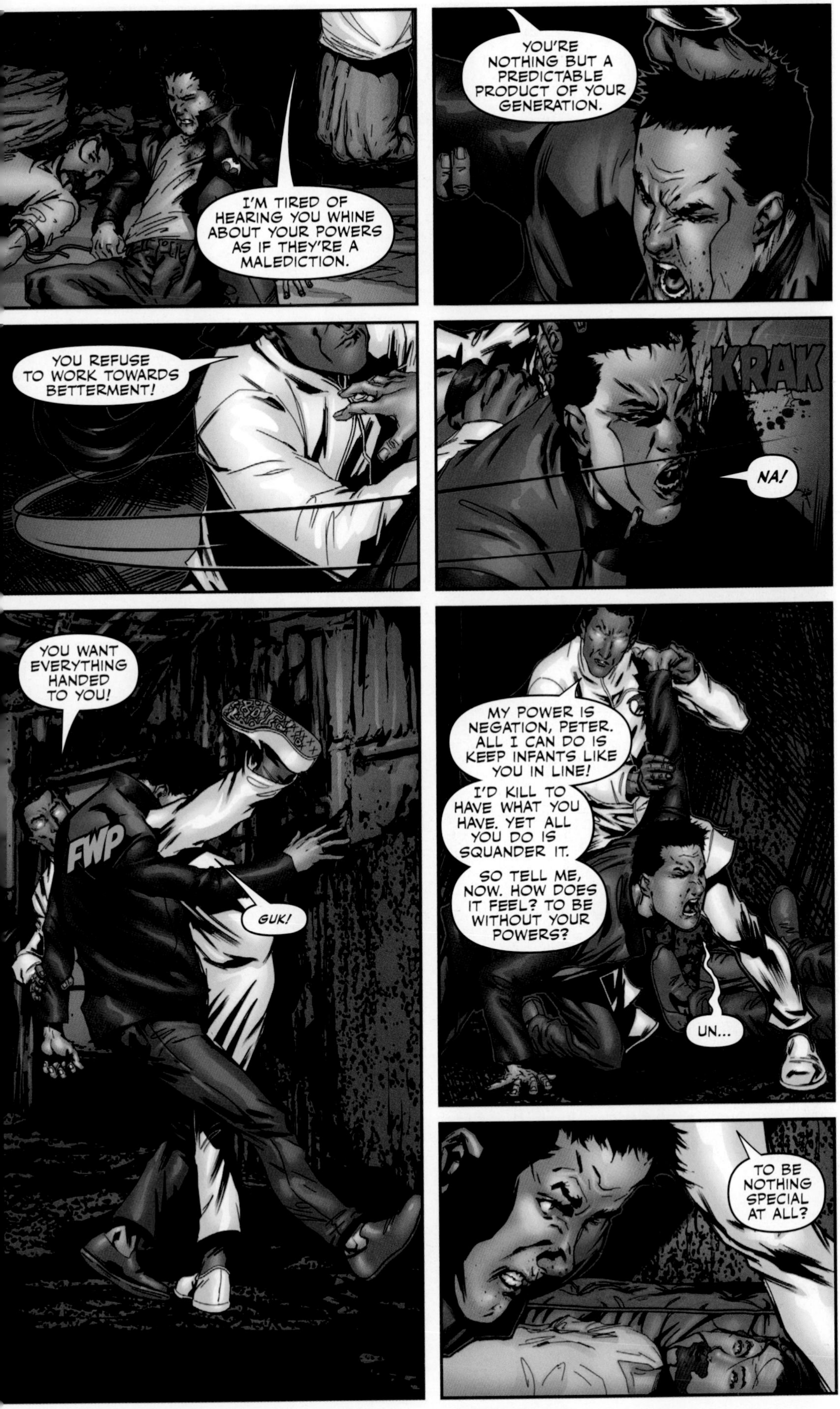
I'M TIRED OF HEARING YOU WHINE ABOUT YOUR POWERS AS IF THEY'RE A MALEDICTION.
YOU'RE NOTHING BUT A PREDICTABLE PRODUCT OF YOUR GENERATION.
YOU REFUSE TO WORK TOWARDS BETTERMENT!
KRAK
NA!
YOU WANT EVERYTHING HANDED TO YOU!
FWP
GUK!
MY POWER IS NEGATION, PETER. ALL I CAN DO IS KEEP INFANTS LIKE YOU IN LINE!
I'D KILL TO HAVE WHAT YOU HAVE. YET ALL YOU DO IS SQUANDER IT.
SO TELL ME, NOW. HOW DOES IT FEEL? TO BE WITHOUT YOUR POWERS?
UN...
TO BE NOTHING SPECIAL AT ALL?

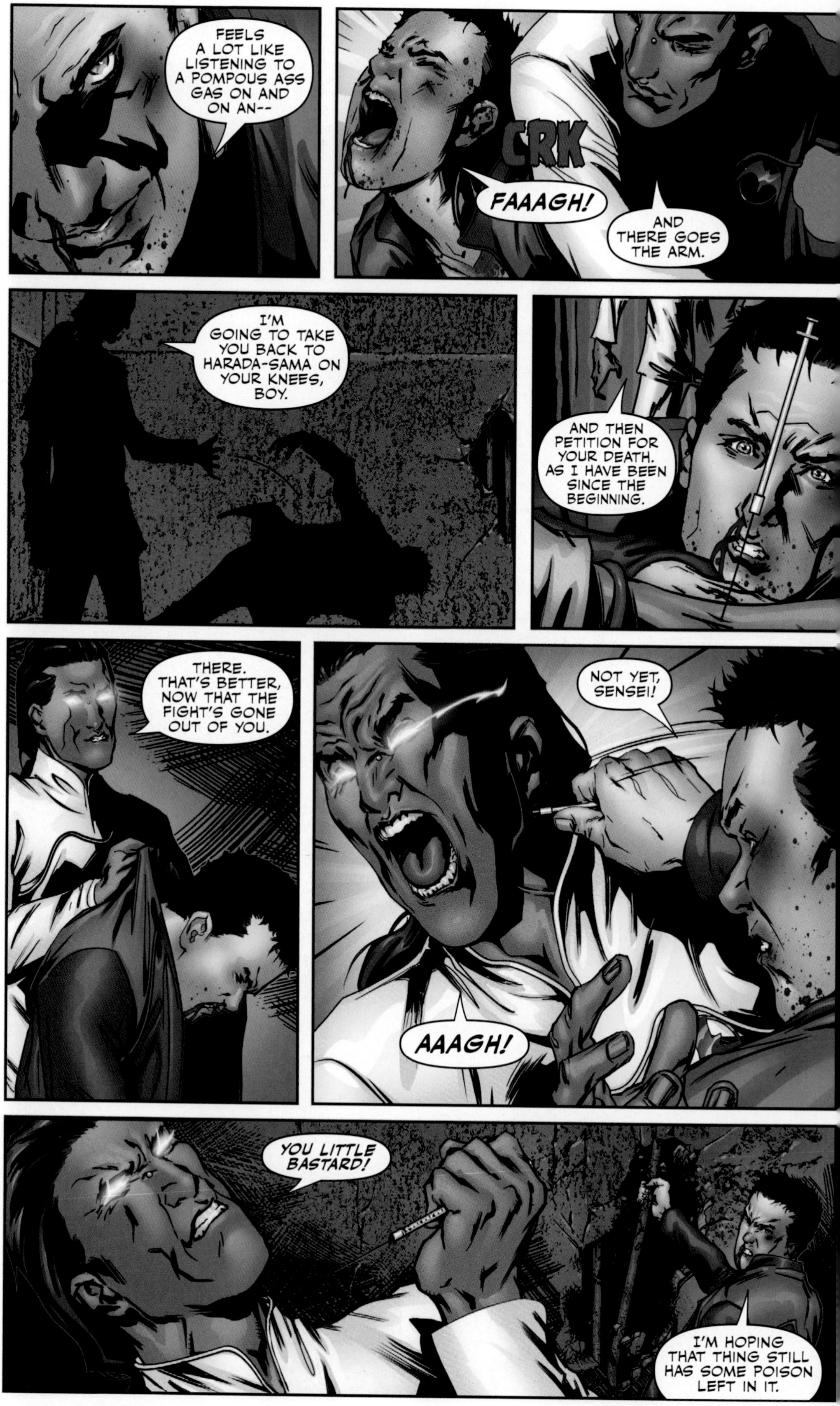
FEELS A LOT LIKE LISTENING TO A POMPOUS ASS GAS ON AND ON AN--
CRK
FAAAGH!
AND THERE GOES THE ARM.
I'M GOING TO TAKE YOU BACK TO HARADA-SAMA ON YOUR KNEES, BOY.
AND THEN PETITION FOR YOUR DEATH. AS I HAVE BEEN SINCE THE BEGINNING.
THERE. THAT'S BETTER, NOW THAT THE FIGHT'S GONE OUT OF YOU.
NOT YET, SENSEI!
AAAGH!
YOU LITTLE BASTARD!
I'M HOPING THAT THING STILL HAS SOME POISON LEFT IN IT.

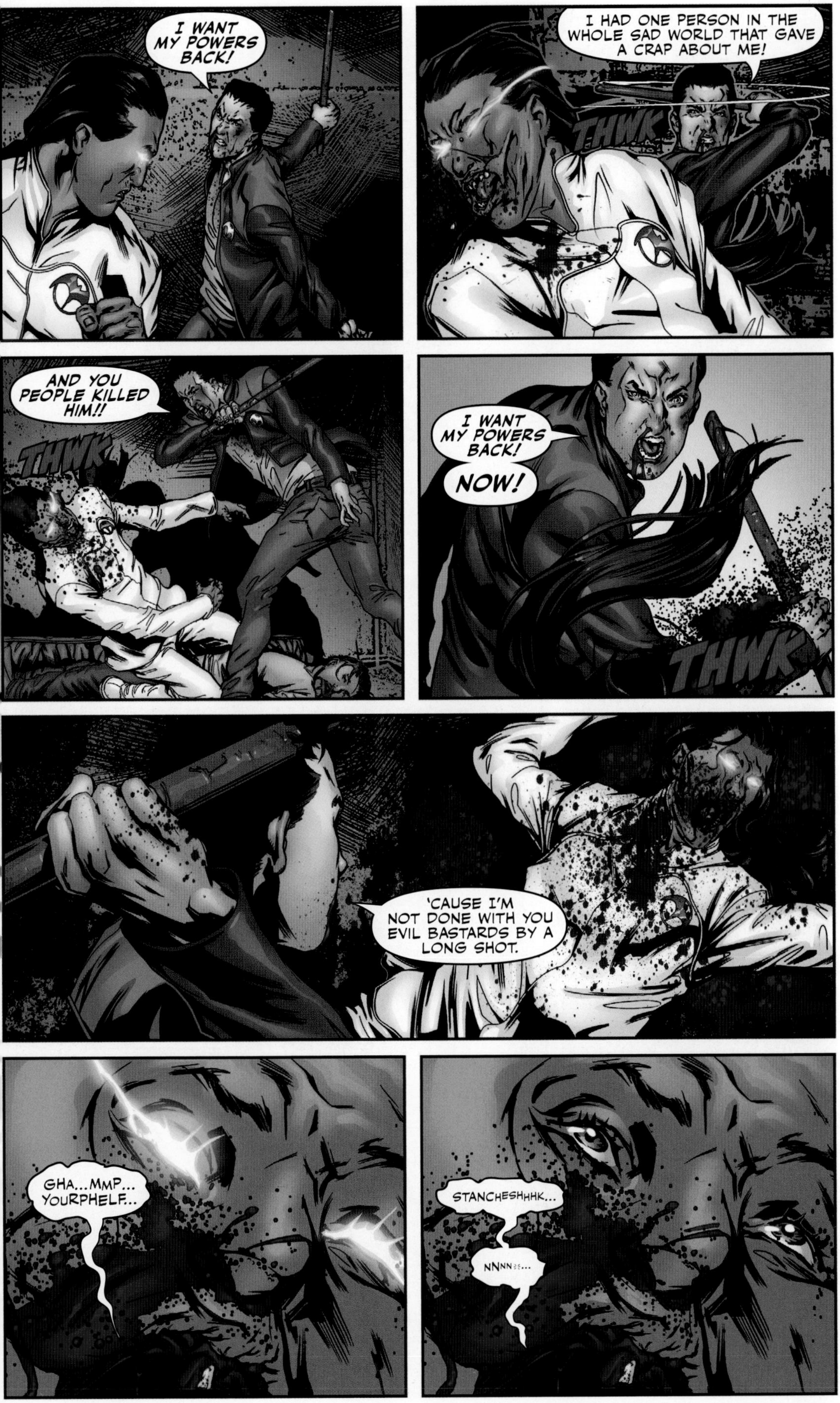
I WANT MY POWERS BACK!
I HAD ONE PERSON IN THE WHOLE SAD WORLD THAT GAVE A CRAP ABOUT ME!
THWK
AND YOU PEOPLE KILLED HIM!!
THWK
I WANT MY POWERS BACK!
NOW!
THWK
'CAUSE I'M NOT DONE WITH YOU EVIL BASTARDS BY A LONG SHOT.
GHA...MMP... YOURPHELF...
STANCHESHHHK...
NNNN...

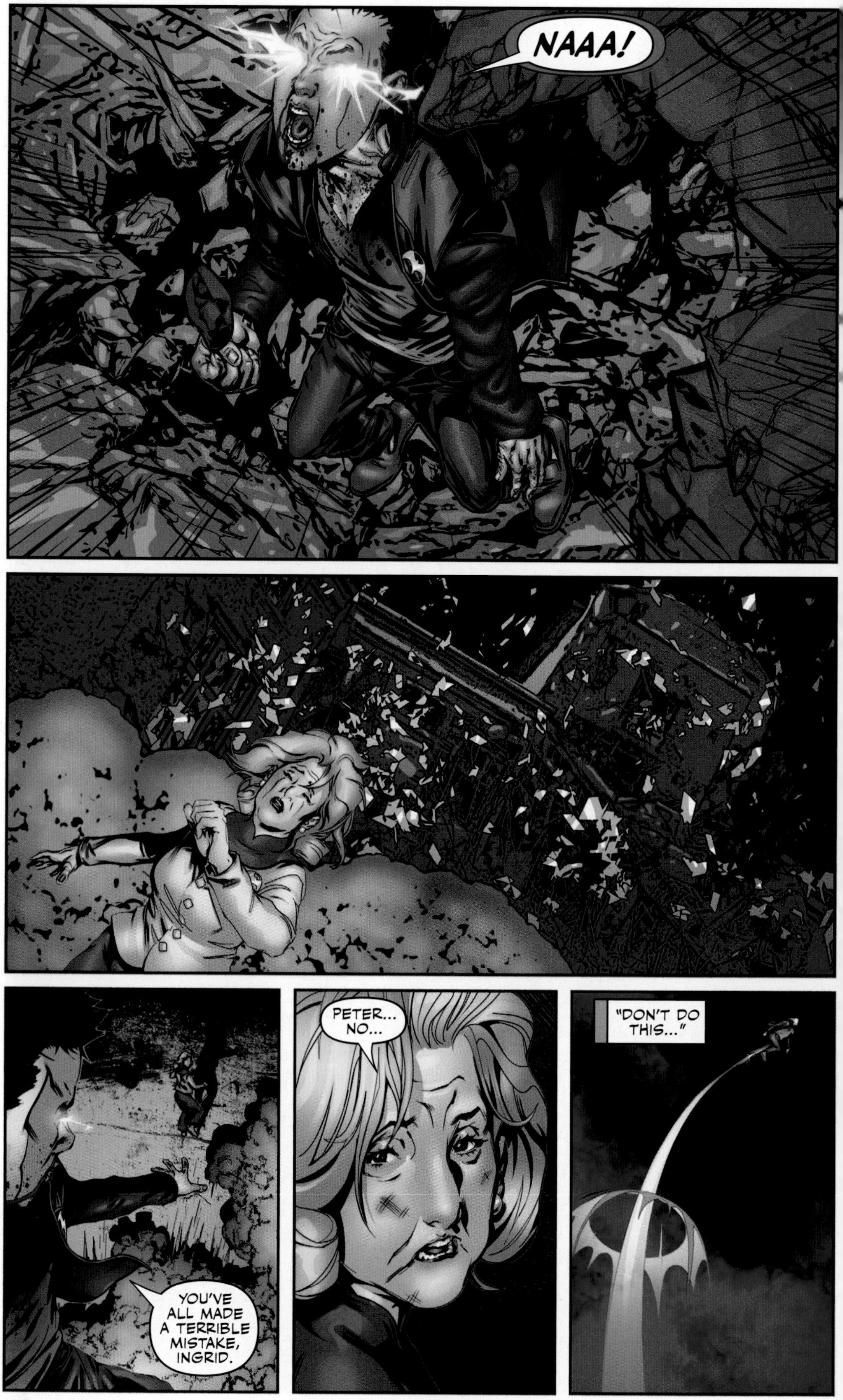
NAAA!
YOU'VE ALL MADE A TERRIBLE MISTAKE, INGRID.
PETER... NO...
"DON'T DO THIS..."

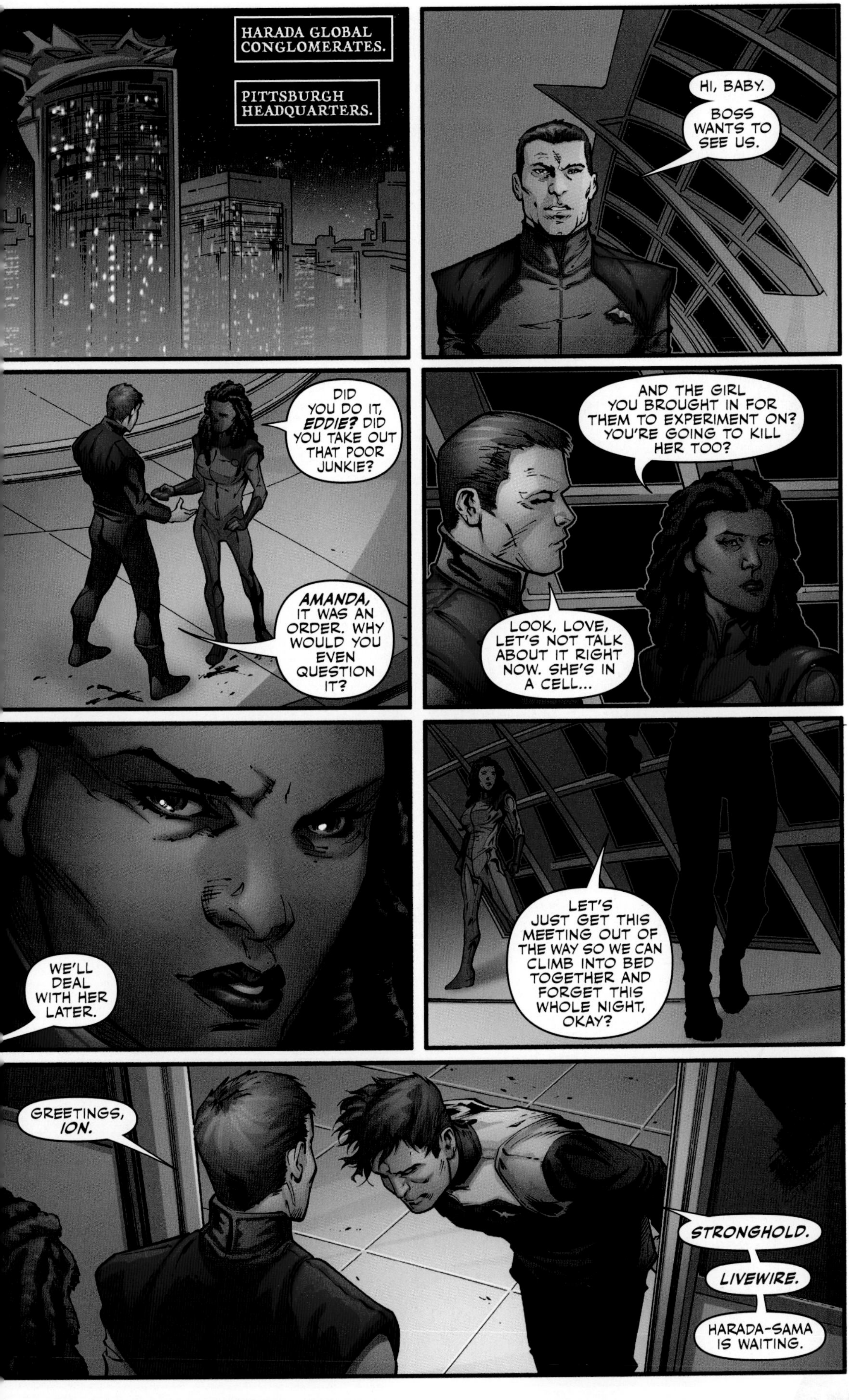
HARADA GLOBAL CONGLOMERATES.
PITTSBURGH HEADQUARTERS.
HI, BABY.
BOSS WANTS TO SEE US.
DID YOU DO IT, EDDIE? DID YOU TAKE OUT THAT POOR JUNKIE?
AMANDA, IT WAS AN ORDER. WHY WOULD YOU EVEN QUESTION IT?
AND THE GIRL YOU BROUGHT IN FOR THEM TO EXPERIMENT ON? YOU'RE GOING TO KILL HER TOO?
LOOK, LOVE, LET'S NOT TALK ABOUT IT RIGHT NOW. SHE'S IN A CELL...
WE'LL DEAL WITH HER LATER.
LET'S JUST GET THIS MEETING OUT OF THE WAY SO WE CAN CLIMB INTO BED TOGETHER AND FORGET THIS WHOLE NIGHT, OKAY?
GREETINGS, ION.
STRONGHOLD.
LIVEWIRE.
HARADA-SAMA IS WAITING.

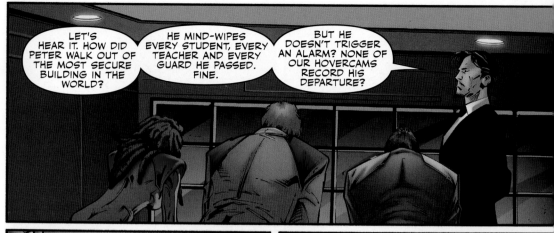

LET'S HEAR IT. HOW DID PETER WALK OUT OF THE MOST SECURE BUILDING IN THE WORLD?

HE MIND-WIPES EVERY STUDENT, EVERY TEACHER AND EVERY GUARD HE PASSED. FINE.

BUT HE DOESN'T TRIGGER AN ALARM? NONE OF OUR HOVERCAMS RECORD HIS DEPARTURE?

LIVEWIRE?

SIR?

ANY SUGGESTIONS ON HOW HE PULLED THAT OFF?

NO, SIR.

I REFRAIN, OUT OF RESPECT FOR YOU...FOR ALL OF YOU, FROM GOING INSIDE YOUR MINDS, BECAUSE LOYALTY MUST BE A CHOICE.

I HOPE YOU RESPECT THAT.

WHAT'S THAT ABOUT?

UPON HIS RETURN TONIGHT, OUR PRIORITY STUDENT WILL HAVE SUFFERED A TRAUMATIC LOSS. TOMORROW WE'LL START FROM SCRATCH AG--

HHHHAARRRRADA

INGRID?

SIR? ARE YOU ALL RIGHT?

HEEEE COMMMMES...

MYYY MIIIND SCRAMBLED... HEEE COOMMMES...

PETER?

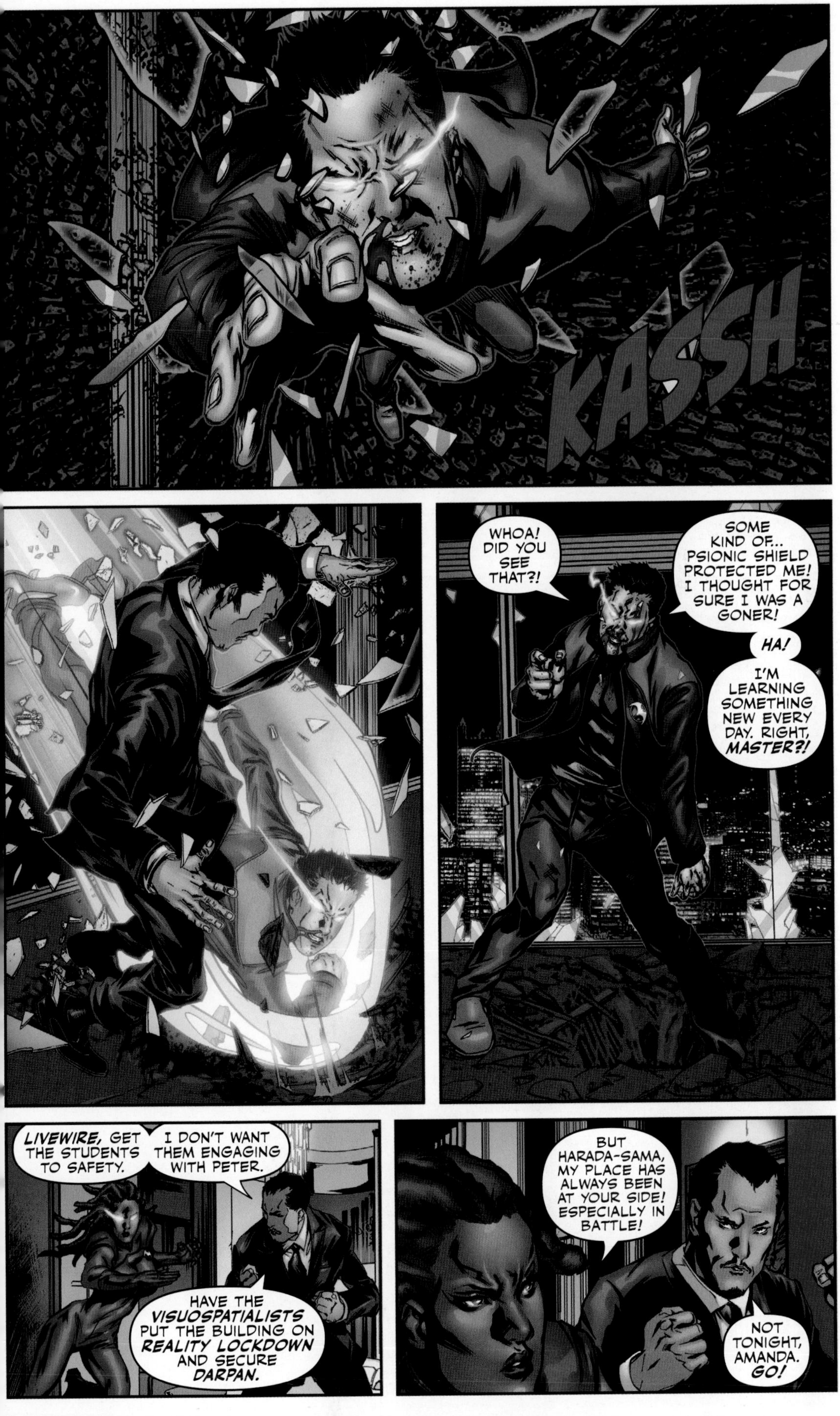
KASSH
WHOA! DID YOU SEE THAT?!
SOME KIND OF... PSIONIC SHIELD PROTECTED ME! I THOUGHT FOR SURE I WAS A GONER!
HA!
I'M LEARNING SOMETHING NEW EVERY DAY. RIGHT, MASTER?!
LIVEWIRE, GET THE STUDENTS TO SAFETY.
I DON'T WANT THEM ENGAGING WITH PETER.
HAVE THE VISUOSPATIALISTS PUT THE BUILDING ON REALITY LOCKDOWN AND SECURE DARPAN.
BUT HARADA-SAMA, MY PLACE HAS ALWAYS BEEN AT YOUR SIDE! ESPECIALLY IN BATTLE!
NOT TONIGHT, AMANDA. GO!

PETER, STOP THIS. LET'S TALK.

YOUR MIND TRICK'S NOT GONNA WORK ON ME.

AND I'M WAY PAST TALKING, BOSS.

A PITY. YOU DON'T LOOK FIT ENOUGH FOR A FIGHT.

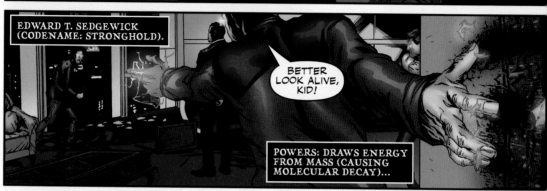

EDWARD T. SEDGEWICK (CODENAME: STRONGHOLD).

BETTER LOOK ALIVE, KID!

POWERS: DRAWS ENERGY FROM MASS (CAUSING MOLECULAR DECAY)...

...LEAVING APPROPRIATED ENERGY FREE FOR PSIONIC MANIPULATION.

YOU'RE IN THE LION'S DEN NOW.

SEE WHAT YOU'RE UP AGAINST? SO LET'S JUST TAKE IT EASY, ALL RIGHT?

I REMEMBER YOU FROM THAT NIGHT, IN THE OTHER VAN. YOU WERE SUPPOSED TO TAKE CARE OF JOE.

YOU MUST BE EDWARD. EDWARD THE KILLER...

WELL, I DON'T KNOW WHAT YOU DID JUST NOW, EDWARD, BUT YOU TOTALLY BONED THE STRUCTURAL INTEGRITY OF THAT CEILING.

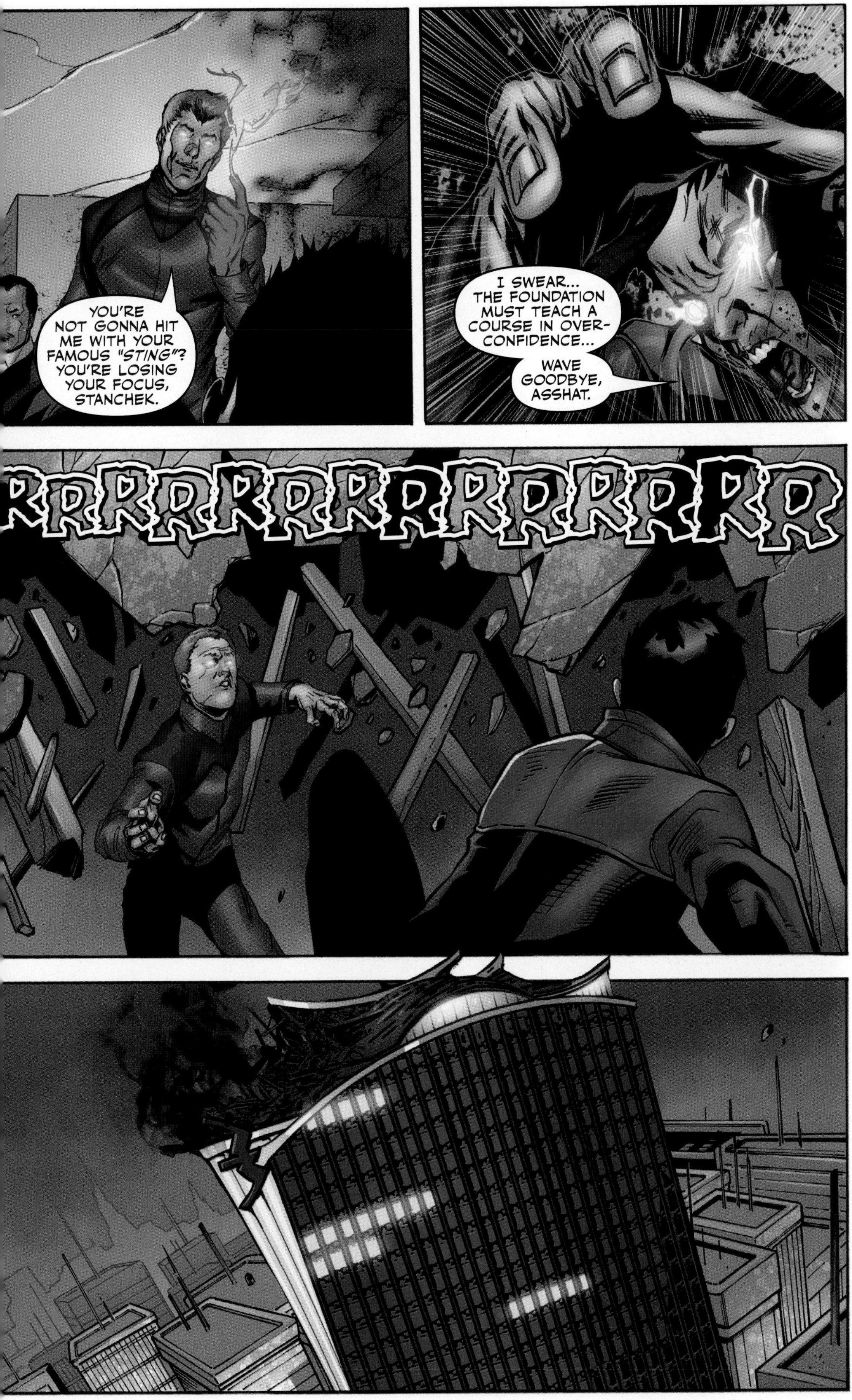

YOU'RE NOT GONNA HIT ME WITH YOUR FAMOUS "STING"? YOU'RE LOSING YOUR FOCUS, STANCHEK.
I SWEAR... THE FOUNDATION MUST TEACH A COURSE IN OVER-CONFIDENCE...
WAVE GOODBYE, ASSHAT.
RRRRRRRRRRRRRR

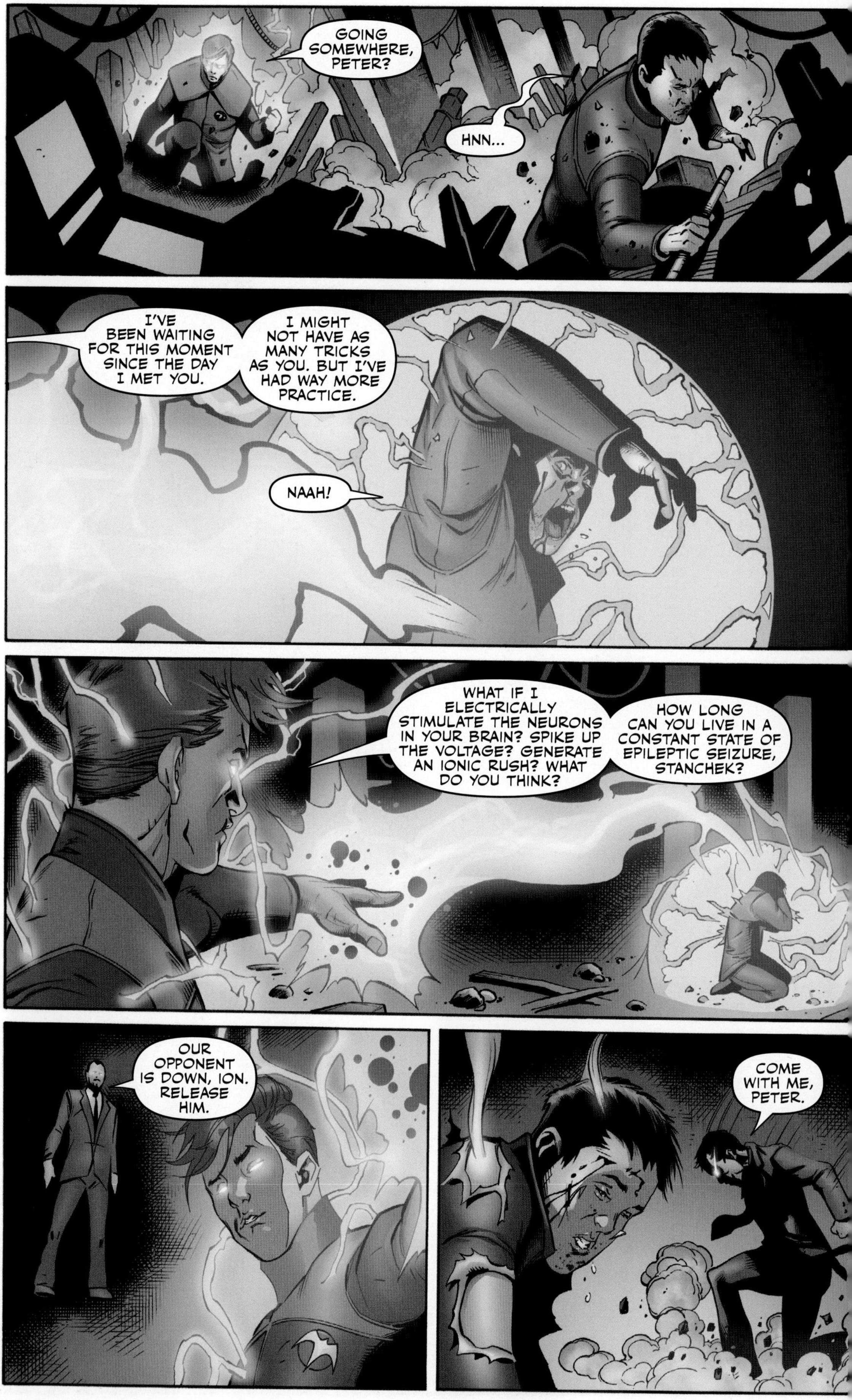
GOING SOMEWHERE, PETER?
HNN...
I'VE BEEN WAITING FOR THIS MOMENT SINCE THE DAY I MET YOU.
I MIGHT NOT HAVE AS MANY TRICKS AS YOU. BUT I'VE HAD WAY MORE PRACTICE.
NAAH!
WHAT IF I ELECTRICALLY STIMULATE THE NEURONS IN YOUR BRAIN? SPIKE UP THE VOLTAGE? GENERATE AN IONIC RUSH? WHAT DO YOU THINK?
HOW LONG CAN YOU LIVE IN A CONSTANT STATE OF EPILEPTIC SEIZURE, STANCHEK?
OUR OPPONENT IS DOWN, ION. RELEASE HIM.
COME WITH ME, PETER.

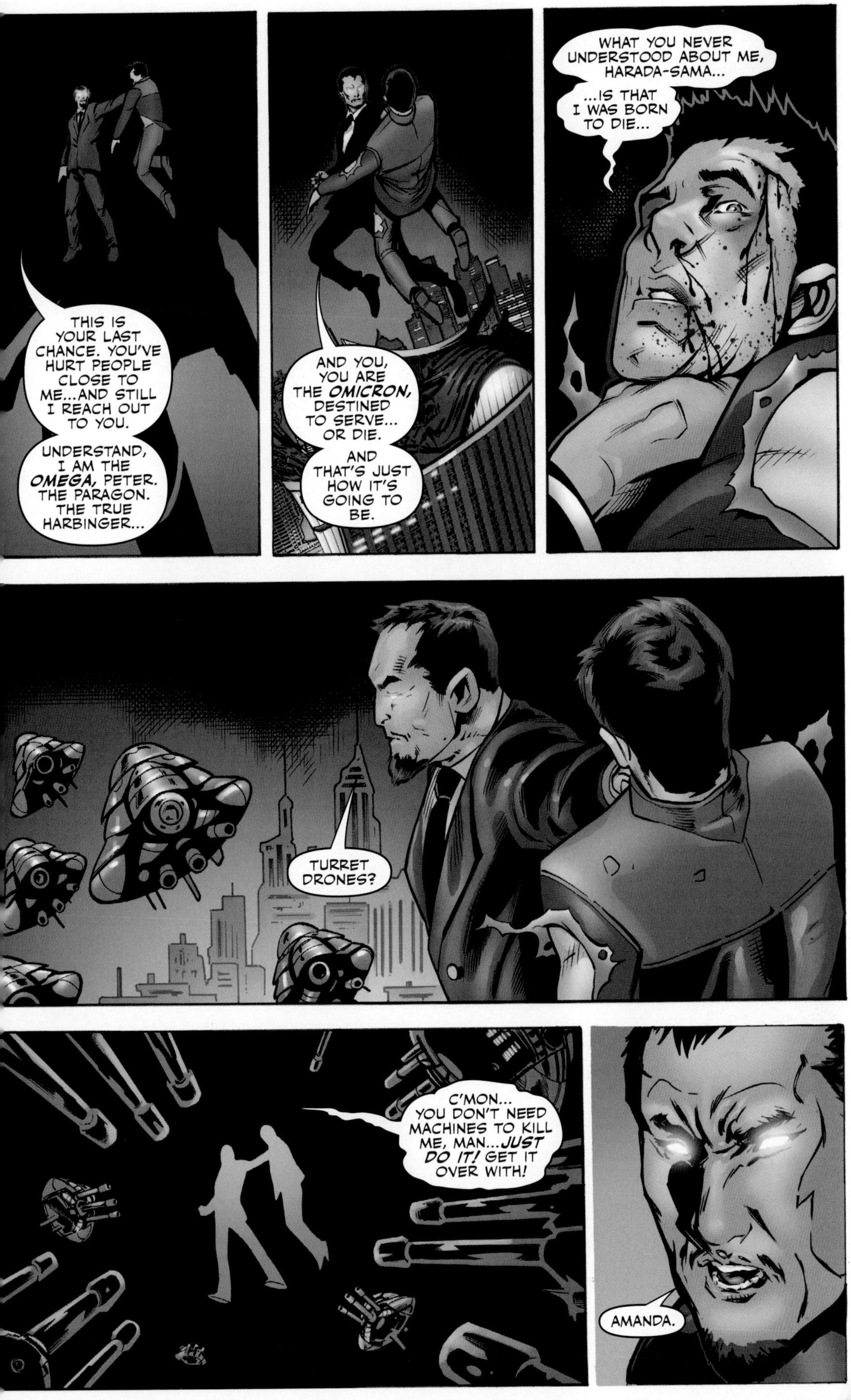
THIS IS YOUR LAST CHANCE. YOU'VE HURT PEOPLE CLOSE TO ME...AND STILL I REACH OUT TO YOU.
UNDERSTAND, I AM THE ***OMEGA,*** PETER. THE PARAGON. THE TRUE HARBINGER...
AND YOU, YOU ARE THE ***OMICRON,*** DESTINED TO SERVE... OR DIE.
AND THAT'S JUST HOW IT'S GOING TO BE.
WHAT YOU NEVER UNDERSTOOD ABOUT ME, HARADA-SAMA...
...IS THAT I WAS BORN TO DIE...
TURRET DRONES?
C'MON... YOU DON'T NEED MACHINES TO KILL ME, MAN...***JUST DO IT!*** GET IT OVER WITH!
AMANDA.

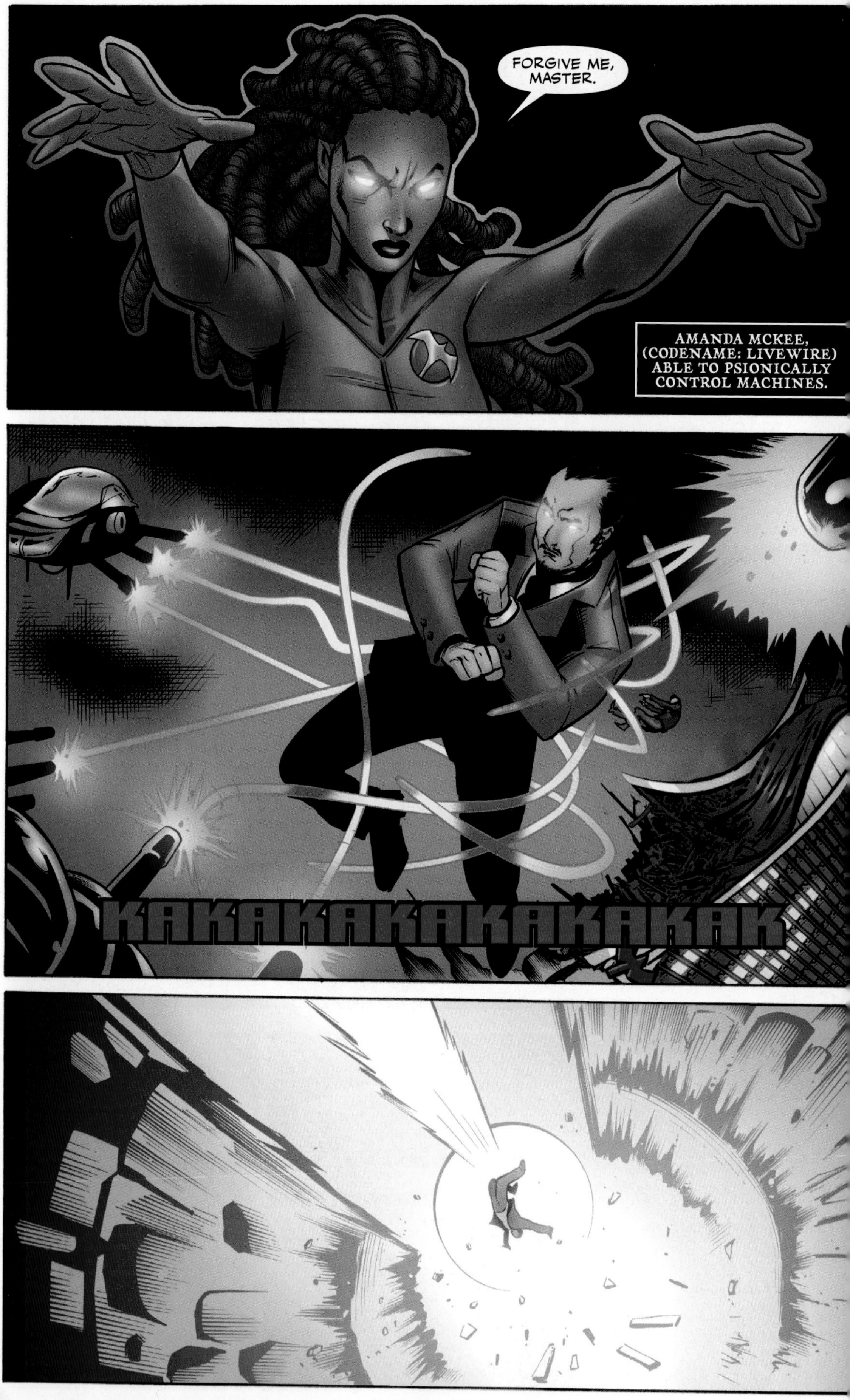

FORGIVE ME, MASTER.
AMANDA MCKEE, (CODENAME: LIVEWIRE) ABLE TO PSIONICALLY CONTROL MACHINES.
KAKAKAKAKAKAKAKAK

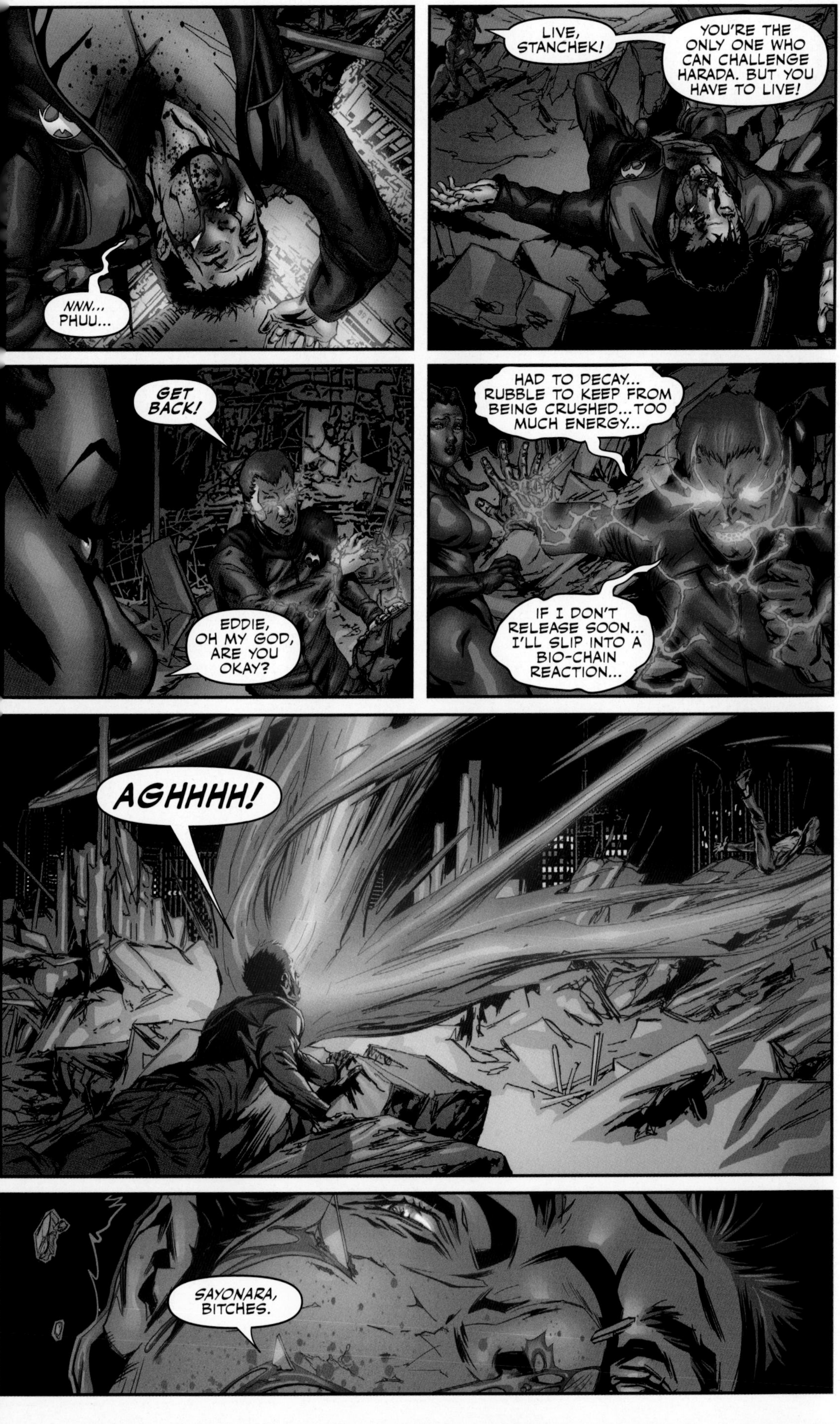
NNN... PHUU...
LIVE, STANCHEK!
YOU'RE THE ONLY ONE WHO CAN CHALLENGE HARADA. BUT YOU HAVE TO LIVE!
GET BACK!
EDDIE, OH MY GOD, ARE YOU OKAY?
HAD TO DECAY... RUBBLE TO KEEP FROM BEING CRUSHED...TOO MUCH ENERGY...
IF I DON'T RELEASE SOON... I'LL SLIP INTO A BIO-CHAIN REACTION...
AGHHHH!
SAYONARA, BITCHES.

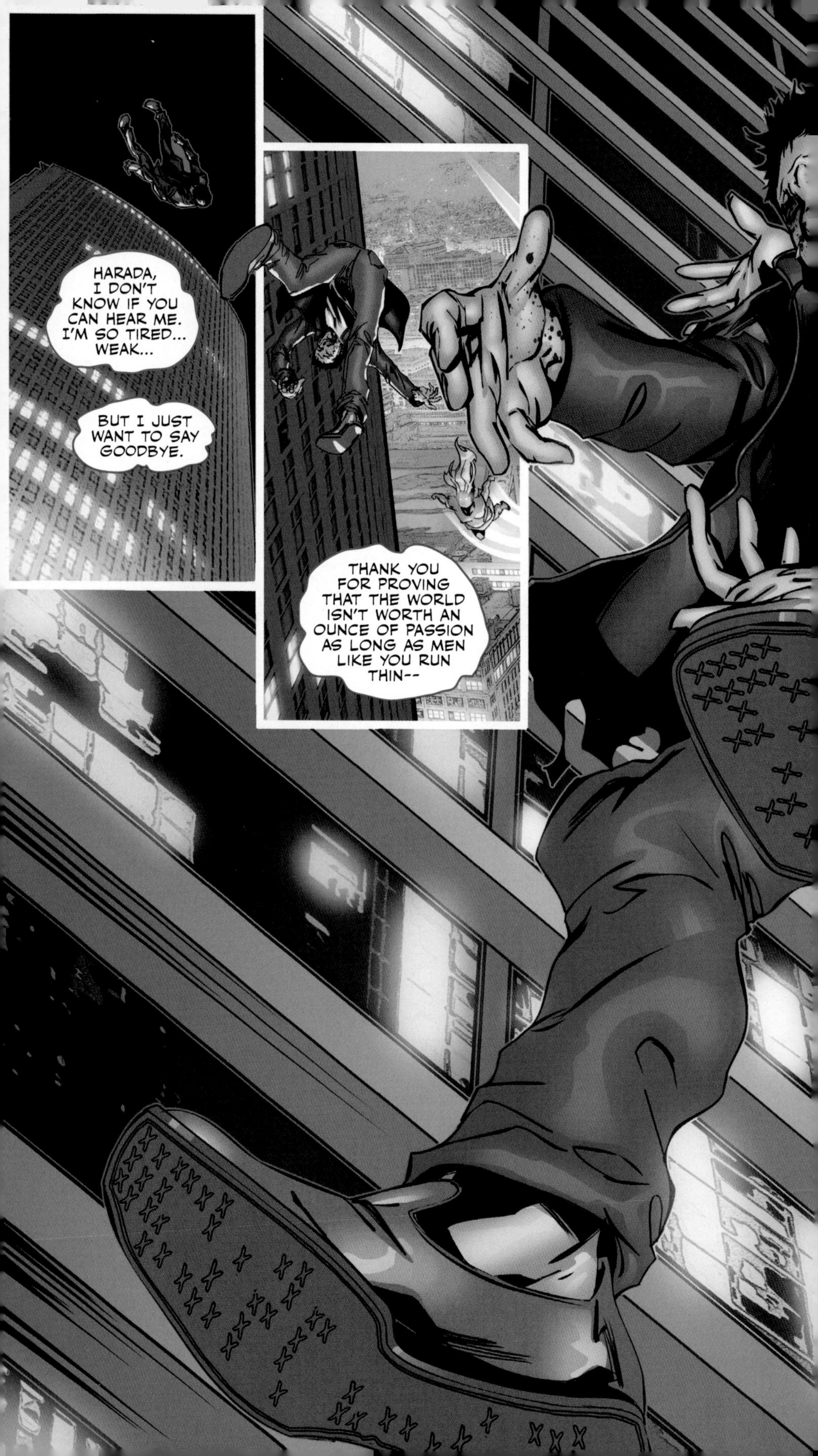
HARADA, I DON'T KNOW IF YOU CAN HEAR ME. I'M SO TIRED... WEAK...
BUT I JUST WANT TO SAY GOODBYE.
THANK YOU FOR PROVING THAT THE WORLD ISN'T WORTH AN OUNCE OF PASSION AS LONG AS MEN LIKE YOU RUN THIN--

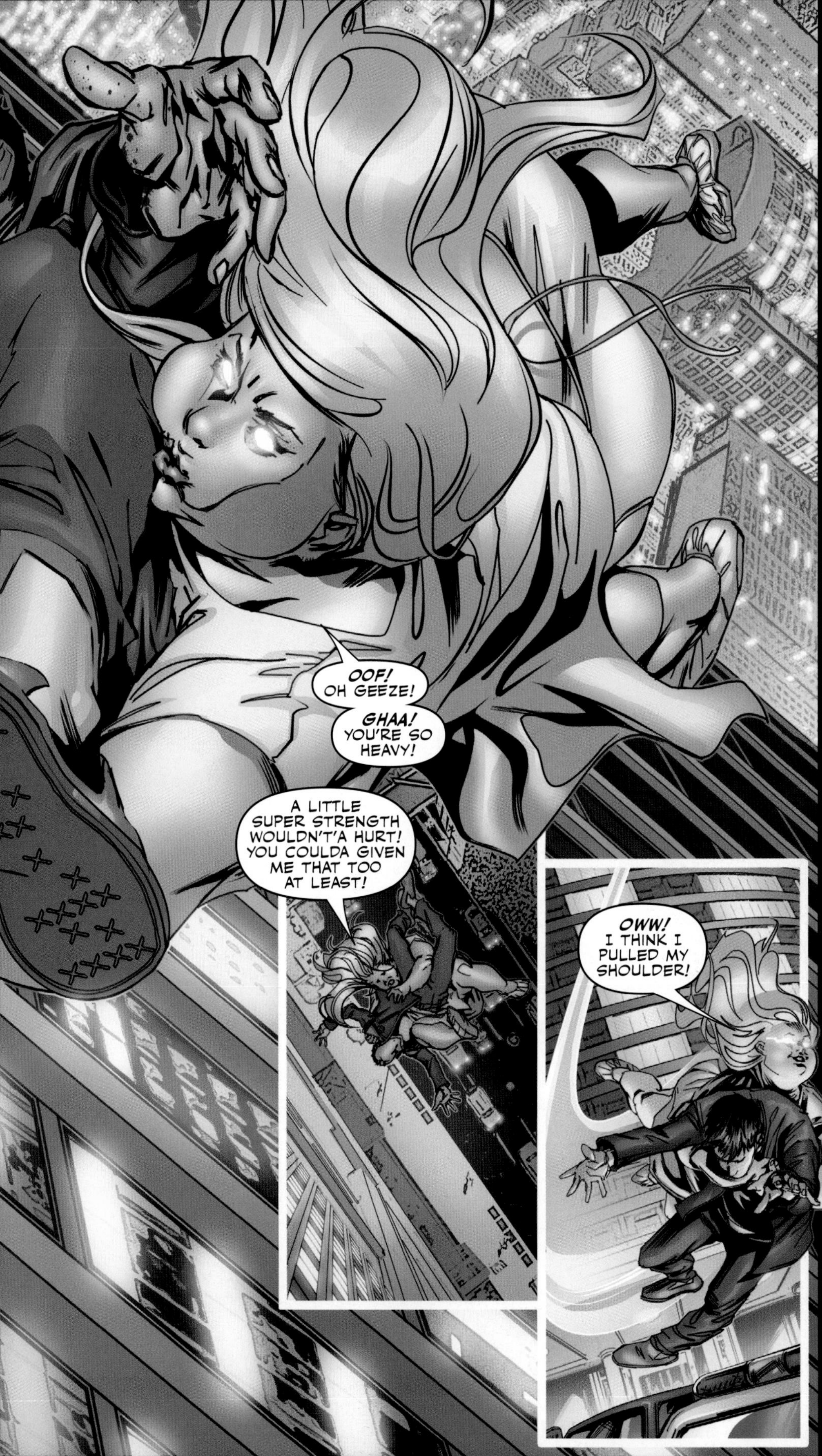
OOF! OH GEEZE!
GHAA! YOU'RE SO HEAVY!
A LITTLE SUPER STRENGTH WOULDN'T'A HURT! YOU COULDA GIVEN ME THAT TOO AT LEAST!
OWW! I THINK I PULLED MY SHOULDER!

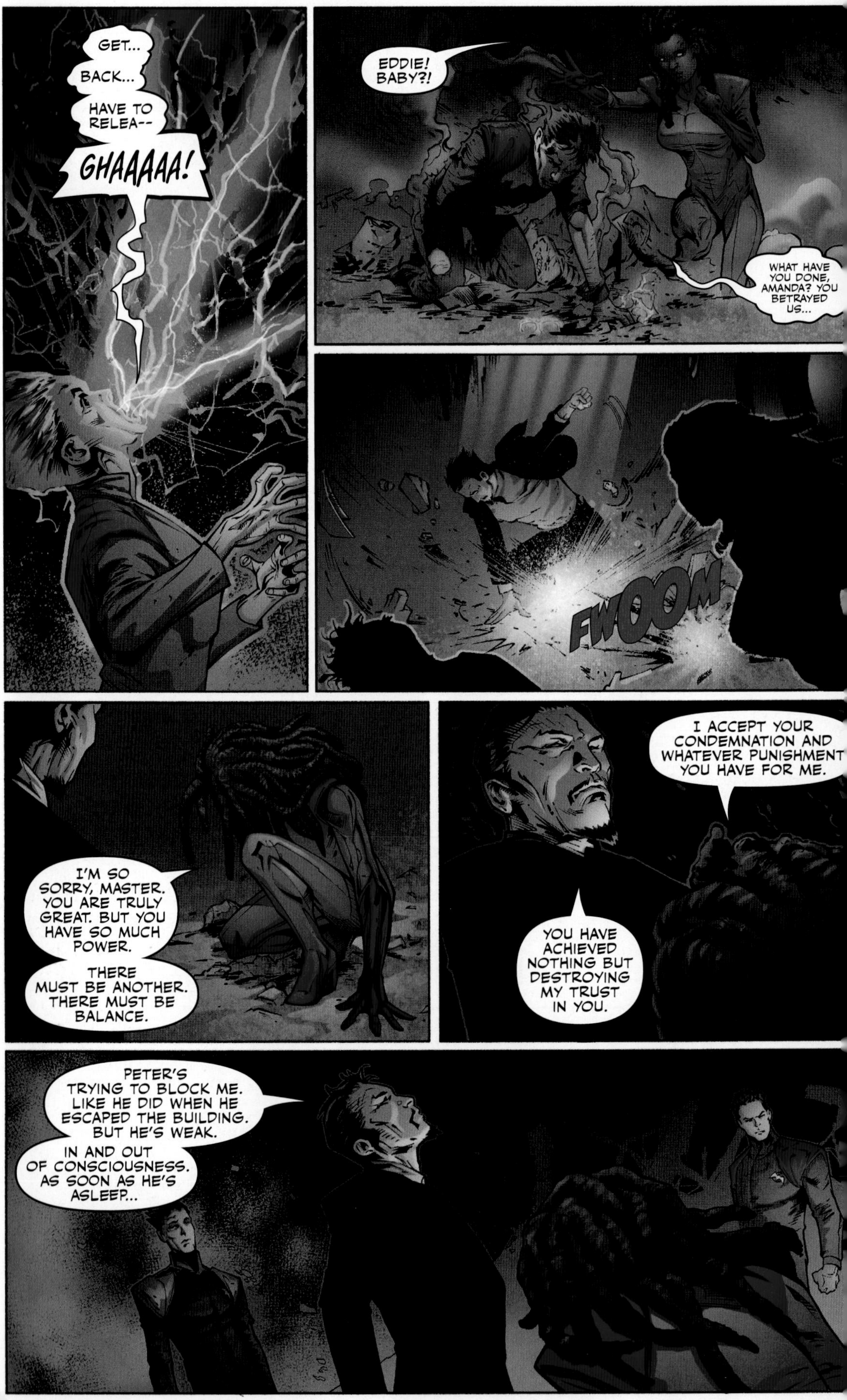
GET...
BACK...
HAVE TO RELEA--
GHAAAAA!
EDDIE! BABY?!
WHAT HAVE YOU DONE, AMANDA? YOU BETRAYED US...
FWOOM
I'M SO SORRY, MASTER. YOU ARE TRULY GREAT. BUT YOU HAVE SO MUCH POWER.
THERE MUST BE ANOTHER. THERE MUST BE BALANCE.
I ACCEPT YOUR CONDEMNATION AND WHATEVER PUNISHMENT YOU HAVE FOR ME.
YOU HAVE ACHIEVED NOTHING BUT DESTROYING MY TRUST IN YOU.
PETER'S TRYING TO BLOCK ME. LIKE HE DID WHEN HE ESCAPED THE BUILDING. BUT HE'S WEAK.
IN AND OUT OF CONSCIOUSNESS. AS SOON AS HE'S ASLEEP...

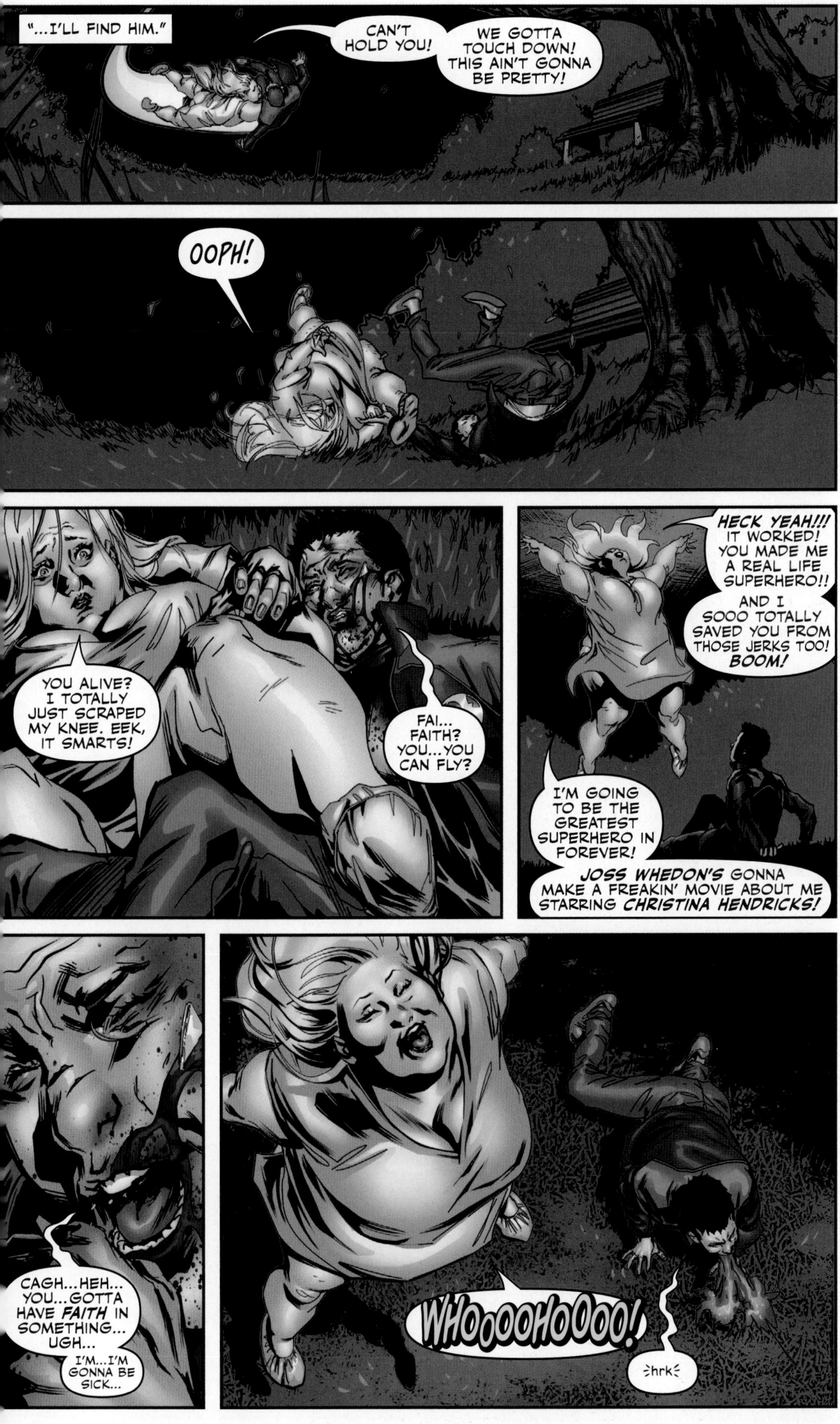

"...I'LL FIND HIM."
CAN'T HOLD YOU!
WE GOTTA TOUCH DOWN! THIS AIN'T GONNA BE PRETTY!
OOPH!
YOU ALIVE? I TOTALLY JUST SCRAPED MY KNEE. EEK, IT SMARTS!
FAI... FAITH? YOU...YOU CAN FLY?
HECK YEAH!!! IT WORKED! YOU MADE ME A REAL LIFE SUPERHERO!!
AND I SOOO TOTALLY SAVED YOU FROM THOSE JERKS TOO! BOOM!
I'M GOING TO BE THE GREATEST SUPERHERO IN FOREVER!
JOSS WHEDON'S GONNA MAKE A FREAKIN' MOVIE ABOUT ME STARRING CHRISTINA HENDRICKS!
CAGH...HEH... YOU...GOTTA HAVE FAITH IN SOMETHING... UGH...
I'M...I'M GONNA BE SICK...
WHOOOOHOOOO!
hrk

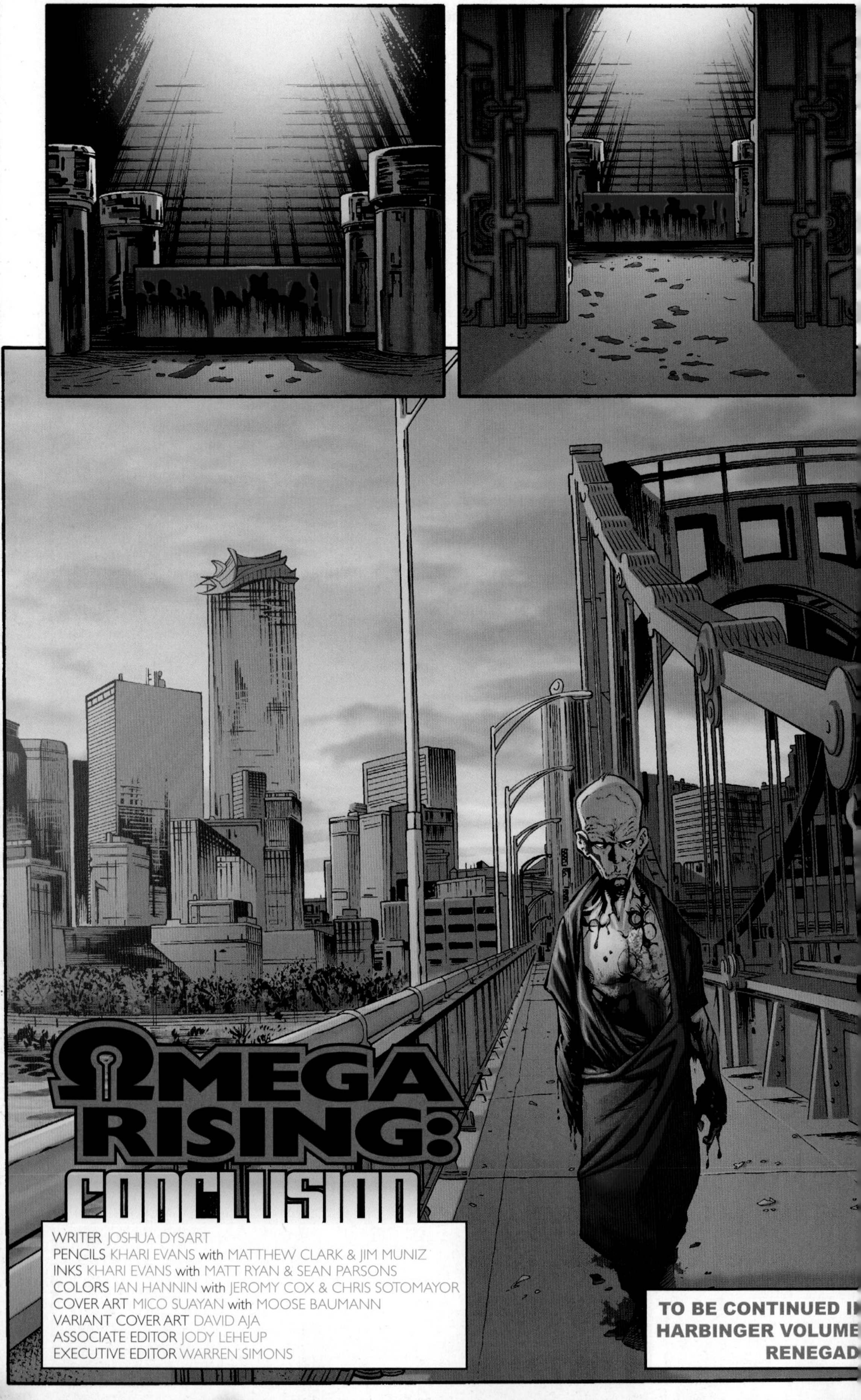
OMEGA RISING:
CONCLUSION
WRITER JOSHUA DYSART
PENCILS KHARI EVANS with MATTHEW CLARK & JIM MUNIZ
INKS KHARI EVANS with MATT RYAN & SEAN PARSONS
COLORS IAN HANNIN with JEROMY COX & CHRIS SOTOMAYOR
COVER ART MICO SUAYAN with MOOSE BAUMANN
VARIANT COVER ART DAVID AJA
ASSOCIATE EDITOR JODY LEHEUP
EXECUTIVE EDITOR WARREN SIMONS
TO BE CONTINUED I
HARBINGER VOLUME
RENEGAD

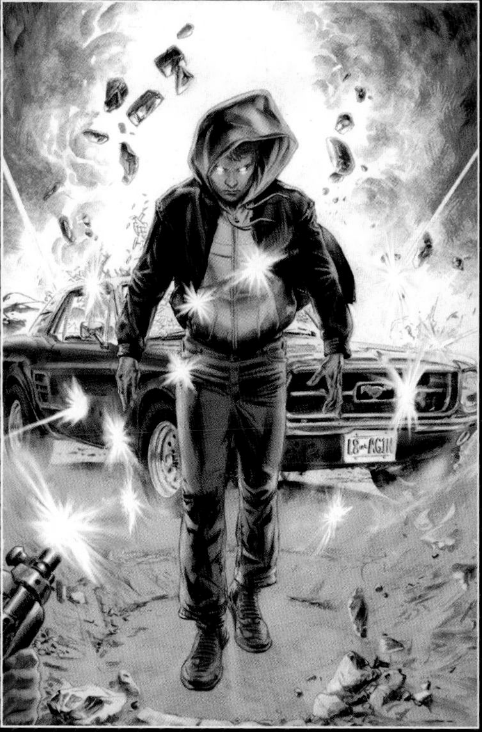

HARBINGER #1 VARIANT
Cover by DOUG BRAITHWAITE

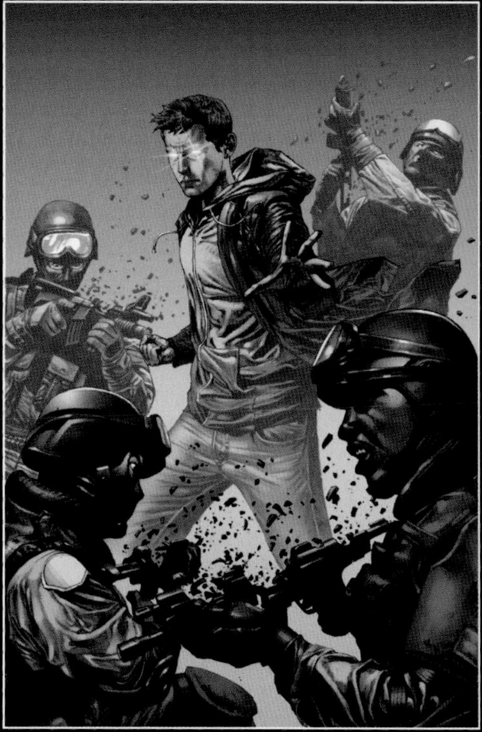

HARBINGER #1 PULLBOX EXCLUSIVE VARIANT
Cover by MICO SUAYAN

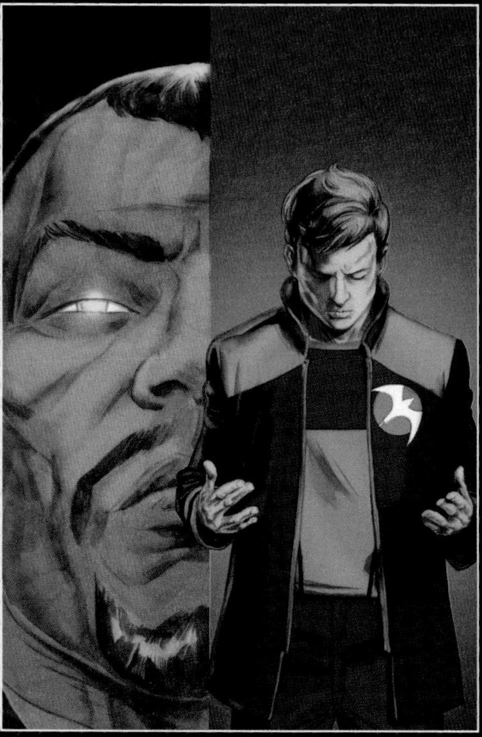

HARBINGER #2 VARIANT
Cover by DOUG BRAITHWAITE

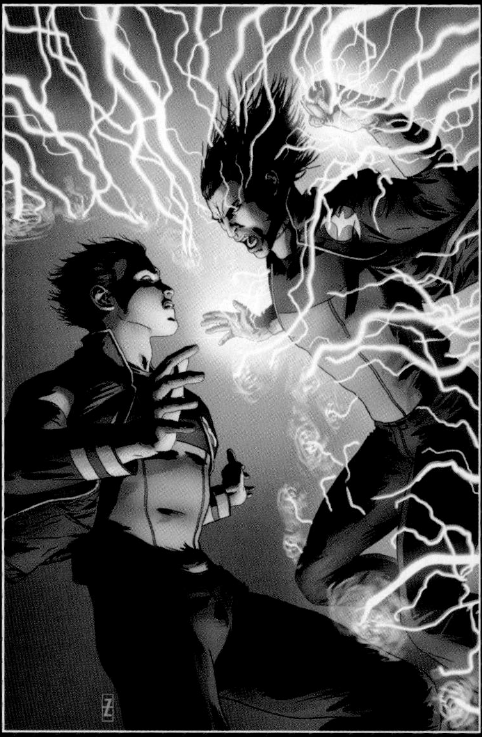

HARBINGER #3 VARIANT
Cover by PATRICK ZIRCHER

VALIANT MASTERS

A NEW LINE OF DELUXE HARDCOVERS COLLECTING THE ORIGINAL ADVENTURES OF VALIANT'S GREATEST HEROES FOR THE FIRST TIME ANYWHERE! FEATURING CLASSIC WORK BY SOME OF COMICS' MOST ACCLAIMED TALENTS.

KEVIN VANHOOK | DON PERLIN
VALIANT
BLOOD OF THE MACHINE
BLOODSHOT
VALIANT MASTERS

VALIANT MASTERS: BLOODSHOT VOL. 1: BLOOD OF THE MACHINE

Written by KEVIN VANHOOK
Art by DON PERLIN
Cover by BARRY WINDSOR-SMITH

- Collecting **BLOODSHOT #1-8 (1993)** and an all-new, in-continuity story from the original **BLOODSHOT** creative team of **Kevin VanHook**, **Don Perlin**, and **Bob Wiacek** available only in this volume
- Featuring Bloodshot's first solo mission in the Valiant Universe and appearances by **Ninjak**, the **Eternal Warrior** and **Rai**

HARDCOVER
ISBN: 978-0-9796409-3-3

MARK A. MORETTI | JOE QUESADA | JIMMY PALMIOTTI
VALIANT
BLACK WATER
NINJAK
VALIANT MASTERS

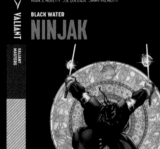

VALIANT MASTERS: NINJAK VOL. 1: BLACK WATER

Written by MARK MORETTI
Art by JOE QUESADA & MARK MORETTI
Cover by JOE QUESADA

- Collecting **NINJAK #1-6 and #0-00 (1994)** with covers, interiors, and rarely seen process art by best-selling artist and creator **Joe Quesada**
- Featuring the complete origin of Valiant's original stealth operative and appearances by **X-O Manowar** and **Bloodshot**

HARDCOVER
ISBN: 978-0-9796409-7-1

VALIANT
SPIRITS WITHIN
SHADOWMAN
VALIANT MASTERS

VALIANT MASTERS: SHADOWMAN VOL. 1: SPIRITS WITHIN

Written by STEVE ENGLEHART, BOB HALL, BOB LAYTON, JIM SHOOTER and MORE
Art by STEVE DITKO, BOB HALL, DAVID LAPHAM, DON PERLIN and MORE
Cover by DAVID LAPHAM

- Collecting **SHADOWMAN #0-7 (1992)** and material from **DARQUE PASSAGES #1 (1994)** with an all-new new introduction by visionary Shadowman writer/artist **Bob Hall**
- The first-ever deluxe hardcover collection to feature the origin and debut solo adventures of Shadowman in the original Valiant Universe!

HARDCOVER
ISBN: 978-1-939346-01-8

EXPLORE THE VALIANT UNIVERSE

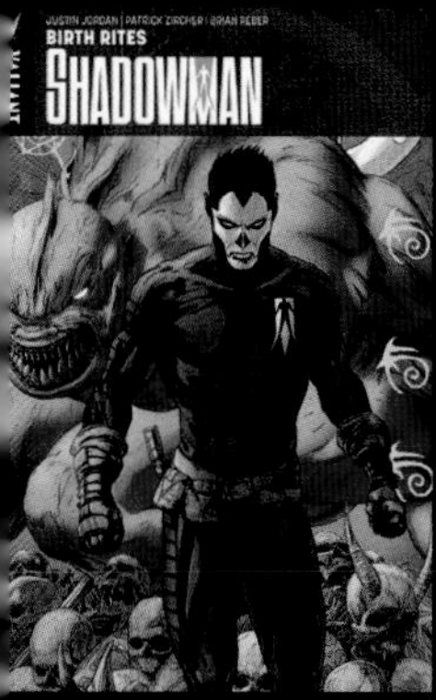
BIRTH RITES
SHADOWMAN

HADOWMAN VOL. 1: BIRTH RITES
ritten by JUSTIN JORDAN &
ATRICK ZIRCHER
t by PATRICK ZIRCHER
ollecting SHADOWMAN #1-4
RADE PAPERBACK
BN: 978-1-939346-00-1

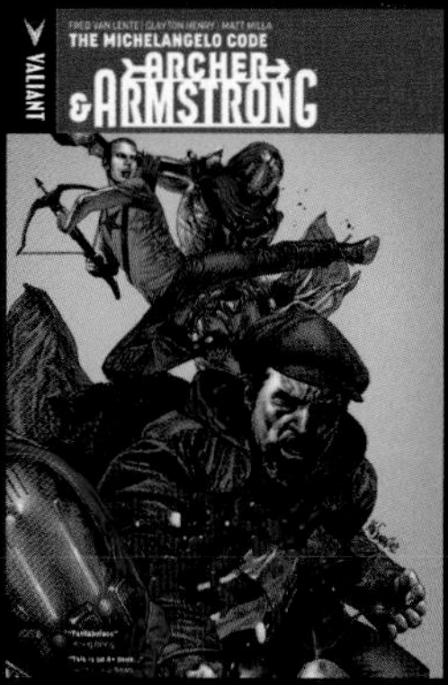
THE MICHELANGELO CODE
ARCHER & ARMSTRONG

ARCHER & ARMSTRONG VOL. 1:
THE MICHELANGELO CODE
Written by FRED VAN LENTE
Art by CLAYTON HENRY
Collecting ARCHER & ARMSTRONG #1-4
TRADE PAPERBACK
ISBN: 978-0-9796409-8-8

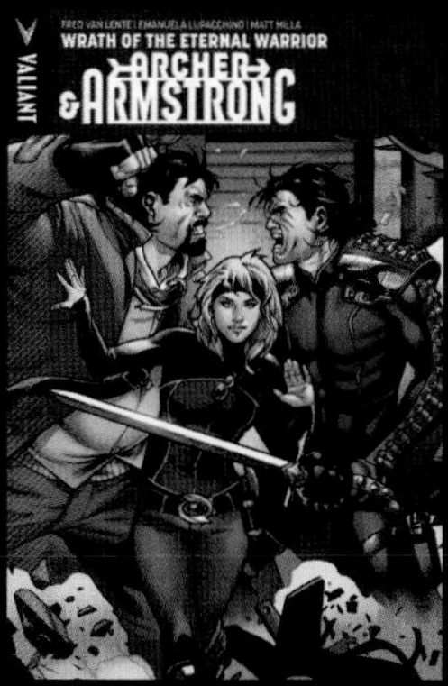
WRATH OF THE ETERNAL WARRIOR
ARCHER & ARMSTRONG

ARCHER & ARMSTRONG VOL. 2:
WRATH OF THE ETERNAL WARRIOR
Written by FRED VAN LENTE
Art by EMANUELA LUPACCHINO
Collecting ARCHER & ARMSTRONG #5-9
TRADE PAPERBACK
ISBN: 978-1-939346-04-9

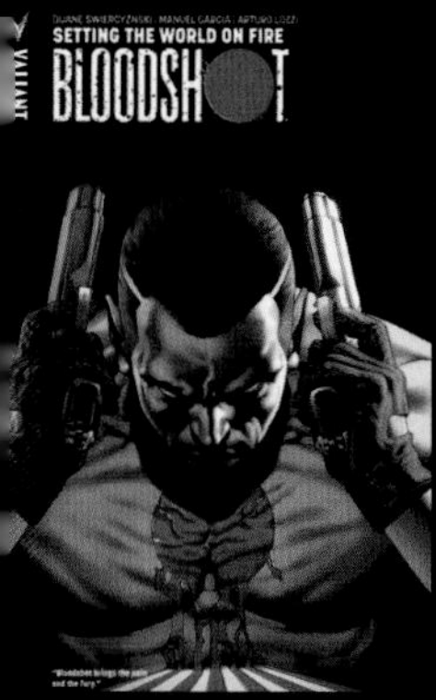
SETTING THE WORLD ON FIRE
BLOODSHOT

LOODSHOT VOL. 1:
ETTING THE WORLD ON FIRE
ritten by DUANE SWIERCZYNSKI
t by MANUEL GARCIA & ARTURO LOZZI
ollecting BLOODSHOT #1-4
RADE PAPERBACK
BN: 978-0-9796409-6-4

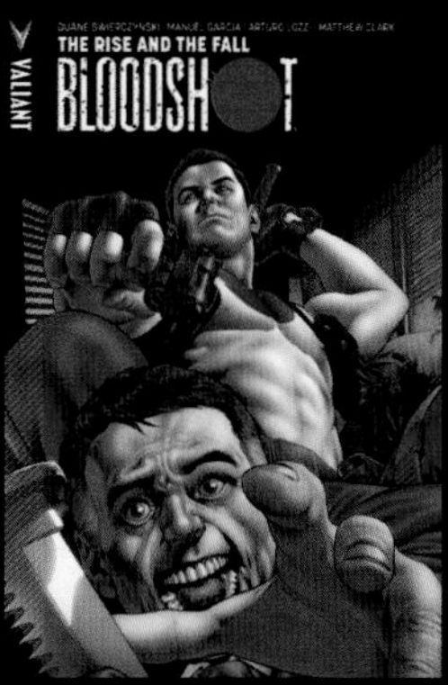
THE RISE AND THE FALL
BLOODSHOT

BLOODSHOT VOL. 2:
THE RISE & THE FALL
Written by DUANE SWIERCZYNSKI
Art by MANUEL GARCIA & ARTURO LOZZI
Collecting BLOODSHOT #5-9
TRADE PAPERBACK
ISBN: 978-1-939346-03-2

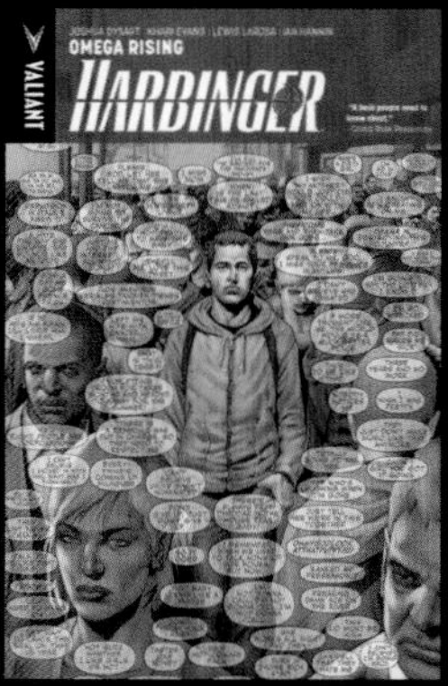
OMEGA RISING
HARBINGER

HARBINGER VOL. 1:
OMEGA RISING
Written by JOSHUA DYSART
Art by KHARI EVANS & LEWIS LAROSA
Collecting HARBINGER #1-5
TRADE PAPERBACK
ISBN: 978-0-979-6409-5-7

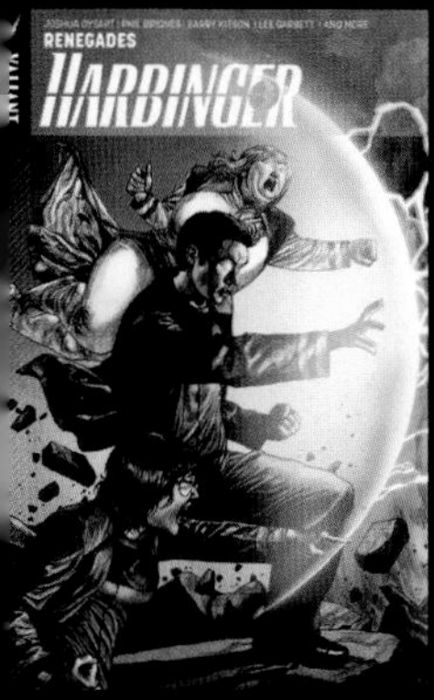
RENEGADES
HARBINGER

ARBINGER VOL. 2: RENEGADES
ritten by JOSHUA DYSART
t by PHIL BRIONES, MATTHEW CLARK,
HARI EVANS, LEE GARBETT, BARRY
TSON and PERE PEREZ
ollecting HARBINGER #6-10
RADE PAPERBACK
BN: 978-1-939346-02-5

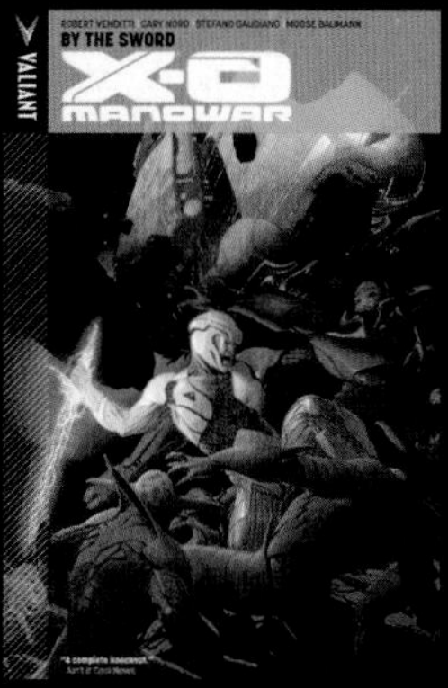
BY THE SWORD
X-O MANOWAR

X-O MANOWAR VOL. 1:
BY THE SWORD
Written by ROBERT VENDITTI
Art by CARY NORD
Collecting X-O MANOWAR #1-4
TRADE PAPERBACK
ISBN: 978-0-9796409-4-0

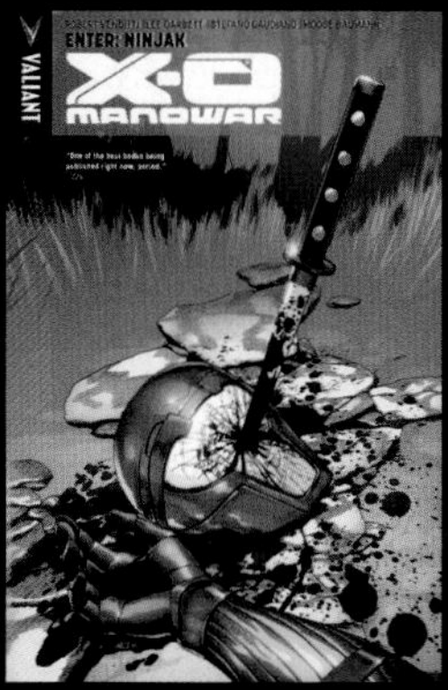
ENTER: NINJAK
X-O MANOWAR

X-O MANOWAR VOL. 2:
ENTER NINJAK
Written by ROBERT VENDITTI
Art by LEE GARBETT
Collecting X-O MANOWAR #5-8
TRADE PAPERBACK
ISBN: 978-1-9393460-0-1

VALIANT®

HARBINGER®

VOLUME TWO: RENEGADES

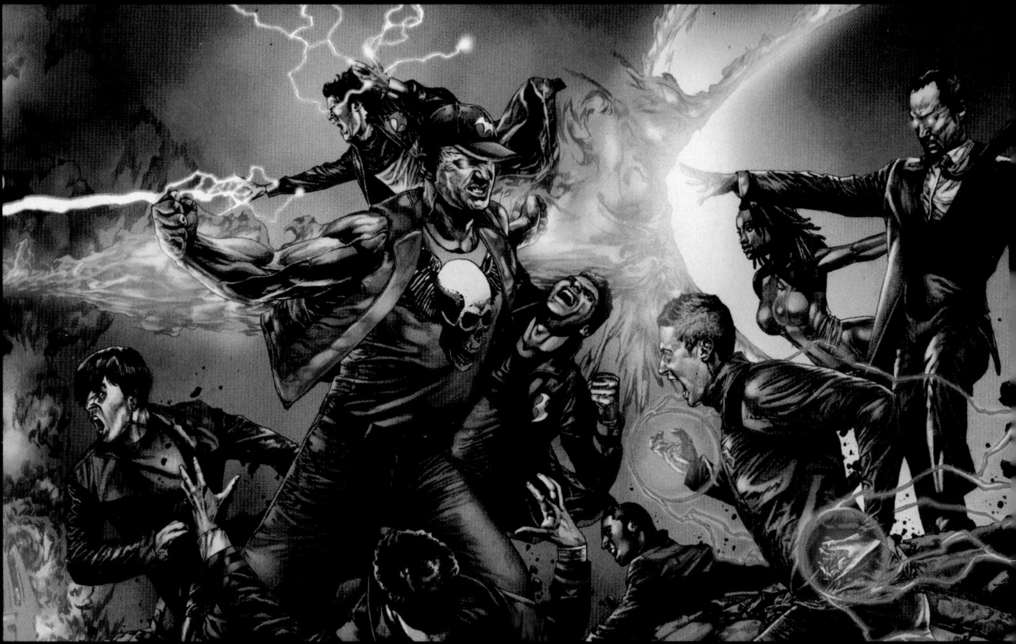

OUTSIDE THE LAW. INSIDE YOUR HEAD.
WELCOME TO THE RENEGADES.

Battered and broken after his escape from the Harbinger Foundation, telekinetic teenager Peter Stanchek only has one option left - run. But he won't have to go it alone. Crisscrossing America with the only two people he can trust, Peter will have to activate a new team of super-powered recruits before Toyo Harada and his Harbinger shock troops can reach them first. Peter Stanchek. Zephyr. Kris. Flamingo. You've never met a team of super-powered teenagers quite like the Renegades. And, together, they'll dismantle Harada's global empire one brick at a time.

HARBINGER VOL. 2:
RENEGADES

Collecting **HARBINGER #6-10** by New York Times best-selling author Joshua Dysart (*Unknown Soldier, BPRD*) and an all-star cast of comics' top artistic talents, get ready for the second stunning volume of the series Ain't It Cool News calls "simply astonishing."

TRADE PAPERBACK
ISBN: 978-1-939346-02-5

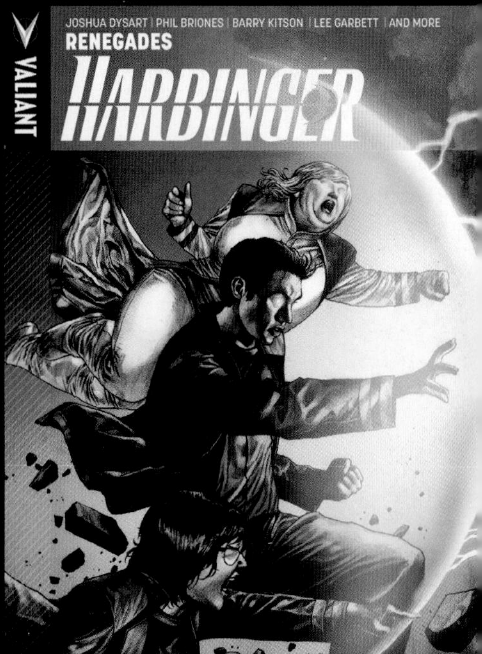
VALIANT
JOSHUA DYSART | PHIL BRIONES | BARRY KITSON | LEE GARBETT | AND MORE
RENEGADES
HARBINGER